MATHS CONNECT 1 B

Dave Kirkby

Lynne McClure

Catherine Roe

Bev Stanbridge

heinemann.co.uk
✓ Free online support
✓ Useful weblinks
✓ 24 hour online ordering

01865 888058

Heinemann

Inspiring generations

Heinemann Educational Publishers
Halley Court, Jordan Hill, Oxford OX2 8EJ
Part of Harcourt Education

Heinemann is the registered trademark of
Harcourt Education Limited

First published 2003

07
10 9 8 7 6

British Library Cataloguing in Publication Data is available
from the British Library on request.

ISBN: 978 0 435534 90 5

Designed by Bridge Creative
Typeset by Tech-Set Ltd, Gateshead, Tyne and Wear
Original illustrations © Harcourt Education Limited, 2003
Illustrated by Tech-Set Ltd and Bigtop Design
Cover design by Miller Craig and Cocking
Printed in China by CTPS

Acknowledgements
Every effort has been made to contact copyright holders of material reproduced in this book. Any omissions
will be rectified in subsequent printings if notice is given to the publishers.

The authors and publishers would like to thank the following for permission to use photographs:
p151 Escher/Cordon art; p143 Autoexpress

Cover photo: Getty images ©

Consultant
Jackie Fairchild

Publishing team

Editorial
Sue Bennett
Amanda Halden
Naomi Anderson   Ian Crane
Lauren Bourque   Carol Harris
John Deans   Katherine Pate
Maggie Rumble   Margaret Shepherd

Design
Phil Leafe

Production
Jason Wyatt

Picture research
Bea Thomas
Jane Hance

Tel: 01865 888058 email: info.he@heinemann.co.uk

MATHS CONNECT 1 B

Contents

Contents

A2 Expressions, formulae and brackets

SSM2 Angles, shapes and coordinates

HD2 Applying statistical skills

N3 Calculating and measuring

A3 General terms and linear graphs

SSM3 Properties of triangles and quadrilaterals

SSM5 Exploring polygons and nets

Matching charts linking the content of the lessons in each unit to the
Sample medium-term plans for mathematics and the Year 7 teaching programme
from the *Framework for teaching mathematics* are available on the web at
www.heinemann.co.uk
They can also be found in the Maths Connect 1B teacher book.

How to use this book

This book is divided up into 18 colour-coded units. Algebra units are green, Number units are orange, **Space, Shape and Measure** units are blue and **Handling Data** units are red. Each unit is divided up into lessons. Each lesson is on its own double page spread.

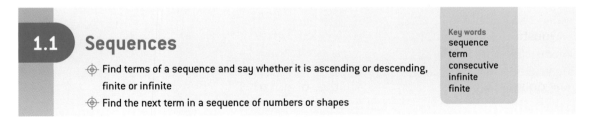

At the top of the page are the **lesson targets**. These tell you what you will learn in the lesson. To help you to remember the important vocabulary, there is a **key words box** here.

A number **sequence** is a set of numbers in a given order, e.g. 1, 2, 3, 4, 5, …

Each number in a sequence is called a **term** .

Terms next to each other are called **consecutive terms** .

Sequences may be **ascending** (e.g. 2, 4, 6, 8, …) or **descending** (e.g. 18, 15, 12, 9, …).

The sequence 1, 2, 3, 4, 5 … is **infinite** . We could go on counting forever.

The sequence 10, 12, 14 … 98 is **finite** . The dots mean that there are missing terms and that the sequence continues in the same way until the final value, 98, is reached.

In the **explanation box**, you can see a summary of the key ideas that are covered in the lesson. The key words are highlighted in yellow.

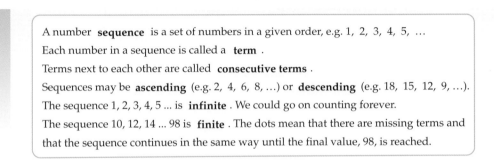

The **worked examples** show you methods of answering the exercise questions. On the blue paper, you can see the kind of working you should be writing in your exercise book. The **hint boxes** help to explain how you can calculate the answers.

The **exercise** for each lesson is made up of three types of question:

- **practice** questions, which allow you to practise the basic skills
- **problem** questions, which encourage you to apply the skills you have learned
- **investigation** questions, which give you practice at solving open-ended problems.

The following features are found in the exercise:

Consecutive terms are terms that are next to each other.

Hint boxes give tips and reminders to help you with the questions

 Questions you should try without the help of a calculator are marked with this symbol

 Questions that require you to use a calculator are marked with this symbol.

If there is no symbol, you can choose whether or not to use a calculator.

Key words
sequence
term
consecutive
infinite
finite

- Find terms of a sequence and say whether it is ascending or descending, finite or infinite
- Find the next term in a sequence of numbers or shapes

A number **sequence** is a set of numbers in a given order, e.g. 1, 2, 3, 4, 5, …

Each number in a sequence is called a **term**.

Terms next to each other are called **consecutive terms**.

Sequences may be **ascending** (e.g. 2, 4, 6, 8, …) or **descending** (e.g. 18, 15, 12, 9, …).

The sequence 1, 2, 3, 4, 5 … is **infinite**. We could go on counting forever.

The sequence 10, 12, 14 … 98 is **finite**. The dots mean that there are missing terms and that the sequence continues in the same way until the final value, 98, is reached.

Example 1 Here is a sequence of diagrams.
Spot the pattern and draw the next two terms in the sequence.

Each time two more dots are added:

This is the 5th term.

This is the 6th term.

Example 2 Here is a sequence of numbers: 3,   6,   9,   12
  a) Is the sequence ascending or descending?
  b) Spot the pattern and write it down.
  c) Write down the next two terms in the sequence.

a) Ascending

b) You count on each time in steps of 3.

   Each term is a multiple of 3.

c) 15, 18

How do you get from 3 to 6 and from 6 to 9?

12 + 3 = 15
15 + 3 = 18

Exercise 1.1

1 Spot the pattern and draw the next two terms in each sequence.

a)

b)

c)

2 4, 7, 10, 13, 16, …

    a) Is this sequence ascending or descending?

    b) What is the difference between consecutive terms?

    c) Write down the next two terms in the sequence.

> Consecutive terms are terms that are next to each other.

3 Write down the next three terms in each of the following sequences:

    a) 10, 11, 12, …   **b)** 80, 72, 64, …

    c) 2, 1.5, 1, …   **d)** 0.7, 0.8, 0.9, …

4 The house numbers on a road go from 1 to 100. The even numbers are on one side of the road, and the odd numbers are on the other side.

    a) You are walking past the odd numbers. The first house you pass is number 1. Write down the numbers of the first five houses you pass.

    b) What is the number on the last house you pass?

    c) You cross the road and walk back past the even numbers. What are the numbers of first five houses you pass?

    d) Is this sequence ascending or descending?

    e) Is this sequence finite or infinite?

5 Copy and complete the following sequences of numbers by spotting the patterns.

    a) 2, 5, 8, ☐, 14, ☐, 20   **b)** 1, ☐, 4, 8, ☐, 32   **c)** 15, ☐, 9, ☐, 3, ☐

    d) 1, 10, 19, 28, ☐, ☐   **e)** 20, ☐, 30, ☐, ☐, 45, 50

6 To make one beach-hut out of matchsticks we used six matchsticks. To make two beach-huts we used eleven matchsticks.

    a) Draw a diagram of how you would make three beach-huts.

    b) How many matchsticks do you need for three beach-huts?

    c) Without drawing, predict how many matchsticks you need for four beach-huts.

    d) Copy and complete the table alongside:

Number of beach-huts	1	2	3	4	5	6	7
Number of matchsticks	6	11					

7 The first few terms of a sequence are: 0, 25, 50, 75

    a) Spot the pattern and write it down.   **b)** How many terms are below 200?

Investigation

8 A detached house has no others attached to it, a semi-detached house is attached to another house on one side, and a terraced house is attached to two other houses: one on either side.

terraced houses   semi-detached houses

Investigate the number of outside walls for rows of detached, semi-detached and terraced houses. You may find a table like this helpful.

Number of houses	1	2	3	4	5	6
Number of outside walls						

Generating sequences

Key words
generate
term
term-to-term rule

⊕ Generate a sequence given a starting point and a rule to go from term-to-term

⊕ Use the rule to find a term in a sequence without finding all the values in between

Generating a sequence means writing down the terms of the sequence. To do this you need to know the pattern that the sequence follows.

To generate a sequence you may be given a starting point and a **rule** that connects one **term** to the next. This is called the **term-to-term rule** .

For example, for the sequence 3, 5, 7 the starting point is 3 and the term-to-term rule is 'add 2'.

Example 1 A sequence starts with 6 and the term-to-term rule is 'add 4'.

Find the first five terms of the sequence.

6, 10, 14, 18, 22 ...

$6 + 4 = \textbf{10}$
$10 + 4 = \textbf{14}$ ... etc.

Example 2 The **third** term of a sequence is 12. The term-to-term rule is 'subtract 5'.
Find the first five terms of the sequence.

22, 17, 12, 7, 2

To find the fourth and fifth terms:
$12 - 5 = \textbf{7}$ $7 - 5 = \textbf{2}$
Remember the inverse of subtraction is addition,
so to find the second and first terms:
$12 + 5 = \textbf{17}$ $17 + 5 = \textbf{22}$

Example 3 The first term of a sequence is 5. The term-to-term rule is 'multiply by 2'.
Write down the first five terms of the sequence.

5, 10, 20, 40, 80

$5 \times 2 = \textbf{10}$
$10 \times 2 = \textbf{20}$ etc.

Exercise 1.2

1 A sequence starts with 100. The term-to-term rule is 'add 6'.
Find the first four terms of the sequence.

2 A sequence starts with 13. The term-to-term rule is 'subtract 3'.
Find the first five terms of the sequence.

3 The first term of a sequence is 1. The term-to-term rule is 'multiply by 2'.
Find the first five terms of the sequence.

4 Given the following starting points and rules, write down the first five terms of each sequence:

	Starting point	Term-to-term rule
a)	7	Add 4
b)	3	Multiply by 2
c)	100	Subtract 6
d)	2	Add 0.5
e)	1	Add 1 then multiply by 3

5 Write down the first three terms of a sequence given the following information:
   a) The first term is 36, to find the next term subtract 12
   b) The first term is 0, to find the next term add 1, then multiply by 2
   c) The first term is 8, to find the next term add 0.5
   d) The first term is 2, to find the next term add 2, then multiply by 3.

6 Sarah has just opened a sandwich shop.
On the first day she has no customers and sells no sandwiches.
On the second day she sells 3 sandwiches and on the third day she sells 6 sandwiches.
If this pattern continues, how many sandwiches do you think Sarah will sell on:
   a) the fourth day?   b) the fifth day?

7 On average days in August have 15 hours of daylight.
Days in September have 13 hours and in October they have 11.
   a) How many hours of daylight do you think there are in days in November?
   b) Why can't this sequence continue in this way?

> Think about how many hours of daylight there would be in April if the sequence continued like this.

8 To get from one term to the next of a sequence, you add 4 and then multiply by 2. If the first term is 3, how many terms are below 100?

9 The term-to-term rule is 'add 3'. The **second** term is 7.
   a) Copy and complete the table below:

1st term	2nd term	3rd term	4th term	5th term	6th term
	7				

> Look back at Example 2.

How many times did you have to add 3 to get from:
   b) the first term to the fourth term?   c) the first term to the sixth term?

Investigation

10 A sequence starts 5, 9, 13, 17 ...
   a) Write down the next five terms in the sequence.
   b) What is the tenth term?
   c) How many times did you have to add 4 to get from the first term to the tenth term?
   d) How many times did you have to add 4 to get from the first term to the sixth term?
   e) Find the twentieth term without finding all the terms in between.

Investigating sequences

⊕ Find a term in a sequence using a rule that connects the term number and the term

Look at this **sequence** :

Term number	1	2	3	4	5
Sequence	5	9	13	17	21

The first **term** is 5, the second term is 9, and so on.

The sequence is going up in 4s so we can break the numbers down into 4s.

Sequence	4 + 1	4 + 4 + 1	4 + 4 + 4 + 1	4 + 4 + 4 + 4 + 1	4 + 4 + 4 + 4 + 4 + 1

The first term is   1 lot of 4 plus 1.
The second term is 2 lots of 4 plus 1.
The fourth term is   4 lots of 4 plus 1.
The fifth term is   5 lots of 4 plus 1.
So the 100th term is 100 lots of 4 plus 1.
$(100 \times 4) + 1 = 401$

Example 1   Find the twentieth term of the sequence below.

Term number	1	2	3	4	5
Sequence	11	14	17	20	23

The twentieth term will be $(20 \times 3) + 8 = \mathbf{68}$

The sequence goes up in 3s so we break the numbers down into 3s.
The first term is 1 lot of 3 plus 8. So the twentieth term is 20 lots of 3 plus 8.

Example 2   The first term of a sequence is 5 and the term-to-term rule is 'add 2'.
Find the fifteenth term.

The first few terms are: 5, 7, 9, 11, 13, …

The first term is 1 lot of 2 plus 3. The second term is 2 lots of 2

plus 3. The fifteenth term will be 15 lots of 2 plus 3.

Fifteenth term = $(15 \times 2) + 3 = \mathbf{33}$

Exercise 1.3 ....

① Copy and complete the following tables, then find the 50th term without calculating all the terms in between.

a)

Term number	1	2	3	4	5	6
Sequence	3	6	9			

b)

Term number	1	2	3	4	5	6
Sequence	3	5	7			

c)

Term number	1	2	3	4	5	6
Sequence	2	6	10			

2 The first term of a sequence is 12 and the term-to-term rule is 'add 3'.
Find the twentieth term.

3 The first few terms of a sequence are: 20, 29, 38, 47

Find: **a)** the eighth term   **b)** the twelfth term   **c)** the fourteenth term.

> Think about what the rule is to go from term-to-term.

4 Find the 60th term of the following sequences:

a) 3, 5, 7, 9 ...   **b)** 9, 19, 29, 39…

c) 5, 8, 11, 14…   **d)** 3, 8, 13, 18…

5 The term-to-term rule for a sequence is 'add 5'. If the first term is 8, what is the nineteenth term?

6 A child's height when it is 1 year old is 60 cm and a year later it is 85 cm.

a)   Assuming the child grows the same amount each year,
find the height of the child when it is 18 years old.

b)   What could be wrong with this pattern?

7 It costs £30 000 for a builder to build one house. Each additional house costs £20 000.
How much will it cost him to build twenty five houses?

8 In the first year of its life a dog needs one injection.
In the second year it needs four and in the third year
it needs seven.

a)   By looking at this as a number pattern can you work out
how many injections a dog will need in its twelfth year?

b)   What could be wrong with this pattern?

Investigation

9 The term-to-term rule for a sequence is 'add 3'.

a)   Write down two possible sequences that follow this rule.

b)   Find a sequence where all the numbers are multiples of 3.

c)   Find a sequence where all the numbers are odd.

d)   Find a sequence where none of the numbers are whole numbers.

e)   Repeat these questions for numbers other than 3 and write down any patterns
you notice.

Function machines

⊕ Find unknown numbers and operations in function machines

⊕ Draw simple mapping diagrams

Key words
input
output
function machine
mapping diagram
unknown

In maths we often need to find an **unknown** number: $1 + \square = 5$

The number we are looking for is 4. $1 + \boxed{4} = 5$

We write this as: $\square = 4$

We can use a **mapping diagram** to show how one number moves to another number by using a rule.

The diagram shows that

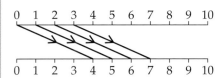

$0 \rightarrow 4$ 0 is mapped onto 4,

$1 \rightarrow 5$ 1 is mapped onto 5,

$2 \rightarrow 6$ 2 is mapped onto 6 and so on.

The rule to get from the first number to the second number is 'add 4'.

A **function machine** for this rule looks like this: Input ⟶ +4 ⟶ Output

Example 1   Find the number represented by $\square$:

  a) $21 - \square = 12$ **b)** $\square \times 5 = 65$

a) $21 - \boxed{9} = 12$

  $\square = 9$

Check: $21 - 9 = 12$ ✓ ──── Always check your answer.

b) $\boxed{13} \times 5 = 65$ ────

  $\square = 13$

Check: $13 \times 5 = 65$ ✓

Count up in fives until you know how many fives make 65.

Example 2   Look at this function machine: Input ⟶ +5 ⟶ Output

  a) If the input is 8, what is the output?

  b) If the output is 6, what is the input?

If you input the number 5, the output is $5 + 5 = 10$

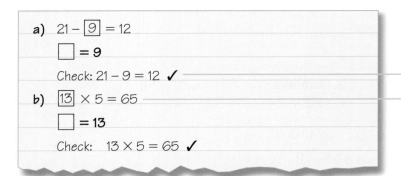

a) $8 \longrightarrow$ +5 $\longrightarrow 13$ the output is 13.

b) $? \longrightarrow$ +5 $\longrightarrow 6$

  The input must be 1. ────

  Check: $1 + 5 = 6$ ✓

You need to work backwards through the function machine here.

Exercise 1.4 ....

1 Draw mapping diagrams for parts **a** to **d** and find the rules that connect the pairs of numbers.

a) $1 \to 7$
$2 \to 8$
$3 \to 9$

b) $10 \to 3$
$11 \to 4$
$12 \to 5$

c) $4 \to 16$
$5 \to 20$
$6 \to 24$

d) $12 \to 4$
$30 \to 10$
$6 \to 2$

> Each pair of numbers is connected by only one operation ($+$, $-$, $\times$ or $\div$).

2 Draw function machines for the rules in Q1.

3 Find ☐ in each of the following:

a) $3 + \square = 12$
b) $7 \times \square = 56$
c) $12 = 144 \div \square$
d) $6 \times 3 = \square \times 6$

e) $\square = 14 - 8$
f) $5 = \square \div 12$
g) $23 \times \square = 4 \times 23$

4 Copy and complete the function machines below:

a)

b)

c)

d)

5 Fill in either $+$, $-$, $\times$ or $\div$ in each of the machines below:

Machine A:

Machine B:

Machine C: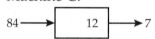

Machine D: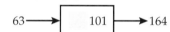

6 ■ $+$ ▲ $= 9$

a) List all the possible positive whole numbers that ■ and ▲ could be.
(For example: ■ $= 2$ and ▲ $= 7$ since $2 + 7 = 9$)

7 One can of cola and one chocolate bar cost 80p.

a) If the chocolate bar costs either 15p or 30p, what are the possible costs of the can of cola?

b) One chocolate bar and two cans of cola cost £1.30.
Use your answers to part **a** to find the cost of a chocolate bar.

Investigation

8 Two whole numbers multiplied together make 12.

a) List as many pairs of numbers as you can which multiply to give twelve.

b) How many pairs of numbers did you find?

c) Try the same with numbers from 12 to 30. Explain any patterns that you find.

> 3×4 is the same as 4×3 so don't count it twice.

More function machines

⊕ Know how to work 'backwards' through a calculation to find the number you started with

⊕ Find unknown numbers in two-step function machines

To calculate the value of **unknown** numbers, find the inverse **operation** : change − to +, and × to ÷.

The **inverse** or opposite of addition is subtraction.

The **inverse** or opposite of multiplication is division.

Look at the function machine below:

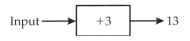

To find out what the input is, work backwards through the machine. The inverse of +3 is −3.
$13 − 3 = 10$ The input is 10.

Now look at this machine:

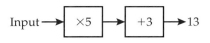

To find out what the input is:
$13 − 3 = 10$ $10 ÷ 5 = 2$
The input is 2.

Example I choose a number, multiply it by 2 and then subtract 7. I get 15.

a) Draw a function machine to show this calculation.

b) What number did I start with?

b) $15 + 7 = 22$ and $22 ÷ 2 = 11$

The number you started with was 11.

Check by using 11 as the input:
$11 × 2 − 7 = 15$ ✓

Exercise 1.5

① Write down the input for the function machines below:

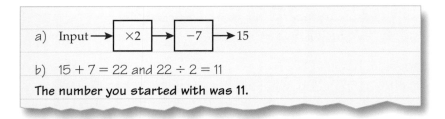

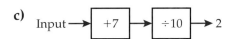

2 What number did I choose?

Look at the Example.

  a) I choose a number, add 4 and get 15.
  b) I choose a number, multiply it by 2, then subtract 8 and get 42.
  c) I choose a number, divide it by 4, then add 3 and get 28.
  d) I choose a number, add 11, then divide by 11 and get 2.
  e) I choose a number, subtract 6, multiply by 5 and get 0.

3 Tom's calculator is broken. When he enters a number, it multiplies that number by 10 and then subtracts 11 and shows the new number instead.

  a) If he enters the number 30, what will the calculator show?
  b) If the calculator shows the number 9, what number did Tom enter?
  c) If Tom enters 7 + 8, which numbers will the calculator try to add together instead?
  d) If the calculator shows the number 1989, what number did Tom enter?

4 Copy and complete these function machines using only the numbers written above them:
  a) 2, 7, 9

  b) 1, 3, 5

  c) 2, 5, 6, 7

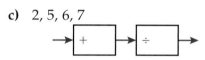

5 Read the box.
  a) What would the combination be on:
     i) 12th January   ii) 24th July
     iii) 7/11/02   iv) 15th May?
  b) What do you notice about the answers to parts i) and iii)?
  c) What is the largest number the combination could be?
  d) What date is it when Lord Number uses this combination?

> Lord Number loves his collection of miniature china vegetables. He keeps them in a safe and changes the combination to the lock every day. He works out his combination according to the date:
> To work out the combination on this day he multiplies the date by 2 and adds on the month number.
> For example, 31st October can be written 31/11. To work out the combination on this day he would calculate: 31 × 2 = 62
>   62 + 11 = 73

Investigations

Read the box above.

6 Lord Number is very forgetful. He has forgotten what date it is. However, he knows the combination on his safe is 34 and that January, February and March have passed.
  a) Write down all the possible days it could be.
  b) He knows that the difference between the date and the month number is 5. What is the date?

> Start by deciding which month you are going to try first.

7 a) Investigate all the combinations that Lord Number uses in January.
  b) What pattern have you noticed?
  c) Repeat this for the other months (you should be able to spot patterns).
  d) Which combinations are only used once a year and what are the dates?
  e) Which combination is used six times in some years and five times in others?

Using letters to stand in for unknown numbers

- Write simple expressions and equations using letters to stand in for unknown numbers
- Solve simple equations by converting them into function machines

In maths we often use a letter to stand in for a number we don't know. This is called **algebra** .

If you chose a number and added 5, you could represent this by writing: $x + 5$
It doesn't matter which letter you use. It is just a method of writing an **unknown** number.

We call $x + 5$ an **expression using algebra** .

The sentence 'I choose a number, subtract 10 and get 12' can be written:
$x - 10 = 12$
This is called an **equation** since it includes an = sign.

If you have more than one unknown number you can use two different letters to stand for the numbers.

Example 1   Write the following as expressions using algebra:

a) I choose a number and multiply it by 5.

b) Janet has some marbles in her pocket. She removes 5 of them. How many marbles are now in her pocket?

c) James has some sweets. If he shares them equally between five people, how many sweets does each person have?

a) $5x$

b) $a - 5$

c) $\dfrac{m}{5}$

> $x \times 5$ using algebra is the same as as $5x$
>
> $m \div 5$ using algebra is the same as $\dfrac{m}{5}$

Example 2   Write the following function machines as equations using algebra and work out the input. Use x to stand in for the input number.

a)   Input → +20 → 30

b)   Input → ÷8 → 3

a) $x + 20 = 30$
   $30 - 20 = 10$ so $x = 10$

b) $\dfrac{x}{8} = 3$
   $3 \times 8 = 24$ so $x = 24$

> The inverse of +20 is −20.

> The inverse of ÷8 is ×8.

Exercise 1.6

1 Write the following expressions, using x to stand in for the number I choose:

    a) I choose a number and subtract 5.   **b)** I choose a number and triple it.

    c) I choose a number and add 32.   **d)** I choose a number and divide it by 7.

2 Georgina, Raashad and Emily are all given the same amount of money. Use the letter b to stand in for the number of pence they are given.

    a) Georgina spends 45p of hers. Write an expression to show how many pence she now has.

    b) Raashad shares his equally with his brother. Write an expression to show how many pence he now has.

    c) Emily is given £1 more. Write an expression to show how many pence she now has.

> Remember £1 = 100p

3 Write the following function machines as equations. Use x to stand in for the input.

    a) Input → | +12 | → 22

    b) Input → | −10 | → 17

    c) Input → | ÷4 | → 5

    d) Input → | ×10 | → 25

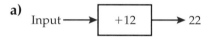 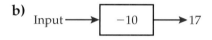

> Look back at Example 2.

4 Find the input for each of the function machines in Q3.

5 Write the following as equations using algebra. Use m to stand in for the number I choose:

    a) I choose a number, add 12 and get 17.

    b) I choose a number, divide it by 5 and get 12.

    c) I choose a number, subtract 70 and get 120.

    d) I choose a number, multiply it by 100 and get 1250.

> For example:
> $m + 12 = 17$

6 Find the unknown number in each part of Q5.

7 Find the value of x in each of these equations:

    a) $x + 12 = 34$ **b)** $x + 71 = 109$

    c) $x - 1 = 0$ **d)** $x - 12 = 144$

8 Find the value of x in each of these equations:

    a) $5x = 35$ **b)** $13x = 143$

    c) $\dfrac{x}{12} = 9$ **d)** $\dfrac{x}{5} = 12$

9 Two whole numbers added together make 15.

    a) Write an equation to show this using letters a and b.

    b) If you multiply the same two whole numbers together you get 50. Write an equation to show this using letters a and b.

    c) Use your equations to find the numbers that a and b must stand in for.

Understanding decimals

Key words
units
tenths
hundredths
thousandths
digit
decimal point

- ⊕ Know the value of each digit in a decimal number with up to 3 decimal places
- ⊕ Read a number written in words, and then write it as a decimal
- ⊕ Add and subtract 0.1 and 0.01 to or from a decimal number

The **decimal point** separates the whole numbers from the parts of whole numbers.

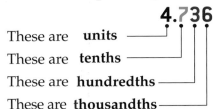

4.736

These are **units**

These are **tenths** — The tenths digit is 7. There are 7 tenths or $\frac{7}{10}$.

These are **hundredths** — The hundredths digit is 3. There are 3 hundredths or $\frac{3}{100}$.

These are **thousandths** — The thousandths digit is 6. There are 6 thousandths or $\frac{6}{1000}$.

Decimal numbers can have different numbers of decimal places:

16.**83** has 2 decimal places;   105.**9** has 1 decimal place.

On a number line, 4.73 is between 4.7 and 4.8.

4.736 is between 4.73 and 4.74.

Example 1   What is the value of the digit underlined in the following numbers:

     a)   5.<u>5</u>32   **b)**   6.05<u>8</u>   **c)**   13.9<u>4</u>

   a)   5 tenths   **b)**   8 thousandths   **c)**   4 hundredths

Example 2   Calculate the value of £0.10 more than £3.62.

   £3.62 + £0.10 = **£3.72**

Add one tenth to six tenths.

Example 3   Write $24 + \frac{6}{10} + \frac{3}{100} + \frac{7}{1000}$ as a decimal number.

$\frac{6}{10}$ is equivalent to 0.6

   $24 + 0.6 + 0.03 + 0.007 = 24 + 0.637$

                        $= \mathbf{24.637}$

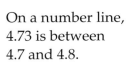

This shows the decimal part of the number with place value cards.

Exercise 2.1

1 What is the value of the digit underlined in the following numbers:
- **a)** 6.3̲87
- **b)** 15̲.96
- **c)** 143.704̲
- **d)** 7.83̲
- **e)** 1̲3.052
- **f)** 0.95̲
- **g)** 249̲.3
- **h)** 1.408̲
- **i)** 26.7̲8
- **j)** 7.56̲0

2 Write the following as decimal numbers:
- **a)** eight, four tenths and seven hundredths
- **b)** eighteen, five tenths and nine hundredths
- **c)** two thousandths, nine hundredths and five tenths
- **d)** fourteen, seven tenths and six thousandths
- **e)** twenty seven and thirty five thousandths
- **f)** eleven and seven hundredths.

> Watch out for numbers which contain the digit zero.

> 35 thousandths is 3 hundredths and 5 thousandths.

3 Write the following numbers in words as units, tenths, hundredths and thousandths:
- **a)** 4.17
- **b)** 8.478
- **c)** 9.056
- **d)** 7.902

> Looking at Q2 might help.

4 Write the following as decimal numbers:
- **a)** $8 + 0.4 + 0.06 + 0.007$
- **b)** $10 + 7 + 0.3 + 0.09$
- **c)** $0.008 + 0.5 + 60$
- **d)** $13 + \frac{5}{100} + \frac{3}{10} + \frac{4}{1000}$
- **e)** $\frac{1}{10} + 9 + \frac{7}{100}$
- **f)** $\frac{6}{1000} + 4 + \frac{7}{100}$

> Convert fractions to decimals first.

5 What is the value of each position on the number lines:

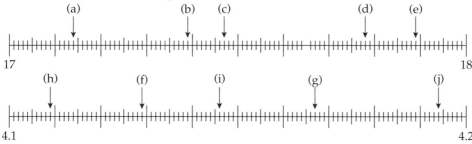

6 Calculate the following:
- **a)** add 0.1 to 7.36
- **b)** add 0.01 to 7.264
- **c)** subtract 0.1 from 5.752
- **d)** £0.01 more than £80.26
- **e)** add $\frac{1}{10}$ to 16.528
- **f)** £0.01 less than £15.70

> The digit 7 can be in the tenths place or in the hundredths.

7 **a)** How many numbers with 2 decimal places between 4.5 and 5.5 contain the digit 7?

b) How many numbers with 2 decimal places between and 7.2 and 8.2 contain the digit 4?

Investigation

8 You need a counter and digit cards. Use the digits 0, 7, 4, 2 and the counter to represent a decimal point.
Investigate how many decimal numbers you can make with up to 3 decimal places.
Each digit can only be used once in each number.

> Be systematic: start with numbers with 1 decimal place, then numbers with 2 decimal places and so on.

Here are three examples: 7.04, 2.407, 74.2

Multiplying and dividing by 10, 100, 1000

⊕ Know how to multiply whole numbers and decimals by 10, 100 or 1000
⊕ Know how to divide whole numbers and decimals by 10, 100 or 1000

When multiplying by 10, 100 or 1000, the digits move one, two or three places to the left on a place value grid.

When dividing by 10, 100 or 1000, the digits move one, two or three places to the right on a place value grid.

Th	H	T	U	t	h	th	
			4	7	8		
		4	7	8			(4.78 × 10)
	4	7	8				(4.78 × 100)
				4	7	8	(4.78 ÷ 10)

Example 1 Multiply 0.76 by 1000.

$0.76 \times 1000 = \mathbf{760}$

The digits move three places to the left on a place value grid.

Example 2 Convert 350 metres into kilometres.

$350 \div 1000 = \mathbf{0.350}$ **kilometres**

1 km = 1000 m.
To change metres into kilometres, divide by 1000.

Exercise 2.2

1 Complete the following calculations:
a) 35.8×10
b) 4.76×100
c) $23.6 \div 10$
d) $400 \div 100$
e) 1000×5.01
f) $736 \div 1000$
g) 100×0.06
h) $0.5 \div 100$

2 Find ☐ in each of the following:
a) $6.49 \times \square = 64.9$
b) $372.4 \div \square = 3.724$
c) $15.35 \div \square = 1.535$
d) $7.64 \times \square = 764$
e) $47.3 \div \square = 0.473$
f) $4.742 \times \square = 4742$
g) $\square \times 4.7 = 4700$
h) $8.5 \div \square = 0.0085$
i) $10 \times \square = 37.1$
j) $1000 \times \square = 4610$

3 Find ☐ in each of the following:
a) $427.3 \times 10 = 42.73 \times \square$
b) $15.8 \div 10 = \square \times 10$
c) $7.34 \times 1000 = \square \times 10$
d) $68.2 \div 100 = \square \div 10$
e) $5.9 \times \square = 5900 \div 100$

Choose numbers so that both sides are equal.

4 Convert:

a) 650 cm into metres
b) 85 cm into millimetres
c) 350 m into kilometres
d) 75 mm into centimetres
e) $\frac{1}{2}$ km into metres
f) 255 ml into litres.

1 m	= 100 cm
1 cm	= 10 mm
1 km	= 1000 m

5 The fun run is 3 km long. What is this in:

a) m
b) cm
c) mm?
d) What are the most sensible units to use?

6 In a DIY shop, a box of ten nails costs £3.20. How much does one nail cost?

7 A bag of 1000 marbles weighs 3720 g. What is the mass of each marble?

8 A pack of ten tennis balls costs £6.45. If I buy 100 balls using four £20 notes, how much change do I get?

9 a) Ten thousand people go to a music concert in Hyde Park. The tickets cost £16.95 each. How much money is raised?

b) The money that is raised is divided equally between 100 charities. How much does each charity receive?

10 Lady Decimal loves her diamonds! She keeps them in an alarmed safe and changes the combination each morning. She chooses a decimal number each Monday.

On Monday Lady Decimal uses:	a new decimal number
On Tuesday she calculates:	Monday's combination × 10
On Wednesday she calculates:	Tuesday's combination × 100
On Thursday she calculates:	Wednesday's combination ÷ 1000
On Friday she calculates:	Thursday's combination × 10
On Saturday she calculates:	Friday's combination × 1000
On Sunday she calculates:	Saturday's combination ÷ 100

One Monday, Lady Decimal chooses 7.4.

a) Work out the combinations for the rest of the week.
b) Work out the combinations for a week when Lady Decimal uses 15.9 on Monday.
c) Another week, she chooses 29.12. Work out that week's combination.
d) What do you notice each time?
e) One Saturday, Lady Decimal has forgotten Friday's combination, so she doesn't know what combination to use! She remembers that on Monday she used 12.01. How can she work out Saturday's combination?

Investigation

11 Use the digits 2 and 4 and a decimal point, together with any of ×1, ÷1, ×10, ÷10, ×100, ÷100, ×1000 or ÷1000. Investigate how many true statements like this you can make:

> Be systematic. For example, try all statements which contain two ÷ signs, then two × signs, then one of each sign.

$$24 \div 100 = 2.4 \div 10$$

Comparing and ordering decimals

⊕ Know how to compare two decimals and decide which is the larger, and which the smaller

⊕ Know how to place a set of decimal numbers in order, smallest to largest

⊕ Know how to order a set of measurements which are in different units

To compare **decimals** , look at the whole number parts first. If they are the same, compare the tenths **digits** . If the tenths are the same, you will need to compare the hundredths digits.

Positions on a number line show the order clearly.

To compare measurements, you may need to change them to a common **unit** first.

$1\,m = 100\,cm$ $1\,cm = 10\,mm$ $1\,km = 1000\,m$

Example 1   Put these decimal numbers in order with the smallest first:

3.25, 3.3, 3.245

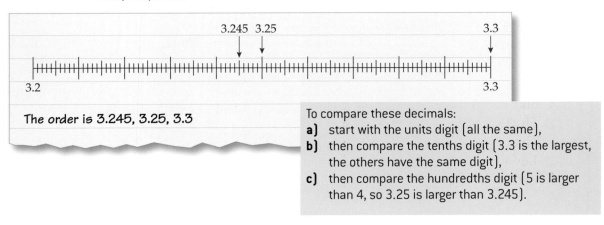

The order is 3.245, 3.25, 3.3

To compare these decimals:
a)   start with the units digit (all the same),
b)   then compare the tenths digit (3.3 is the largest, the others have the same digit),
c)   then compare the hundredths digit (5 is larger than 4, so 3.25 is larger than 3.245).

Example 2   Put these measurements in order with the smallest first:

$36\,cm, 450\,mm, \frac{1}{2}\,m, 0.4\,m$

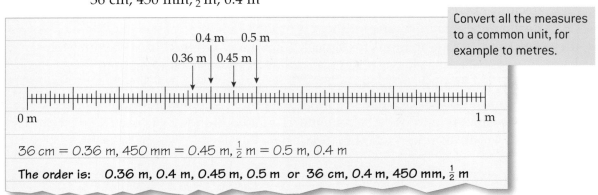

Convert all the measures to a common unit, for example to metres.

$36\,cm = 0.36\,m, 450\,mm = 0.45\,m, \frac{1}{2}\,m = 0.5\,m, 0.4\,m$

The order is: $0.36\,m, 0.4\,m, 0.45\,m, 0.5\,m$ or $36\,cm, 0.4\,m, 450\,mm, \frac{1}{2}\,m$

Example 3   Write this pair of numbers with either $<$ or $>$ between them: 2.35 and 2.53.

2.35 < 2.53

2.35 is less than 2.53

Exercise 2.3

1 Put the following sets of numbers in order, smallest first:
  a) 25, 46, 18, 75, 34
  b) 2.3, 3.1, 5.2, 2.7, 3.7
  c) 5.25, 5.34, 5.19, 5.31, 5.29
  d) 4.1, 5.2, 3.8, 6.1, 4
  e) 3.2, 3.26, 3.206, 3.001, 3.5
  f) 17.7, 17.63, 17.9, 17.07, 17.80
  g) 0.04, 0.6, 0.12, 0.4, 0.62
  h) 9.94, 10.471, 10.5, 19.9, 10.01

2 Write each pair of numbers, with either < or > between them.
  a) 4.32 and 4.23
  b) 18.34 and 18.09
  c) 17.234 and 17.243
  c) 6.013 and 6.12
  e) 5.2 and 5.201
  f) 6.05 and 6.1
  g) 9.308 and 9.31
  h) 1.71 and 1.171
  i) 7.15 and 7.146
  j) 3.029 and 3.03

> < means 'less than'
> > means 'more than'

3 Put the following sets of measurements in order, largest first:
  a) 0.43 m, 45 cm, 420 mm, $\frac{1}{2}$ m
  b) 0.015 km, 1.4 m, 16 m, 145 cm
  c) 650 mm, 0.7 m, 75 cm, $\frac{1}{2}$ m
  d) 0.07 km, 75 m, 0.065 km, 80 m

> Remember to change to a common unit first.

4 These are the times for the Women's 200 m semi-finals in the 2002 Athletic Championships in Munich. Put them in order, first to eighth.

C. Sheehy (Ireland) 23.47 secs
K. Mayr (Austria) 22.99 secs
S. Anderson (GB) 23.60 secs
A. Bikar (Slovenia) 23.18 secs
M. Hurtis (France) 22.46 secs
C. Khabarova (Russia) 23.59 secs
M. Levorato (Italy) 22.93 secs
E. Mashova (Bulgaria) 23.48 secs

5 $14.7 \leqslant x \leqslant 14.9$
  What possible values can x have if it has:
  a) 1 decimal place?
  b) 2 decimal places?
  c) 3 decimal places?
  For parts **b** and **c** give five answers only.

> ≤ means 'less than or equal to'. x could be any value from 14.7 up to 14.9.

Investigation

6 Use the four digit cards 3, 5, 2, 9, together with a decimal point card. Make as many decimal numbers as you can between 3 and 4. The numbers can have 1, 2 or 3 decimal places. Finally, put them in order, smallest first.

> Be systematic. For example: start with numbers with 1 decimal place, then with 2 decimal places, and so on.

Order of operations

⊕ Know which operation [×, ÷, +, −] you should do first
⊕ Understand the commutative law

Key words
addition
subtraction
multiplication
division
operation
commutative

When rearranging a written calculation, it is important to keep the sign or **operation** with the number.

$1 + 2 - 7 + 3$ can be rearranged as $1 - 7 + 3 + 2$.

$1 \times 6 \div 4 \times 2$ can be rearranged as $1 \times 2 \div 4 \times 6$.

When an expression includes **addition** and **subtraction** and **multiplication** and **division**, work from left to right. Do the divisions and multiplications first, then the additions and subtractions.

$6 + 4 \times 7 - 13$

↓

$6 + 28 - 13$

Addition and multiplication are **commutative**.
It does not matter which order you do them in: $2 + 3 = 3 + 2$ and $2 \times 3 = 3 \times 2$
Subtraction and division are **not** commutative.
The order in which you do them is important: $4 - 2 \neq 2 - 4$ and $4 \div 2 \neq 2 \div 4$

Example Calculate $8 \times 7 - 12 \div 3$

$8 \times 7 - 12 \div 3$

$56 - 4 = \mathbf{52}$

Do the division and multiplication first, then do the subtraction.

Exercise 2.4

❶ Work out the answer to these calculations. Rewrite each calculation in a different order, and check that the answers are the same.

a) $8 + 7 + 3$
b) $4 + 5 + 9 + 6$
c) $47 + 21 + 33 + 19$
d) $17 - 5 - 6 - 1$
e) $12 - 3 - 4 - 5$
f) $19 - 1 - 6 - 2$
g) $14 - 5 + 2$
h) $11 + 2 - 8$

❷ Work out the answer to these calculations. Rewrite each calculation in a different order, and check that the answers are the same.

a) $5 \times 2 \times 3$
b) $6 \times 4 \times 2$
c) $7 \times 3 \times 2$
d) $8 \times 5 \times 3$
e) $16 \div 2 \div 4$
f) $48 \div 3 \div 4$
g) $160 \div 5 \div 10$
h) $144 \div 4 \div 12$

❸ Thinking carefully about the rules, rewrite each calculation in a different order, and check that the answers are the same.

a) $4 \times 8 - 1$
b) $7 + 6 \times 8 - 3$
c) $12 - 8 \div 2 + 3$
d) $3 \times 9 + 8 \times 6$
e) $4 \times 2 - 3 \div 1 + 6$
f) $14 \times 8 - 1 + 7$

4 These are the answers to the calculations in the questions below:

18	19	40	27	9	4	19	6
25	7	8	20	15	44	5	

However, an extra answer has been included by mistake. Complete each calculation and find the extra answer.

a) $6 \times 4 + 3$ **b)** $3 \times 5 + 10$ **c)** $16 - 5 \times 2$ **d)** $4 \times 2 - 1$

e) $2 \times 8 + 3$ **f)** $12 + 3 \times 2$ **g)** $11 - 6 \times 1$ **h)** $4 \times 2 + 7$

i) $5 \times 4 - 1$ **j)** $24 - 2 \times 10$ **k)** $37 + 35 \div 5$ **l)** $29 - 27 \div 3$

m) $8 + 4 \times 0$ **n)** $10 + 6 \times 5$

5 Write 'True' or 'False' for each of these. First, guess what the answer will be. Then do the calculations and compare the answers with your guesses.

a) $12 - 7 + 6 = 12 + 6 - 7$ **b)** $7 \times 12 \div 6 = 12 \div 6 \times 7$

c) $9 + 8 - 5 - 2 = 9 - 8 + 5 + 2$ **d)** $12 \div 6 + 30 = 12 + 30 \div 6$

e) $11 - 7 \times 3 = 11 \times 3 - 7$ **f)** $35 \div 5 \div 2 = 35 \div 2 \div 5$

g) $24 \div 2 \times 4 = 24 \times 4 \div 2$ **h)** $16 + 4 \times 3 - 2 = 16 + 3 \times 4 - 2$

> Remember to work from left to right.

6 Complete these calculations:

a) $5 \times 4 + 2 \times 3$ **b)** $9 \times 2 + 3 \times 4$ **c)** $6 \times 2 + 5 \times 3$ **d)** $8 \times 4 + 15 \div 3$

e) $12 \div 6 - 10 \div 5$ **f)** $7 \times 2 - 18 \div 3$ **g)** $24 \div 2 + 4 \times 4$ **h)** $18 \div 1 - 3 \times 4$

i) $7 \times 5 - 4 \times 6$ **j)** $3 \times 8 + 40 \div 5$ **k)** $60 \div 10 - 40 \div 5$ **l)** $9 \div 9 + 4 \times 7$

7 Insert the missing operation signs to make the following correct:

a) $5 - 4 + 1 = 5 \ \square \ 1 \ \square \ 4$

b) $8 - 6 + 4 - 2 = 8 \ \square \ 2 \ \square \ 4 \ \square \ 6$

c) $19 + 7 - 12 + 5 = 19 \ \square \ 12 \ \square \ 5 \ \square \ 7$

d) $12 \times 3 \div 2 = 12 \ \square \ 2 \ \square \ 3$

e) $18 \div 3 \times 6 = 18 \ \square \ 6 \ \square \ 3$

f) $120 \div 6 \times 2 \div 10 = 120 \ \square \ 10 \ \square \ 6 \ \square \ 2$

Investigation

8 Calculate $3 \times 7 + 4 \times 8$.

Investigate different ways of writing this calculation without changing the value of the answer, for example: $8 \times 4 + 7 \times 3$.

Choose your own calculation with mixed operations, and investigate different ways of writing the same calculation.

Brackets and powers

⊕ Understand the meaning of a bracket

⊕ Know the order of mixed operations in a calculation involving

$+, -, \times, \div$, brackets and powers

3^2 is read as 'three squared' or 'three to the power of 2'.
It is shorthand for 3 multiplied by itself, i.e. $3 \times 3 = 3^2$.

A bracket tells you that the contents must be worked out first, before any other operations. Examples of calculations involving brackets are: $(3 + 5) \times 2$ or $(4 + 1)^2 - 6$.

A horizontal line acts like a bracket. For example: $\dfrac{3 + 5}{2}$ means $(3 + 5) \div 2$.

The order for operations is:

brackets

↓

powers

↓

division and **multiplication**

↓

addition and **subtraction**

Example 1 Calculate $7 + (32 + 3) \div 5$

$7 + (32 + 3) \div 5$
$= 7 + 35 \div 5$
$= 7 + 7$
$= 14$

First do the calculation in the brackets. There are no powers so do the division next. Finally, do the addition.

Example 2 Calculate $(3 + 5)^2 - 8 \times 4$

$(3 + 5)^2 - 8 \times 4$
$= 8^2 - 8 \times 4$
$= 64 - 8 \times 4$
$= 64 - 32$
$= 32$

First do the calculation in the brackets. Next, work out 8^2. Do the multiplication and then finally the subtraction.

Exercise 2.5

1 Complete the following calculations:

a) $4 + (7 - 5) \times 3$

b) $2 + 5 \times (6 - 4)$

c) $58 - (4 + 3) \times 6$

d) $5 + (28 + 5) \div 3$

e) $(17 + 10) - (16 - 10)$

f) $15 + 14 - (13 + 7)$

g) $(5 + 2) \times (4 - 1)$

h) $(4 + 3) \times (11 - 4)$

i) $(17 + 3) \div (8 - 4)$

j) $(9 + 3) \div (17 - 5)$

k) $100 - 5 \times (6 + 7)$

l) $(51 + 39) \div 9 + 17$

m) $\dfrac{7 + 9}{2}$

n) $\dfrac{12 - 2}{5}$

2 Copy these statements, putting in brackets to make them true.

a) $3 + 5 \times 2 = 16$

b) $4 \times 5 + 7 = 48$

c) $12 \div 3 \times 2 = 2$

d) $14 \div 10 - 3 = 2$

e) $16 - 4 \div 3 = 4$

f) $12 + 3 \times 0 = 12$

g) $8 + 6 \div 3 + 4 = 2$

h) $28 - 4 \times 3 - 14 = 58$

i) $27 - 5 \times 9 - 5 = 88$

j) $100 - 3 \times 6 + 4 = 78$

3 Calculate the value of:

a) $4^2 - 10$

b) $8 + 9^2$

c) 4×10^2

d) $2^2 \times 3$

e) $2^2 + 3^2$

f) $7^2 - 4^2$

g) $6^2 \div 9$

h) $8^2 + 5^2 - 6^2$

i) $100^2 - 10^2$

j) $\dfrac{8^2}{16}$

4 Calculate the value of:

a) $(2 + 4)^2$

b) $(8 - 3)^2$

c) $2 + (4 + 3)^2$

d) $28 - (9 - 7)^2$

e) $(2 + 5) \times 2^2$

f) $(4 + 3^2) - 1$

g) $2 \times (2 + 5^2) - 5$

h) $\dfrac{4 \times 12}{(1 + 3)^2}$

i) $9 + (7 - 6)^2$

j) $72 \div (5 - 2)^2$

k) $\dfrac{(4^2 - 1)}{6 + 3^2}$

l) $(7 + 3)^2 \div 25$

m) $(3^2 - 2^2)^2$

n) $(5^2 - 4^2)^2$

Remember to calculate the contents of the bracket first.

5 Use $0 - 9$ digit cards.

Deal two cards to make a 2-digit target number such as 47.

Deal four more cards to use as 'ammunition' such as 1, 3, 8 and 5.

Using different operations, brackets and powers, see how close you can get to the target, and score points for the difference. You are trying to get a low score.

For example $(8 \times 5) + 1 + 3 = 44$ scores 3 points because $47 - 44 = 3$

but $(1 + 8) \times 5 + 3 = 48$ scores 1 point because $48 - 47 = 1$.

Shuffle the cards and play again.

Play ten rounds. What is your total score?

Can you get a score under 20?

Investigation

6 Choose the digit 2 and any other three digits, for example 3, 4 and 7.

You may use any of the four operations: $+, -, \times, \div$.

You can make square numbers using the digit 2.

Using each operation and sign only once each time, investigate how many different answers you can make, for example:

$(2 + 4) \times 3 - 7 = 11$

$7 \times (4 - 3) + 2 = 9$

$7 + (3 \times 4)^2 = 151$

Adding

◈ Add whole numbers using a standard written method

◈ Add decimal numbers using a standard written method

◈ Estimate answers to addition by rounding

Key words
column method
estimate
rounding
carrying

When adding using a **column method** :
- write an **estimate** of the answer by **rounding** each value
- write the numbers in columns underneath each other, making sure each digit is in its correct column
- start adding from the right, **carrying** into the next column on the left if necessary
- compare the answer with the estimate as a check.

Example 1 Add 3568, 809 and 3814

Choose numbers close to the ones given that are easy to add up.

```
Estimate: 4000 + 1000 + 4000 = 9000
   3568
 +  809
   3814
   8191
    2 2
```

8191 is close to 9000.

Write the digits in columns making sure the unit digits line up.

Start adding from the right.

8 + 9 + 4 = 21: 2 tens and 1 unit.

Compare the answer with the estimate as a check.

Example 2 Add 5.86, 3.8 and 15.66

```
Estimate: 6 + 4 + 16 = 26
    5.86
 +  3.8
   15.66
   25.32
   12 1
```

25.32 is close to 26.

Choose numbers that are close to the ones given that are easy to add up.

Make sure the decimal points line up to check that the place value of the digits in each column is right.

Compare the answer with the estimate as a check.

Exercise 2.6

1 Work out the following additions:

a) 741 + 203 + 76

b) 5691 + 387 + 204

c) 27 514 + 38 629 + 7813

d) 173 + 4158 + 934

e) 2671 + 3428 + 1795

Remember to write the estimate of the answer first.

2 Work out the following additions:

a) 5.36 + 11.78 + 12.4

b) 0.86 + 17.59 + 1.01

c) 52.17 + 8.3 + 9.89

d) 5.7 + 14.26 + 9.73

e) 3.85 + 15.6 + 27.34

3 Copy and complete the following addition pyramids.
The number in each brick is found by adding the two directly below it:

a)

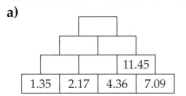

b)

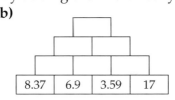

4 Copy the boxes below.

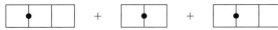

Roll a dice eight times, and after each roll, write the number on the dice in one of the boxes. After the eighth roll, add the three numbers together using the column method.

Play three rounds. What is your total score?

5 At a toy shop, a pack of elves costs £3.87, a pack of goblins costs £7.19, and a pack of orcs costs £5.26. What is the total cost of:

a) a pack of orcs and a pack of goblins

b) a pack of elves and a pack of orcs

c) one pack each of elves, orcs and goblins

d) two packs of elves and a pack of goblins?

6 When a 5-digit integer is added to a 4-digit integer the total is 41 814. What are two possible integers?

Use 1–9 digit cards to help you.

7 Invent problems to match these additions:

a) 1436 + 2351 + 378

b) 15.35 + 9.72 + 8.9

Then give the problem to someone else to solve.

Investigation

8 Use a set of 1–9 digit cards, and three counters.
Shuffle the cards, and deal them out to create three numbers with 2 decimal places, using the counters as decimal points.
Add them together.
Find the total of the digits in the answer, then add the digits in this answer.
Continue adding the digits until you make a 1-digit number.
See the example on the right.

Repeat the activity several times.
What do you notice?

estimate = 17

```
   6 . 3 9
   7 . 6 1
   2 . 8 5
 1 6 . 8 5
     1
```

Total of digits: 1 + 6 + 8 + 5 = 20
                          2 + 0 = 2

Length and perimeter

- ⊕ Know and use the names and abbreviations for units of length
- ⊕ Be able to measure and make a sensible estimate of length
- ⊕ Find out and use the formula for the perimeter of a rectangle
- ⊕ Know how to calculate the perimeter of a shape made from rectangles

Key words
metre (m)
centimetre (cm)
kilometre (km)
millimetre (mm)
perimeter

The unit of length is the **metre (m)** .
Milli means thousandth so a **millimetre (mm)** is a thousandth of a metre(m).
Centi means hundredth so a **centimetre (cm)** is a hundredth of a metre (m).
Kilo means thousand so there are a thousand metres (m) in a **kilometre (km)** .

10 mm = 1 cm
1000 mm = 100 cm = 1 m
1 000 000 mm = 100 000 cm = 1000 m = 1 km

The thickness of this line is about 1 mm:
The length of this line is about 1 cm:
The width of an ordinary door is about 1 m.
A kilometre is about ten times the length of a football pitch.
We still sometimes use miles to measure distance. A mile is longer than a kilometre.
5 miles is about the same as 8 kilometres.
 Perimeter means the distance all the way around the edge of a shape.
The perimeter of a rectangle is: 2 × length + 2 × width

Example 1 Find the perimeter of this shape:

Perimeter = 10 cm + 10 cm + 4 cm + 3 cm + 6 cm + 7 cm
= 40 cm

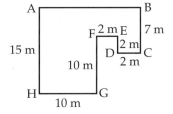

Example 2 Find the perimeter of this shape:

AB = HG + FE + DC
= 10 m + 2 m + 2 m
= 14 m
Perimeter = AB + BC + CD + DE + EF + FG + GH + HA
= 14 m + 7 m + 2 m + 2 m + 2 m + 10 m + 10 m + 15 m
= 62 m

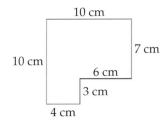

Find the missing lengths first. AB means the line joining A and B.

Exercise 3.1

1 Calculate the perimeters of these shapes:

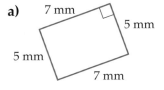

a)
7 mm
5 mm
5 mm
7 mm

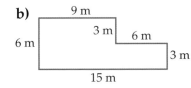

b)
9 m
3 m
6 m
6 m
3 m
15 m

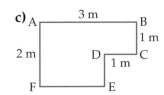

c) A
3 m
B
2 m
1 m
D
C
F
1 m
E

2 Calculate the perimeter of these shapes:
  a) a rectangular carpet, width 2 m and length 3 m
  b) a rectangular garden, length 12 m, width 5 m
  c) a square of side 2.3 cm
  d) a square of side 4.2 cm.

3 Write down the unit you would use to make the following measurements. You can choose from mm, cm, m and km.
  a) Distance around a football pitch
  b) Length of a matchstick
  c) Length of the tape in a video
  d) Width of a staple
  e) Distance a mobile phone signal travels
  f) Thickness of an electric cable
  g) Length of a javelin throw
  h) Height of a high jump.

4 Play with a partner. Copy the table. Estimate the length of each line to the nearest mm and record both your answers. Measure each line (use a piece of string to help you) and calculate the difference

Line	Estimate	Measure	Difference	My points
A				
B				

between your estimate and the accurate measurement. Compare your answer. Whoever has the smaller difference gains one point. If you estimate exactly, score two points.

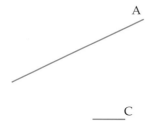
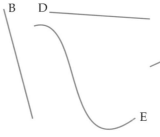

5 Calculate the perimeter of the shape.
AB = 120 mm, BC = 6 cm, CD = 5 cm, DE = 1 cm, FG = 80 mm and GH = 5 cm.

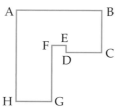

Change all the measurements to cm first.

6 This swimming pool has a perimeter of 120 m. The length is twice the width.
  a) What is the length of this pool?
  b) What is the width of this pool?

Investigation

7 Use squared paper.
  a) How many different rectangles can you draw using 12 whole squares?
  b) Do they all have the same perimeter?
  c) What other shapes can you make using 12 whole squares?
  d) Calculate or count the squares in their perimeters.
  e) Do they all have the same perimeter?
  f) Write a hint for someone who is trying to make a rectangle from 100 squares with the smallest possible perimeter.

Areas of rectangles

Key words
square centimetre (cm²)
square metre (m²)
square millimetre (mm²)
square kilometre (km²)
area

- ⊕ Know and use the names and abbreviations for units of area
- ⊕ Be able to measure and make a sensible estimate of area
- ⊕ Know the formulae for the areas of a rectangle and of a right-angled triangle
- ⊕ Know how to calculate the areas of shapes made from rectangles
- ⊕ Solve problems in everyday life involving length and area

The **area** is the space inside a two dimensional shape.
Units most often used are:

square millimetre (mm²)

square centimetre (cm²)

square metre (m²)

square kilometre (km²) ·

We can calculate the area of a rectangle by multiplying the length by the width.

Area = length × width

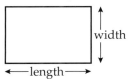

We can calculate the area of a right-angled triangle by imagining it is half of a rectangle.

Area = ½ (length × width)

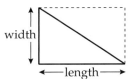

Example   Find the area of this shape:

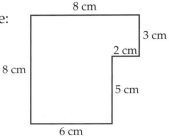

This can be done in different ways. Either break the shape down into rectangles or take the missing rectangle out of the corner of the large rectangle.

Breaking the shape into two rectangles:

Area of rectangle A	
= 8 cm × 3 cm	
= 24 cm²	
Area of rectangle B	
= 6 cm × 5 cm	
= 30 cm²	
Total area of A + B	
= 24 cm² + 30 cm²	
= **54 cm²**	

Take a rectangle away from the large rectangle:

Area of large rectangle	
= 8 cm × 8 cm	
= 64 cm²	
Area of rectangle C	
= 2 cm × 5 cm	
= 10 cm²	
Total area of whole − C	
= 64 cm² − 10 cm²	
= **54 cm²**	

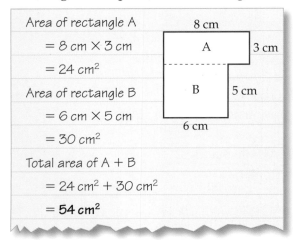

Exercise 3.2

1 Calculate or count squares to find the areas of these rectangles.
Make sure you record the units too.

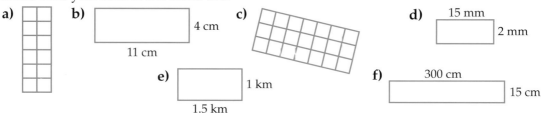

a)
b) 11 cm, 4 cm
c)
d) 15 mm, 2 mm
e) 1.5 km, 1 km
f) 300 cm, 15 cm

2 Which units would you use to measure the areas of the following shapes?
Choose from: mm² cm² m² or km²

a) the sole of your foot
b) the cover of this book
c) the top of the table
d) the floor of this room
e) a mouse's footprint
f) Spain.

3 These shapes are made from rectangles. Find the areas of the shaded parts.

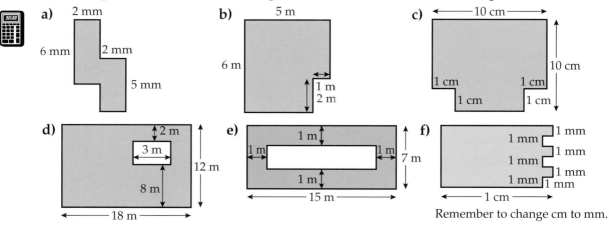

a) 2 mm, 6 mm, 2 mm, 5 mm

b) 5 m, 6 m, 1 m, 2 m

c) 10 cm, 10 cm, 1 cm, 1 cm, 1 cm, 1 cm

d) 2 m, 3 m, 12 m, 8 m, 18 m

e) 1 m, 1 m, 1 m, 1 m, 7 m, 15 m

f) 1 mm, 1 mm, 1 mm, 1 mm, 1 mm, 1 mm, 1 mm, 1 cm
Remember to change cm to mm.

4 a) Estimate the area of the palm of your hand in cm².
b) Draw around your hand onto centimetre
squared paper.
c) Record the number of square centimetres covered.
How accurate was your estimate? Compare your result with your partner.

> Count part squares less than half as zero, and parts bigger than half as one.

5 Find the width and length of rectangles which have:

a) area 10 cm², perimeter 14 cm
b) area 24 cm², perimeter 22 cm
c) area 16 mm², perimeter 16 mm
d) area 7.5 km², perimeter 13 km

Explain how you worked these out.

> You might find it helpful to sketch the rectangles.

6 Play with a partner. You will need one normal dice, and a piece of squared paper each.
In one game, you have four turns each. Take turns to throw the dice and shade in that
number of squares on your piece of paper. The squares must be joined to each other by at
least one side. At the end of the game the winner is the one whose shape has the largest
perimeter.

Investigation

7 On squared paper draw these shapes and cut them out. Join
them in as many different ways as you can and record the shapes
you make. For each shape, note down the area and the perimeter.
Do you always get the same area? Does the perimeter stay the same?

Connecting 2-D and 3-D

Key words
face
edge
vertex
vertices
cube
cuboid
3-D

- Know that cubes and cuboids have square and rectangular faces
- Use other 2-D shapes to visualise and describe 3-D shapes and consider their properties
- Be able to draw 2-D representations of 3-D shapes

A **face** is the flat surface of a solid.

An **edge** is where two faces meet.

A **vertex** is where three or more edges meet.

Vertices is the plural of vertex.

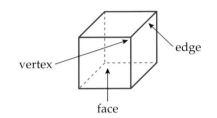

A **cube** has six identical square faces.

A **cuboid** has three pairs of rectangular faces. Opposite faces are the same shape and size.

A **tetrahedron** has four triangular faces.

A **prism** has two identical faces that are parallel.

A **hemisphere** has one circular face and one curved face.

A **cylinder** has two circular faces and one curved face.

cube   cuboid   tetrahedron

triangular prism   hemisphere   cylinder

We sometimes use isometric paper to draw representations of **3-D** shapes.

cube

Example   Describe the 3-D shapes that these drawings represent:

> This shape is made from six cubes. There are three in a line on the bottom layer, two together on the middle layer and one on the top layer.

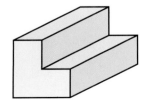

> This shape is a prism. It has two L-shaped faces and six rectangular faces. It has 18 edges and 12 vertices.

Exercise 3.3

1 Work with a partner. Take a handful of cubes each. Take it in turns to make a 3-D shape and describe it so that your partner can make it. If your cubes are coloured, try not to use colour as a clue!

> Think about how many edges, faces and vertices your shapes have.

2 Use isometric paper to draw these shapes. Shade the front faces.

i)   **ii)**   **iii)** 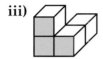 **iv)**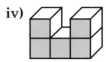

> Draw all the front faces first.

3 Build-a-shape game. You will need a normal dice and some isometric paper.
Take turns to throw the dice. 1 = square; 2 = rectangle; 3 = triangle; 4 = circle; 5 = hexagon; 6 = another throw. Collect a face for each number you throw. The winner is the first to collect enough 2-D faces to make a 3-D shape and to sketch that shape.

4 This skeleton 3-D shape is made from four 10 cm lengths of wire and eight 5 cm lengths of wire.

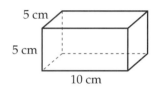

a) Write the list of lengths of wire for each of the skeletons shown below:

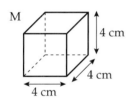

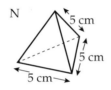

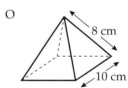

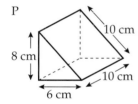

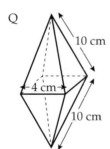

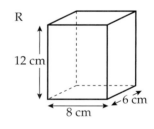

b) How many faces, edges and vertices does each shape have?

Investigation

5 Lucy made some models using five cubes each time. She dipped her models in paint and used them to print the shapes below.

i)   **ii)**   **iii)**

What could her models have looked like? Use cubes to make all the possible models. Draw your models using isometric paper.

3.4 Cubes and cuboids

- Know what the nets of cubes and cuboids look like
- Find out and use the formula for the surface area of a cube and cuboid
- Calculate the surface area of shapes made from cubes and cuboids

The **surface area** of a three dimensional shape is the total area of all its faces.
Drawing the net helps us to make sure we have added up the areas of all of the faces.

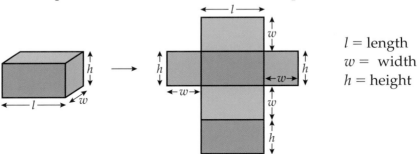

l = length
w = width
h = height

You can see that there are two blue rectangles, two green rectangles and two red rectangles.

Example 1 Find the surface area of this cuboid.

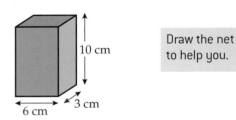

10 cm

6 cm   3 cm

Draw the net to help you.

Area of purple rectangle = 6 × 10 cm = 60 cm²

Area of pink rectangle   = 3 × 10 cm = 30 cm²

Area of brown rectangle = 6 × 3 cm = 18 cm²

Total surface area   = 2 × 60 cm² + 2 × 30 cm² + 2 × 18 cm²

                          = **216 cm²**

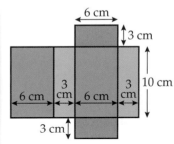

Example 2 Find the surface area of these steps:

Area of red face = 2 × 2 − 1 × 1 = 3,

but there are 2 of these so area of red faces = **6**.

Area of the 2 green sides = 1 × 1 + 1 × 1 = **2**

Area of the 2 blue sides = 1 × 1 + 1 × 1 = **2**

Area of the base = 2 × 1 = **2**

Area of the back = 2 × 1 = **2**

Total surface area = 6 + 2 + 2 + 2 + 2 = **14 square units**

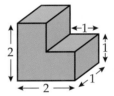

You may find it helpful to sketch the different faces of the steps with their dimensions.

Exercise 3.4

1 Here are the nets of different cuboids. For each one, find the area of the yellow, blue and green shapes. Then find the total surface area for each net.

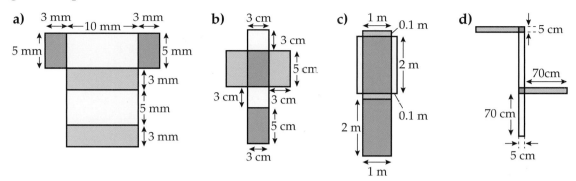

2 Find the areas of the front, side and top faces of the following shapes:

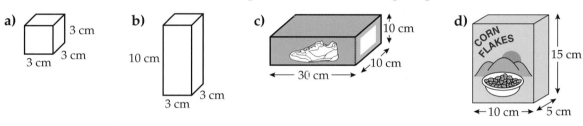

3 Find the surface area for each of the shapes in Q2.

4 These shapes are made from cuboids.
   a) Find the areas of the faces which are NOT rectangular.
   b) Find the total surface areas of the shapes.

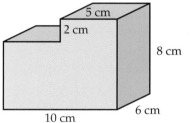 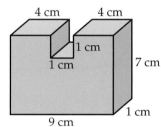

5 Eight cubes with 1 cm edges are individually covered in sticky paper.
   a) How much paper is needed?
   b) The eight cubes are then wrapped in a single parcel. What arrangement of cubes would need the least wrapping paper?

Investigation

6 Jani has been given a garden stick of length 120 cm, and eight corner connectors.

She cuts the stick into twelve lengths and uses the corner connectors to make a cuboid. She records her results in a table:

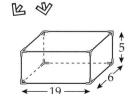

Length (cm)	Width (cm)	Height (cm)	Total surface area
19	6	5	

She only uses whole number values. What other cuboids could she make? Keep a table of your results and write down what you notice.

4.1 Fractions

⊕ Know how to use fractions to describe part of something

⊕ Write an improper fraction as a mixed number

⊕ Write a mixed number as an improper fraction

Key words
fraction
denominator
numerator
proper fraction
improper fraction
mixed number

One way to think of a **fraction** is as a number of parts of a whole.

The bottom number in a fraction is the number of parts we divide the whole into. These parts are the same size. The bottom number is called the **denominator**.

The top number in a fraction is the number of these parts we are counting. The top number is called the **numerator**.

These are **proper fractions**: the denominator is greater than the numerator. So the fraction is made of some of the parts of the whole.

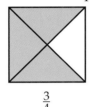

$\frac{3}{4}$

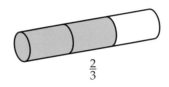

$\frac{2}{3}$

These are **improper fractions**: the denominator is less than the numerator. An improper fraction can be converted to a **mixed number** – part whole number and part fraction. $\frac{5}{2}$ as a mixed number is $2\frac{1}{2}$.

$\frac{5}{2}$ or $2\frac{1}{2}$

$\frac{7}{4}$ or $1\frac{3}{4}$

Example 1 Convert $3\frac{5}{8}$ into an improper fraction.

$3 \times \frac{8}{8} = \frac{24}{8}$.

$\frac{24}{8} + \frac{5}{8} = \frac{29}{8}$

Start by finding the number of eighths in 3 wholes by multiplying 8 by 3.

Example 2 Convert $\frac{32}{5}$ into a mixed number.

$32 \div 5 = 6$ remainder 2

therefore $\frac{32}{5} = 6\frac{2}{5}$

Divide 32 by 5 to find how many wholes can be made from $\frac{32}{5}$.

Exercise 4.1 .... Fractions ...

1 a) Look at each shape. Write the fraction which is shaded.

i) 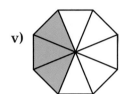   **ii)** 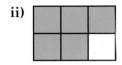   **iii)**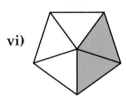

iv)   **v)**   **vi)**

b) Write the fraction of the unshaded part of each shape.

2 Convert these mixed numbers into improper fractions:

  a) $2\frac{3}{4}$ **b)** $3\frac{1}{3}$ **c)** $5\frac{2}{5}$ **d)** $4\frac{1}{6}$ **e)** $1\frac{5}{8}$

  f) $1\frac{4}{7}$ **g)** $4\frac{1}{2}$ **h)** $2\frac{3}{10}$ **i)** $3\frac{11}{15}$ **j)** $6\frac{2}{3}$

3 Convert these improper fractions into mixed numbers:

  a) $\frac{11}{5}$ **b)** $\frac{22}{3}$ **c)** $\frac{7}{4}$ **d)** $\frac{18}{7}$ **e)** $\frac{9}{2}$

  f) $\frac{11}{6}$ **g)** $\frac{32}{9}$ **h)** $\frac{43}{11}$ **i)** $\frac{27}{8}$ **j)** $\frac{40}{12}$

4 Write your answers to the following as mixed numbers:

  a) How many hours equal 90 minutes?   **b)** How many weeks equal 10 days?

  c) How many minutes in 130 seconds?   **d)** How many metres in 130 cm?

5 Copy the pairs of numbers, writing $<$, $>$ or $=$ between each pair:

  a) $\frac{11}{2}$ and $\frac{25}{7}$ **b)** $2\frac{1}{5}$ and $3\frac{1}{5}$ **c)** $6\frac{3}{8}$ and $\frac{53}{8}$ **d)** $\frac{17}{4}$ and $4\frac{3}{4}$

  e) $5\frac{4}{5}$ and $\frac{27}{5}$ **f)** $\frac{31}{12}$ and $2\frac{7}{12}$ **g)** $6\frac{2}{3}$ and $\frac{22}{3}$ **h)** $\frac{46}{10}$ and $4\frac{3}{5}$

  i) $8\frac{1}{2}$ and $\frac{33}{4}$ **j)** $\frac{23}{11}$ and $2\frac{3}{11}$

> Try converting both numbers to a mixed number to compare them.

6 Choose any odd number between 20 and 40, for example 23.
Now halve it. Write it as a number of halves: $\frac{23}{2}$, and then as a mixed number: $11\frac{1}{2}$.
Next write it as a number of thirds: $\frac{23}{3} = 7\frac{2}{3}$.
Continue like this, up to tenths.
Repeat for a different number.

7 Oranges are cut into quarters. At half-time in a hockey match,
eleven players and four substitutes each have a quarter of orange.
How many oranges do they have between them? How many
are left from a bag of ten oranges?

Equivalent fractions

Key words
numerator
denominator
equivalent fraction
cancel
lowest terms

- Recognise sets of equivalent fractions
- Simplify a fraction by cancelling
- Reduce a fraction to its lowest terms

The fractions $\frac{1}{3}$, $\frac{2}{6}$ and $\frac{4}{12}$ are **equivalent**. The same fraction of each grid is shaded.

You can use fraction walls to find sets of **equivalent fractions**.

1 whole							
$\frac{1}{2}$				$\frac{1}{2}$			
$\frac{1}{4}$		$\frac{1}{4}$		$\frac{1}{4}$		$\frac{1}{4}$	
$\frac{1}{8}$	$\frac{1}{8}$	$\frac{1}{8}$	$\frac{1}{8}$	$\frac{1}{8}$	$\frac{1}{8}$	$\frac{1}{8}$	$\frac{1}{8}$
$\frac{1}{16}$	$\frac{1}{16}$ $\frac{1}{16}$ $\frac{1}{16}$ $\frac{1}{16}$ $\frac{1}{16}$ $\frac{1}{16}$ $\frac{1}{16}$ $\frac{1}{16}$ $\frac{1}{16}$ $\frac{1}{16}$ $\frac{1}{16}$ $\frac{1}{16}$ $\frac{1}{16}$ $\frac{1}{16}$ $\frac{1}{16}$						

This fraction wall illustrates the following sets of equivalent fractions:

$\frac{1}{2} = \frac{2}{4} = \frac{4}{8} = \frac{8}{16}$, $\frac{1}{4} = \frac{2}{8} = \frac{4}{16}$, $\frac{3}{4} = \frac{6}{8} = \frac{12}{16}$

You can also use a multiplication square to find sets of equivalent fractions.

1	2	3	4	5	6	7	8	9	10
2	4	6	8	10	12	14	16	18	20
3	6	9	12	15	18	21	24	27	30
4	8	12	16	20	24	28	32	36	40
5	10	15	20	25	30	35	40	45	50
6	12	18	24	30	36	42	48	54	60

The two highlighted rows show the following set of equivalent fractions: $\left(\frac{2}{5}, \frac{4}{10}, \frac{6}{15}, \frac{8}{20}, \ldots \right)$ Some of these fractions can be simplified by dividing both numerator and denominator by the same number – this is called **cancelling**. When a fraction can't be simplified by cancelling (e.g. $\frac{2}{5}$), we say it is in its **lowest terms**.

Example 1   Find the missing number: $\frac{3}{4} = \frac{\square}{20}$

The denominator has been multiplied by 5. (4 × 5 = 20)

The numerator, 3, must also be multiplied by 5 (5 × 3 = 15), giving $\frac{3}{4} = \frac{15}{20}$

Example 2 Write $\frac{16}{40}$ in its lowest terms.

$\frac{16}{40} = \frac{4}{10}$

$\frac{4}{10} = \frac{2}{5}$

Cancel by dividing both the numerator and denominator by 4. Divide again by 2. Now the fraction is in its lowest terms.

Exercise 4.2

1 Copy each pair of equivalent fractions and find the missing numbers:

a) $\frac{2}{3} = \frac{\square}{6}$ b) $\frac{3}{5} = \frac{6}{\square}$ c) $\frac{\square}{12} = \frac{2}{6}$ d) $\frac{5}{6} = \frac{\square}{24}$ e) $\frac{3}{4} = \frac{\square}{12}$

f) $\frac{5}{8} = \frac{10}{\square}$ g) $\frac{\square}{10} = \frac{21}{30}$ h) $\frac{6}{\square} = \frac{18}{21}$ i) $\frac{5}{\square} = \frac{15}{27}$ j) $\frac{\square}{20} = \frac{35}{100}$

2 Write the following, in their lowest terms:

a) $\frac{6}{10}$ b) $\frac{12}{16}$ c) $\frac{16}{24}$ d) $\frac{20}{25}$ e) $\frac{15}{18}$ f) $\frac{18}{60}$ g) $\frac{28}{49}$ h) $\frac{11}{33}$ i) $\frac{35}{45}$ j) $\frac{20}{32}$

3 In each set four fractions are equivalent. Write down the fraction which is not.

a) $\frac{6}{8}, \frac{3}{4}, \frac{30}{40}, \frac{15}{24}, \frac{9}{12}$ b) $\frac{6}{9}, \frac{12}{18}, \frac{4}{6}, \frac{14}{27}, \frac{16}{24}$ c) $\frac{12}{15}, \frac{4}{5}, \frac{8}{10}, \frac{24}{35}, \frac{40}{50}$ d) $\frac{5}{6}, \frac{35}{42}, \frac{20}{24}, \frac{10}{12}, \frac{15}{20}$

e) $\frac{42}{60}, \frac{56}{70}, \frac{21}{30}, \frac{14}{20}, \frac{7}{10}$ f) $\frac{9}{21}, \frac{18}{42}, \frac{15}{28}, \frac{3}{7}, \frac{6}{14}$ g) $\frac{4}{18}, \frac{8}{36}, \frac{14}{63}, \frac{16}{54}, \frac{2}{9}$ h) $\frac{6}{16}, \frac{15}{40}, \frac{24}{72}, \frac{12}{32}, \frac{3}{8}$

4 Use a set of 1–30 number cards. Shuffle them and deal out ten pairs of cards. For each pair, place the smaller number as the numerator and the larger as the denominator of a fraction. Reduce each of the ten fractions to its lowest terms.

$$\frac{1\ 0}{2\ 4}$$

5 Who am I?

a) I am a fraction equivalent to $\frac{3}{4}$. My denominator is 12.

b) I am a fraction equivalent to $\frac{4}{5}$. My numerator is 20.

c) I am a fraction equivalent to $\frac{2}{3}$. My numerator and denominator have a total of 15.

d) I am a fraction. You'll need four digits to write me down. My digits are all even. My numerator and denominator have a total of 22. I reduce to $\frac{7}{12}$ in my lowest terms.

Investigation

6 You need a set of 1–9 digit cards.
Draw a large version of this 'equivalent fractions board'.
Investigate different ways of placing the cards to create pairs of equivalent fractions.
Here is one example:

$$\frac{\square}{\square\ \square} = \frac{\square}{\square}$$

$$\frac{9}{1\ 2} = \frac{3}{4}$$

Work systematically. For example: keep the denominator of the right hand fraction fixed, and explore different ways of arranging the cards to make a fraction which is equivalent.

Comparing fractions

⊕ Convert a simple fraction to a decimal

⊕ Convert a decimal to a fraction

⊕ Put a set of fractions in order

To **convert** a fraction to a decimal, find an **equivalent fraction** with a denominator of 10 or 100. For example: $\frac{2}{5} = \frac{4}{10}$; four tenths = 0.4

$\frac{21}{50} = \frac{42}{100}$; forty two hundredths is four tenths and two hundredths = 0.42

The fractions $\frac{3}{5}, \frac{3}{4}, \frac{7}{10}$ and $\frac{1}{2}$ can be ordered by either:

converting each to a decimal by first converting to tenths or hundredths:

$\frac{3}{5} = \frac{6}{10}$; $\frac{6}{10} = 0.6$ $\frac{7}{10} = 0.7$

$\frac{3}{4} = \frac{75}{100}$; $\frac{75}{100} = 0.75$ $\frac{1}{2} = \frac{5}{10}$; $\frac{5}{10} = 0.5$

or

changing them to equivalent fractions with the same denominator and placing them on a number line:

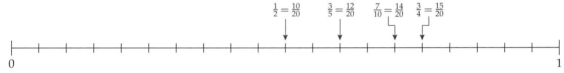

$\frac{1}{2} = \frac{10}{20}$ $\frac{3}{5} = \frac{12}{20}$ $\frac{7}{10} = \frac{14}{20}$ $\frac{3}{4} = \frac{15}{20}$

0   1

In both cases, the order is: $\frac{1}{2}, \frac{3}{5}, \frac{7}{10}, \frac{3}{4}$.

Example 1   Write $<$ or $>$ between the pair of fractions $\frac{4}{5}$ and $\frac{17}{20}$. Convert each one to a decimal first.

$\frac{4}{5} = \frac{8}{10} = 0.8$ ——————————— Multiply numerator and denominator by 2.

$\frac{17}{20} = \frac{85}{100} = 0.85$ ———————— Multiply numerator and denominator by 5.

0.8 is less than 0.85, so $\frac{4}{5} < \frac{17}{20}$

Example 2   Convert 0.35 to a fraction in its lowest terms.

0.35 is 3 tenths and 5 hundredths or 35 hundredths.

$\frac{35}{100} = \frac{7}{20}$

Divide numerator and denominator by 5.

Exercise 4.3

1 Draw each of the following number lines. Mark the position of each fraction, then write them out in order, smallest first:

First change them to equivalent fractions with the same denominator.

a)

$\frac{3}{10}$ $\frac{1}{2}$ $\frac{2}{5}$
$\frac{3}{4}$ $\frac{1}{4}$

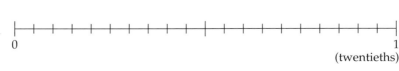

0   1
(twentieths)

b)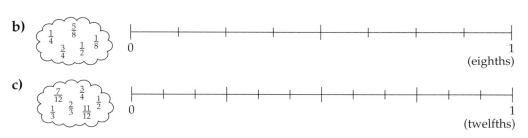

c)

$\frac{7}{12}$ $\frac{3}{4}$ $\frac{3}{4}$
$\frac{1}{3}$ $\frac{2}{3}$ $\frac{11}{12}$ $\frac{1}{2}$

0 ————————————— 1
(twelfths)

2 Write $<$ or $>$ between each pair of fractions, by placing them on a number line.

   a) $\frac{3}{4}$ and $\frac{2}{3}$ **b)** $\frac{4}{5}$ and $\frac{7}{10}$ **c)** $\frac{1}{2}$ and $\frac{1}{3}$ **d)** $\frac{5}{12}$ and $\frac{1}{3}$ **e)** $\frac{2}{3}$ and $\frac{5}{6}$

   f) $\frac{3}{8}$ and $\frac{1}{4}$ **g)** $\frac{17}{20}$ and $\frac{8}{10}$ **h)** $\frac{36}{50}$ and $\frac{7}{10}$ **i)** $\frac{11}{15}$ and $\frac{3}{5}$ **j)** $\frac{1}{6}$ and $\frac{3}{24}$

3 Convert each fraction to a decimal:

   a) $\frac{7}{10}$ **b)** $\frac{3}{10}$ **c)** $\frac{1}{5}$ **d)** $\frac{4}{5}$ **e)** $\frac{1}{2}$ **f)** $\frac{3}{4}$ **g)** $\frac{3}{100}$ **h)** $\frac{1}{4}$ **i)** $\frac{18}{25}$ **j)** $\frac{11}{50}$

4 Write $<$ or $>$ between each pair of fractions, by first converting each fraction to a decimal:

   a) $\frac{2}{5}$ and $\frac{1}{2}$ **b)** $\frac{8}{10}$ and $\frac{3}{4}$ **c)** $\frac{1}{4}$ and $\frac{2}{5}$

   d) $\frac{19}{100}$ and $\frac{2}{10}$ **e)** $\frac{11}{50}$ and $\frac{1}{10}$ **f)** $\frac{2}{5}$ and $\frac{41}{100}$

5 Convert each decimal to a fraction in its lowest terms:

   a) 0.3   **b)** 0.6   **c)** 0.42   **d)** 0.64   **e)** 1.32   **f)** 2.78   **g)** 5.08   **h)** 7.12

6 Put these in order, smallest to largest:

   a) $\frac{1}{2}, \frac{1}{4}, 0.3, \frac{31}{100}, 0.2$ **b)** $\frac{3}{5}, \frac{59}{100}, \frac{3}{4}, 0.7, \frac{1}{2}$ **c)** $0.34, 0.43, \frac{4}{10}, \frac{6}{20}, \frac{19}{50}$

   d) $0.91, \frac{4}{5}, \frac{19}{20}, 0.85, \frac{9}{10}$ **e)** $1\frac{3}{4}, 1.35, 1\frac{7}{10}, 1.4, 1\frac{16}{20}$

7 Use a set 1 – 10 number cards. Shuffle them and deal out five pairs of cards. For each pair place the smaller number as the numerator and the larger as the denominator of a fraction. Write the five fractions in order, smallest to largest.
Reshuffle and repeat several times.

8 Who am I?

   a) I am a proper fraction. My decimal equivalent is 0.6. My denominator is 20.

   b) I am an improper fraction. My decimal equivalent is 1.75. My numerator and denominator have a total of 55.

   c) I am a number with 2 decimal places equivalent to a fraction with a denominator of 20. Its numerator is the total of my tenths and hundredths digits.

Investigation

9 You need a set of 0 – 9 digit cards.
Draw a large version of this diagram.
Investigate different ways of placing the cards to create a fraction and its equivalent decimal.
Here are two examples:

$$\frac{1}{4} = 0.25 \qquad\qquad \frac{4}{5} = 0.8$$

Adding and subtracting fractions

Key words
equivalent fraction
lowest terms
improper fractions
mixed number
denominator

- ⊕ Add two fractions
- ⊕ Subtract two fractions
- ⊕ Break up a calculation into steps

If fractions have the same denominator, drawing grids or number lines can help when adding and subtracting them.

$$\frac{3}{8} + \frac{1}{8} = \frac{4}{8}$$

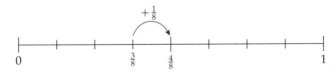

If the fractions have different denominators, convert them to **equivalent fractions** that have the same denominator:

Rewrite $\frac{3}{4} + \frac{1}{2}$ as $\frac{3}{4} + \frac{2}{4}$

$$\frac{3}{4} + \frac{2}{4} = \frac{5}{4}$$

$$\frac{5}{4} = 1\frac{1}{4}$$

So $\frac{3}{4} + \frac{1}{2} = 1\frac{1}{4}$.

Example 1   Work out $\frac{7}{8} + \frac{5}{8}$

$$\frac{7}{8} + \frac{5}{8} = \frac{12}{8}$$
$$\frac{12}{8} = 1\frac{4}{8}$$
$$1\frac{4}{8} = 1\frac{1}{2}$$

Once you have the answer $\frac{12}{8}$, change the improper fraction to a mixed number $(1\frac{4}{8})$. Reduce the fraction to its lowest terms $(1\frac{1}{2})$.

Example 2   Work out $\frac{3}{4} - \frac{1}{8}$

$$\frac{3}{4} - \frac{1}{8} = \frac{6}{8} - \frac{1}{8}$$
$$\frac{6}{8} - \frac{1}{8} = \frac{5}{8}$$
So $\frac{3}{4} - \frac{1}{8} = \frac{5}{8}$

Find an equivalent fraction to $\frac{3}{4}$ so that both fractions in the subtraction have the same denominator.

Exercise 4.4

1 Work these out, and express the answer in its lowest terms:

a) $\frac{3}{5} + \frac{1}{5}$ **b)** $\frac{7}{8} - \frac{1}{8}$ **c)** $\frac{8}{10} + \frac{4}{10} - \frac{3}{10}$ **d)** $\frac{5}{6} + \frac{1}{6} + \frac{4}{6}$

e) $1\frac{1}{8} + \frac{3}{8}$ **f)** $2\frac{7}{10} - \frac{3}{10}$ **g)** $3\frac{5}{6} + \frac{5}{6}$ **h)** $4\frac{1}{4} - \frac{3}{4}$

i) $3\frac{1}{5} - 2\frac{2}{5}$ **j)** $1\frac{3}{4} + 2\frac{3}{4}$

2 Find ☐ in each of the following:

a) $\frac{3}{4} + ☐ = 1$

b) $\frac{7}{10} - ☐ = \frac{6}{10} = \frac{3}{5}$

c) $\frac{3}{8} + ☐ + \frac{1}{8} = 1\frac{1}{8}$

d) $\frac{7}{12} - \frac{1}{12} - ☐ = \frac{1}{12}$

e) $1\frac{1}{5} + ☐ = 2\frac{3}{5}$

f) $3\frac{11}{12} - ☐ = 2\frac{1}{2}$

g) $☐ + \frac{3}{4} = 4$

h) $☐ - \frac{2}{3} = 3\frac{2}{3}$

> What is $2\frac{1}{2}$ as an improper fraction with 12 as the denominator?

3 Work out:

a) $\frac{3}{4} + \frac{1}{2}$

b) $\frac{2}{3} + \frac{1}{6}$

c) $\frac{5}{8} - \frac{1}{4}$

d) $\frac{7}{10} - \frac{1}{5}$

e) $\frac{3}{5} + \frac{1}{5} + \frac{1}{10}$

f) $\frac{1}{2} + \frac{1}{4} + 1\frac{1}{4}$

g) $1\frac{1}{2} + \frac{3}{4}$

h) $\frac{1}{8} + 1\frac{3}{4}$

i) $\frac{1}{3} + \frac{2}{3} + \frac{1}{6}$

j) $\frac{3}{5} + \frac{1}{4} + \frac{2}{5}$

> Remember to convert to equivalent fractions first. For example in part **a**, $\frac{1}{2} = \frac{2}{4}$.

4 In Mary's flowerbed there are red, yellow and purple flowers. $\frac{3}{10}$ of the flowerbed is filled with red flowers and $\frac{2}{10}$ of the flowerbed is filled with yellow flowers. The remainder of the flowerbed is filled with purple flowers. What fraction of the flowerbed is filled with purple flowers?

5 We ate half of my birthday cake on Saturday, and one third of it on Sunday. What fraction is left?

6 Janice went on a two-week holiday. She spent $\frac{3}{5}$ of her holiday money in the first week, and only $\frac{1}{10}$ in the second week. What fraction of her holiday money did she bring home?

7 Who am I?

a) I am a fraction. I am $\frac{1}{2}$ more than $\frac{1}{3}$.

b) I am a fraction. I am $\frac{1}{4}$ less than $\frac{5}{8}$.

c) I am an odd number of fifths. When $\frac{1}{2}$ is subtracted from me the result is equivalent to $\frac{2}{20}$.

Investigations

8 Start with a number, for example $1\frac{3}{4}$.

Explore different additions which have this number as an answer.

For example: two fractions with the same denominator: $1\frac{1}{4} + \frac{2}{4}$ or $\frac{7}{8} + \frac{7}{8}$

three fractions with the same denominator: $\frac{3}{4} + \frac{3}{4} + \frac{1}{4}$ or $\frac{7}{8} + \frac{3}{8} + \frac{4}{8}$

two fractions with different denominators: $\frac{1}{2} + 1\frac{1}{4}$

9 Here are some pairs of fractions which have a difference of $\frac{1}{2}$:

$\frac{3}{4}$ and $\frac{1}{4}$ $\frac{7}{8}$ and $\frac{3}{8}$ $1\frac{1}{6}$ and $\frac{2}{3}$

Investigate pairs of fractions which have a difference of $\frac{1}{3}$.

Repeat for $\frac{3}{4}$.

> Start with thirds and write down about five pairs. Then look at sixths, ninths, twelfths, and so on.

Fractions of amounts

⊕ Calculate fractions of numbers, quantities and measures

⊕ Multiply a fraction by a whole number

$\frac{1}{4}$ of 20 kg is the same as 20 kg ÷ 4 which is 5 kg.

To find $\frac{3}{4}$ of 32 kg, start by finding $\frac{1}{4}$ of 32 kg, then multiply by 3:

$\frac{1}{4}$ of 32 kg = 8 kg

$\frac{3}{4}$ of 32 kg = 3 × 8 kg. So 3 × 8 kg = 24 kg

$\frac{1}{4} \times 20$ and $\frac{1}{4}$ of 20 are identical; $\frac{3}{4}$ of 32 and $\frac{3}{4} \times 32$ are identical **expressions** .

Example 1 Find **a)** $\frac{1}{9}$ of £54 **b)** $\frac{5}{9}$ of £54.

a) £54 ÷ 9 = **£6**

b) $\frac{5}{9}$ of £54 = 5 × £6 = **£30**

Example 2 Find the value of ☐ when $\frac{\square}{6}$ of 42 = 35.

$\frac{1}{6}$ of 42 = 7

35 ÷ 7 = 5, so ☐ is equal to 5

$\frac{5}{6}$ of 42 = 35

What do you need to multiply 7 by to get 35?

Exercise 4.5

1 Work out:

a) $\frac{1}{2}$ of 48 litres **b)** $\frac{1}{4}$ of 32 kg **c)** $\frac{1}{10}$ of 700 ml **d)** $\frac{1}{3}$ of 27 cm

e) $\frac{1}{5}$ of 45p **f)** $\frac{1}{6}$ of 30 hours **g)** $\frac{1}{9}$ of 54 days **h)** $\frac{1}{7}$ of 49 minutes

i) $\frac{1}{8}$ of 88 m **j)** $\frac{1}{100}$ of £60

2 Work out:

a) $\frac{3}{4}$ of 24 km b) $\frac{2}{3}$ of 21 litres c) $\frac{4}{5}$ of 65 cm d) $\frac{7}{10}$ of 110 m

e) $\frac{3}{8}$ of 48p f) $\frac{5}{6}$ of £36 g) $\frac{3}{7}$ of 63 weeks h) $\frac{2}{9}$ of 45 kg

i) $\frac{13}{20}$ of 800 ml j) $\frac{27}{100}$ of £300

3 For each of the following lists, put the expressions in order, smallest to largest.

a) $20 \times \frac{2}{5}$, $\frac{44}{4}$, $\frac{2}{3}$ of 15, $54 \div 6$, $\frac{3}{4} \times 16$

b) $\frac{3}{5}$ of 25, $24 \times \frac{1}{2}$, $48 \div 3$, $\frac{65}{5}$, $\frac{2}{7} \times 49$

c) $\frac{2}{3} \times 27$, $\frac{150}{10}$, $35 \times \frac{4}{7}$, $70 \div 7$, $\frac{7}{10}$ of 20

d) $\frac{66}{6}$, $63 \div 9$, $45 \times \frac{2}{9}$, $\frac{2}{5} \times 20$, $\frac{1}{6}$ of 54

e) $\frac{8}{9}$ of 36, $\frac{9}{10}$ of 40, $\frac{6}{11} \times 77$, $160 \div 4$, $\frac{250}{5}$

> **a)** $20 \times \frac{2}{5}$, $54 \div 6$, $\frac{2}{3}$ of 15, $\frac{44}{4}$, $\frac{3}{4} \times 16$

4 Find □ in each of the following:

> Look back at Example 2.

a) $\frac{\square}{5}$ of 15 = 9 b) $\frac{\square}{3}$ of 24 = 16 c) $\frac{4}{\square}$ of 21 = 12 d) $\frac{3}{\square} \times 44 = 33$

e) $\frac{\square}{6} \times 36 = 30$ f) $\frac{\square}{10}$ of 110 = 99 g) $72 \times \frac{\square}{8} = 27$ h) $\frac{11}{\square} \times 120 = 66$

i) $500 \times \frac{19}{\square} = 500$ j) $\frac{\square}{9}$ of 81 = 36

5 Copy and complete each multiplication table:

×	20	60	50
$\frac{1}{2}$			
$\frac{3}{5}$			
$\frac{7}{10}$			

$\frac{1}{2} \times 20 = 10$

×	24	60	96
$\frac{2}{3}$			
$\frac{3}{4}$			
$\frac{5}{6}$			

6 In a survey, 120 pupils were asked to vote for their favourite subject from English, science and maths. $\frac{1}{5}$ voted for english, $\frac{1}{4}$ voted for science, and the remainder voted for maths. How many more votes did maths receive than English?

7 At a test match there were 16 000 spectators. $\frac{3}{4}$ supported the home team, $\frac{1}{5}$ supported the away team, and the remainder were neutral. How many neutral spectators were there?

8 Who am I?

a) I am a number of days. One quarter of me is one week.

b) I am an amount of money. Three-quarters of me is one half of £48.

c) I am a proper fraction. When I am multiplied by £20, the result is £8.

Investigation

9 Start with a whole number, for example 6.
Here are six different expressions, using multiplication, whose answer is 6:

$\frac{1}{3}$ of 18 $\frac{1}{3} \times 18$ $18 \times \frac{1}{3}$

$\frac{2}{3}$ of 9 $\frac{2}{3} \times 9$ $9 \times \frac{2}{3}$

Choose your own numbers, and write six different expressions for each.
Give an example of a number that has nine (or more) different expressions.

Percentages

⊕ Understand percentage as the number of parts per 100

⊕ Convert a percentage to a decimal

⊕ Convert a percentage to a fraction

⊕ Recognise the equivalence of percentages, fractions and decimals

⊕ Break up a calculation into steps

Key words
per cent
percentage
hundredths
convert
equivalent

% is shorthand for **per cent** .

A **percentage** is the number of parts in every 100.

40% means '40 out of every 100' or $\frac{40}{100}$

18% means '18 out of every 100' or $\frac{18}{100}$

Percentages can be written as **equivalent** fractions or decimals.

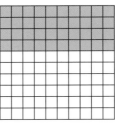

40 out of 100

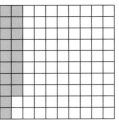

18 out of 100

Percentage	Fraction	Decimal
90%	$\frac{90}{100} = \frac{9}{10}$	0.90
45%	$\frac{45}{100} = \frac{9}{20}$	0.45
68%	$\frac{68}{100} = \frac{17}{25}$	0.68

Example 1 Convert 72%   **a)** to a fraction in its lowest terms
b) to a decimal.

a) $72\% = \frac{72}{100} = \frac{36}{50} = \frac{18}{25}$

b) $72\% = \frac{72}{100} = 0.72$

Divide the numerator and denominator by 2, then by 2 again.

Example 2 Find the value of ☐ when $70\% = \frac{\square}{40}$

$70\% = \frac{70}{100} = \frac{7}{10}$

so $\frac{7}{10} = \frac{\square}{40}$

$10 \times 4 = 40$ and $7 \times 4 = 28$ so $70\% = \frac{28}{40}$.

Write the fraction in its lowest terms. The denominator has been multiplied by 4, so multiply the numerator by 4 to get 40.

Exercise 4.6

1 Write the shaded amount in each shape as a percentage:

a)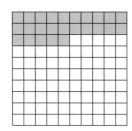

b)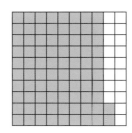

c)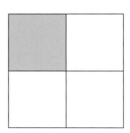

2 Convert each percentage to a fraction in its lowest terms:

    a) 50%   **b)** 25%   **c)** 75%   **d)** 60%   **e)** 120%

    f) 85%   **g)** 135%   **h)** 72%   **i)** 64%   **j)** 24%

3 Find the decimal equivalent of each percentage:

    a) 40%   **b)** 90%   **c)** 35%   **d)** 42%   **e)** 164%

    f) 78%   **g)** 92%   **h)** 6%   **i)** 11%   **j)** 102%

4 Find the value of $\square$ in each of the following:

    a) $40\% = \frac{\square}{5}$ **b)** $30\% = \frac{\square}{10}$ **c)** $60\% = \frac{\square}{20}$ **d)** $75\% = \frac{\square}{12}$

    e) $25\% = \frac{3}{\square}$ **f)** $80\% = \frac{12}{\square}$ **g)** $50\% = \frac{\square}{4}$ **h)** $28\% = \frac{\square}{25}$

    i) $76\% = \frac{19}{\square}$ **j)** $5\% = \frac{1}{\square}$

> Look back at Example 2.

5 Copy and complete this table, writing all the fractions in their lowest terms:

Percentage	50%			190%			48%	
Decimal		0.75				0.85		1.24
Fraction			$\frac{3}{5}$		$\frac{1}{4}$			

6 Roll a normal dice 25 times and record the number thrown each time in a table. Write the percentage of throws for each number. Repeat the activity, but this time roll the dice 40 times. Write a few sentences comparing the two sets of results.

7 48% of the pupils in a school are boys. What fraction of the pupils are girls? Give your answer in its lowest terms.

> Work out the percentage of girls first, then convert to a fraction.

8 Harry saves money by collecting coins in a bottle. 25% of the coins are 5p pieces, $\frac{2}{5}$ of the coins are 10p pieces, and the rest are 20p pieces.

    a) What percentage of the coins are 20p pieces?

    b) What fraction of the coins are 20p pieces?

9 Who am I?

    a) I am a percentage. I am $\frac{1}{2}$ less than 0.72.

    b) I am a percentage. When I am doubled, I am equivalent to $\frac{21}{25}$.

The mode, median and range

⊕ Calculate the mode, median and range for a set of data

Key words
data
mode
median
range
average

An **average** gives information that is typical of a set of data.

The **mode** is a type of average. In a set of data it is the value or values that happen most often:

  1   1   2   2   2   3   4   4   6   9

The mode is 2 as there are more 2s than any other number.

The **median** is another type of average. In an **ordered** set of data, it is the middle value:

  1   2   2   3   4   6   9

The median is 3 as it is the middle value.

The **range** is not an average. It is the smallest value subtracted from the largest value and shows how spread out the data is:

  1   2   2   3   4   6   9

The range is 8 because $9 - 1 = 8$

Example   Work out   **a)**   the median
              b)   the mode
              c)   the range for this set of numbers:

              21   8   12   17   8   21   15   19

a) 8   8   12   15 ↑ 17   19   21   21

The median is **16** as the middle is halfway between 15 and 17.

b) There are two modes: **8** and **21**

c) The range equals **13** because $21 - 8 = 13$

Put the numbers in order.

Exercise 5.1

1 Find the median, mode and range for each of the following sets of numbers.

a) 1   1   3   3   3   4   5
b) 6   6   6   7   9   9   10   10   11
c) 11   11   12   13   15   16
d) 0.4   0.9   1.1   1.3   1.5   1.5

2 Ravi asks his friends what mark they got for their last piece of homework.

| 4 | 4 | 5 | 6 | 6 | 7 | 8 | 8 | 8 | 9 | 9 |

a) What is the median mark?
b) What is the mode?
c) What is the range?
d) Ravi wants to include his mark of 7. Write all twelve marks out in order and find the new median mark.

3 Find the median, mode and range for each of the following set of numbers:

a) 4   1   8   3   7   1   2
b) 6   8   3   7   1   8   2   5
c) 0   0   4   1   2   3   5   4
d) 2.5   2.8   2.1   2.4   2.6   2.5   2.4   2.5   2.2
e) 1.15   1.26   1.19   1.18   1.23   1.19   1.24   1.25

> Order the numbers first.

4 Sharon has collected some information about the heights in centimetres of her friends:

119   121   123   125   128   124   119   121   119   126

a) What is the mode?   b) What is the median?

5 The table shows the number of days that rain fell each month in London:

Month	Jan	Feb	Mar	Apr	May	Jun	Jul	Aug	Sep	Oct	Nov	Dec
Number of days	12	10	10	11	12	12	15	14	13	16	15	12

Find the mode, median and range of the data over the year.

6 Information that is not to do with numbers (called categorical data) can only have the mode as an average.
Which of these cannot have a median value, only a mode?

> Can the information be put into order?

a) Colour of hair   b) Time it takes to get to school
c) Number of pets   d) Height
e) Age   f) Type of car
g) Favourite colour   h) Amount of spending money

7 Which **three** consecutive whole numbers have a median of 9?

> 3, 4, 5 are consecutive and have a median of 4 and a range of 2.

8 Which consecutive whole numbers have a median of 8 and a range of 6?

9 Which consecutive whole numbers have a total of 15 and a median of 3 ?

The mean

⊕ Calculate the mean for a set of data

The **mean** is an average. Like the median, it can only be used for data which is numerical. In everyday language, when people say 'average' they usually mean 'the mean'.

The mean is calculated as: $\dfrac{\text{The } \textbf{total sum} \text{ of all the data}}{\text{The number of items of data}}$

Example 1   Juan asked his teachers how many pieces of fruit they ate yesterday and got the following results: 3   5   1   2   3   3   4

What was the mean number of pieces of fruit eaten by Juan's teachers?

The mean $= \dfrac{3+5+1+2+3+3+4}{7} = \dfrac{21}{7}$

        $= 3$ pieces of fruit

The total number of pieces of fruit eaten

The number of teachers asked

Example 2   The mean height of six children is 1.5 metres. What is the sum of the six heights?

The mean $= 1.5$ m

The total height of all six children $= 6 \times 1.5$

                          $= 9$ m

To find the mean height of six children, you divide the total sum by 6. So, to find the total sum, multiply the mean by 6.

Exercise 5.2

1 Find the mean for each of these sets of data.

a) the number of videos hired in the previous week by a group of pupils:
3   7   4   9   1   6

b) the ages in years of a group of people at a swimming pool:
28   31   17   33   27   20   19

c) the distance in kilometres from school to home for ten pupils:
2.4   5.1   0.5   3.9   4.7   1.1   0.7   3.2   6.8   5.6

2 The ten fastest times in seconds for Dwain Chambers of Great Britain to run the 100 m are: 9.87   9.94   9.96   9.98   10.02   10.03   10.04   10.05   10.06   10.08

What is his mean time?

3 The dawn temperatures in °C in London for ten days in December were:
5   3   1   2   0   4   2   1   4   3

What was the mean temperature?

4 Kate asks her friends how many times they were late for school last term. She puts her results in a spreadsheet.

	A	B	C
1		Number of times late for school	Ordered number of times late for school
2		3	0
3		0	0
4		2	1
5		0	2
6		1	3
7	Total		
8	Mean		

a) Look at column B. What will Kate enter in cell B7 to find the total number of times her friends were late?

b) What will Kate enter in cell B8 to find the mean number of times her friends were late?

c) Explain how she could use column C to find the median, mode and range of her data.

5 Melissa has recorded the number of bags of crisps eaten by her friends over the past week.

Meg	Nii	Owen	Sue	Jack	Luke	Jenny	Sam	Huw	Ian
1	2	0	3	1	4	1	2	1	1

Find the mean number of bags of crisps eaten.

6 a) If the mean of four numbers is 10, what is the total sum of the four numbers?

Look back at Example 2.

b) If the mean of ten numbers is 17.3, what is the total sum of the ten numbers?

7 Find the missing numbers, shown by ☐. They are all whole numbers, greater than 0. Each set of numbers has a mean of 7.

a) 7   7   ☐
b) 5   5   ☐
c) 14   ☐   ☐   or   14   ☐   ☐

8 Ian needs a mean of 75% in his three tests for an A grade. So far, his marks have been 62% and 81%. What percentage does he need for his last test to gain an A?

Start by finding the **total** sum he needs in the 3 tests.

9 The Hargreaves family are on a walking holiday for a week. During the week they need to walk a mean distance of 25 km per day to return to their car. This is how far they have walked:

Day	Saturday	Sunday	Monday	Tuesday	Wednesday	Thursday	Friday
Distance	28	21	25	26	19	29	

The most they can walk in a day is 30 km. Can they complete the holiday on Friday? Explain your answer.

Investigation

10 Make a list showing how many days there are in each month during a year that is not a leap year. Find the mode and the median number of days in a month.
What is the mean number of days in a month in a leap year?
What is the mean number of days in a **year** over a period of four years?

Frequency tables

- Record data in frequency tables
- Use frequency tables to calculate the mean

The word **event** is used to describe something in particular that happens. For example, an event is that I roll a dice.

We use the word **frequency** to describe the number of times an event happens.

A **frequency table** is a way of sorting this data into groups. To find the **mean**, instead of adding up all the bits of data separately we can find the totals for each group.

Example   Thirty people were asked how many pets they owned. These are the results:

0 3 4 1 1 3 1 2 4 1 2 2 5 1 1
1 1 2 2 1 3 3 2 3 2 2 1 3 2 1

a) Draw a frequency table to show this data.
b) Use the table to work out the mean number of pets owned.

Record the results in a tally column.

a)

Number of pets owned	Tally	Frequency	Total number of pets owned
0	l	1	$0 \times 1 = 0$
1	llll llll l	11	$1 \times 11 = 11$
2	llll llll	9	$2 \times 9 = 18$
3	llll l	6	$3 \times 6 = 18$
4	ll	2	$4 \times 2 = 8$
5	l	1	$5 \times 1 = 5$
		30	60

9 people own 2 pets, so 18 pets in total.

The number of pets owned in total.

b) Mean = $\dfrac{\text{total number of pets owned}}{\text{total frequency}} = \dfrac{60}{30} = 2$

The number of people asked. (total frequency)

Exercise 5.3

1   The table shows the number of magazines bought by pupils in one class, in the last month.

Find the mean number of magazines bought by pupils in the class.

Number of magazines bought last month	Frequency	Number of magazines × frequency
0	4	
1	5	
2	3	
3	5	
4	1	
5	2	
Total number of pupils =	Total number of magazines =	

2 This data shows the number of goals scored in the Premiership in 20 matches. Put the data into a frequency table and find the mean number of goals per match.

5   2   1   0   0   0   1   2   1   1   1   3

1   1   1   3   0   0   1   1

Draw a tally chart first.

3 Sharon is collecting information about the size of shoes worn by pupils in her class.

| 4 | 6 | 2 | 6 | 5 | 9 | 3 | 5 | 4 | 8 | 4 | 6 |
| 5 | 7 | 5 | 3 | 6 | 7 | 4 | 5 | | | | |

Put the data into a frequency table. Find the mean shoe size using this table.

4 Jake is collecting information about how many complete books his friends read in one week. He records the results for 15 friends. Unfortunately, he has lost some of the numbers. Can you help him?

Number of books	Frequency	Number of books × frequency
0	3	0
1		3
2	2	
3	4	12
4		
5	2	10
	Total =	Total =

The frequency column must add up to 15 as his survey was for a total of 15 people.

a) Copy the frequency table and fill in the missing numbers.

b) Calculate the mean number of books read in one week.

5 This frequency table shows the ages in years and complete months of people at a youth club. Find the mean age of these people, in years and months.

Age	Frequency
11 years 4 months	1
11 years 5 months	2
11 years 7 months	2
11 years 8 months	4
11 years 11 months	1
12 years	1
12 years 1 month	1

You could change each age into months. For example, 11 years is 11 × 12 = 132 months.

Investigation

6 Draw a frequency table to show how many letters are in the first names of the people in your maths group. For example, the name David has five letters.
Find the range, mode, median and mean for the number of letters in the names.

Interpreting diagrams

◈ Interpret diagrams, graphs and charts

◈ Find simple statistics from diagrams

Key words
pictogram
bar chart
bar-line graph
pie chart
compound bar chart

Pictograms, **bar charts**, **bar-line graphs** and **pie charts** can all be used to represent data. Showing data in this way makes it easier to interpret and to spot trends.

Example 1 For each diagram write down the mode and total frequency of data.

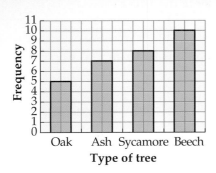

The mode is **beech**.

The total frequency of trees

$= 5 + 7 + 8 + 10 = \mathbf{30}$

It has the greatest frequency.

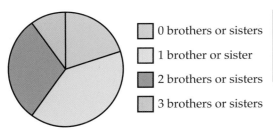

- ☐ 0 brothers or sisters
- ☐ 1 brother or sister
- ☐ 2 brothers or sisters
- ☐ 3 brothers or sisters

The mode is **1** brother or sister.

The total frequency cannot be found, as the frequencies are not given.

The mode is the biggest slice.

Example 2 This compound bar chart shows how many pupils from each form took part in a sponsored swim.

The first bar shows a total of 9 pupils, 3 girls and 6 boys

a) Which group has the most girls taking part?

b) Which group had the same number of boys and girls taking part?

c) How many pupils took part in total?

d) What is the mean number of pupils taking part per form group?

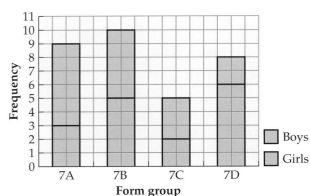

☐ Boys
☐ Girls

a) **7D** has the most girls taking part.

b) **7B** has 5 boys and 5 girls.

c) **7A** has 9 pupils, **7B** has 10, **7C** has 5 and **7D** has 8.

$9 + 10 + 5 + 8 = \mathbf{32}$ **pupils**

d) From c) there are 32 pupils, so $32 \div 4 = \mathbf{8}$

Number of form groups

Exercise 5.4

1 a) Which sport was the most popular?

b) Which sports did more boys than girls choose?

c) How many girls took part in the survey?

d) Can you work out the median favourite sport? Explain your answer.

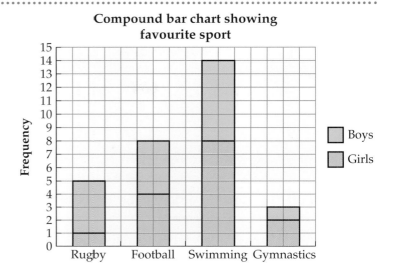

Compound bar chart showing favourite sport

2 This pictogram shows the number of CDs sold each week. Each symbol represents 1000 CDs. How many CDs were sold in:

a) Week 1   **b)** Week 2   **c)** Week 3?

d) 1250 CDs were sold during Week 4. How would this figure be shown on the pictogram?

e) What is the mean number of CDs sold in a week? Include Week 4 in your calculation.

Week 1 ⊙ ⊙ ⊙

Week 2 ⊙ ⊙ ⊙ ⊙ (

Week 3 ⊙ (

3 This table shows different items in the bedrooms of six children:

Name	TV	Computer	CD player	Games console
Lynn	✓	✓	✗	✗
Malcolm	✗	✗	✓	✗
Toby	✓	✗	✓	✓
Nikki	✗	✓	✓	✗
Fiona	✓	✗	✗	✓
Eddy	✓	✓	✓	✓

Which data has not been included on the bar chart? Explain your answer.

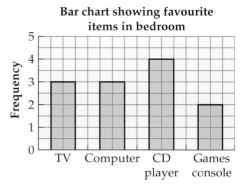

Bar chart showing favourite items in bedroom

4 The bar chart shows the grades obtained by a class in their last mathematics test.

a) Which of the mean, median and mode can be calculated to give an average grade? Explain your answer.

b) Can the range be calculated?

c) How many pupils took the test?

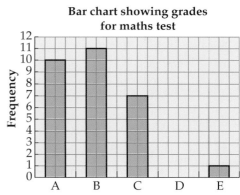

Bar chart showing grades for maths test

Investigation

5 Choose a bar or pie chart from a newspaper, magazine or travel brochure. Make up some questions about the information it shows. Give them to a friend to answer.

Describing probabilities

Key words
probability
certain
impossible
unlikely
likely
even
chance
outcome

⊕ Use words to describe probabilities
⊕ Compare events using words describing probabilities

An **event** such as rolling a standard dice can have different outcomes. When a dice is rolled the different **outcomes** are 1, 2, 3, 4, 5 or 6.

We often use words to describe the **probability** or **chance** of an outcome.

Example 1 Decide if each of the following is:

IMPOSSIBLE   UNLIKELY   EVEN   LIKELY   CERTAIN

a) Ten coins are spun and all land showing *heads*.
b) There will be 32 days in the next month.
c) An odd number is shown when a standard dice is rolled.

a) It is **unlikely** that all 10 coins will land showing *heads*.

b) It is **impossible** for there to be 32 days next month.

c) There is an **even chance** of getting an odd number or an even number.

Example 2 Here are three spinners: A   B   C

i) Which spinner gives the greatest chance of landing on:
   a) blue   **b)** green   **c)** orange   **d)** blue **or** orange?
ii) Which spinner gives the smallest chance of landing on green or orange?

i)	**a)**	Spinner A
	b)	Spinner B
	c)	Spinner C
	d)	Spinner C
ii)		Spinner A

First look for the spinner that has the most blue area.

If spinners B and C were split into six sections they would look like this:

B   C

Exercise 5.5

❶ Say whether the following are: IMPOSSIBLE UNLIKELY EVEN LIKELY CERTAIN
  a) Getting a total of 13 when throwing two dice.
  b) When a coin is spun, it shows *heads*.
  c) You are getting older.
  d) It will rain next month.
  e) Four dice are thrown and all land showing sixes.
  f) You get a 1, 2 or 3 when you roll a dice.

2 For each of the following pairs, write down which outcome is more likely.
   a) On a dice: throwing a 6 or an even number.
   b) On a dice: throwing an odd number or a number bigger than 4.
   c) On two dice: getting a 'double' or not getting a 'double'.
   d) From a chess set: picking a king or a pawn.
   e) From a chess set: picking a knight or a rook.

> Each chess set includes 2 kings, 4 knights, 4 rooks and 16 pawns.

3 Dan and Ellie have designed some spinners.
Which spinner gives the **greatest** chance of landing on
   a) blue   **b)** green   **c)** red or blue?
   d) Which spinner gives the **smallest** chance of landing on green or red?

Dan's spinner   Ellie's spinner

> Look back at Example 2.

4 Copy and complete the spinner so it gives an equal chance of landing on a red or green **and** a greater chance of landing on black than red.

5 Decide if each of the following are fair ways to start a game using a standard dice.
If they are not fair, which player is most likely to start each time?

	Player 1	Player 2
a)	Odd	Even
b)	6	Not a 6
c)	Less than 4	4 or more
d)	Prime number	Not a prime

6 Ruth has these digit cards:

She shuffles the cards and turns the top one over.
She gets a 4.
   a) Is the next card she turns over more likely or less likely to be a number greater than 4?
   b) The card she got was a 3. Is the next card she turns over more likely or less likely to be a greater number than 3?

> Remember, she has already turned over 4.

7 Mehdi has some different colour counters in a bag. He picks one without looking, notes the colour and returns it to the bag. He does this 16 times.
Here is a table of his results:
   a) He picks another counter without looking. What colour is it most likely to be?
   b) Mehdi says that the colour he was least likely to get was green. Can this be true? Explain your answer.

Colour	Frequency
Red	3
Blue	6
Yellow	1
White	4
Black	2

8 An ordinary coin is tossed three times and each time a *head* shows it is tossed again. Is the chance of another *head* less likely, more likely or even? Explain your answer.

Key words
outcome
event
random
probability scale
equally likely

⊕ Understand and use the probability scale from 0 to 1
⊕ Find probabilities of equally likely outcomes
⊕ Identify all the outcomes of a single event

As well as using words to show the probability of an **outcome** , we can use numbers. A probability expressed in numbers will always be between 0 and 1. It can be a fraction, a decimal or a percentage.

$$\begin{array}{ccc} \underset{\text{Impossible}}{0} & \underset{\text{Even}}{\frac{1}{2}} & \underset{\text{Certain}}{1} \end{array}$$

Probability of an outcome $= \dfrac{\text{Number of ways the outcome could happen}}{\text{Total number of possible outcomes}}$

Example 1 For this spinner, what is the probability of it landing on:

a) a 1 b) an odd number c) not a 3?

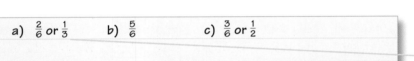

a) $\frac{2}{6}$ or $\frac{1}{3}$ b) $\frac{5}{6}$ c) $\frac{3}{6}$ or $\frac{1}{2}$

There are 6 possible outcomes and 2 of these are '1'. So the probability of scoring 1 is $\frac{2}{6}$ or $\frac{1}{3}$.

Example 2 The labels have fallen off ten similar tins of food. Six tins contain soup, three contain beans and one contains oranges. A tin is chosen.

i) What is the probability that it will contain

a) beans b) soup c) beans or soup d) not soup?

ii) Mark these probabilities on a probability scale.

a) The probability it contains beans is $\frac{3}{10}$ or **0.3** or **30%**.

b) The probability it contains oranges is $\frac{1}{10}$ or **0.1** or **10%**.

c) The probability it contains beans or soup is $\frac{9}{10}$ or **0.9** or **90%**.

d) The probability it does not contain soup is $\frac{4}{10}$ or **0.4** or **40%**.

e)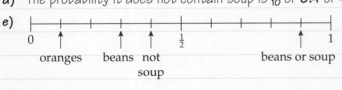

3 tins of beans out of a total of 10.

1 tin of oranges out of a total of 10.

3 tins of beans + 6 tins of soup = 9 tins out of a total of 10.

If 6 tins are soup, then 4 tins are not soup.

Mark a probability scale in tenths to record the above information.

Exercise 5.6

1 A spinner has eight equal sections. What is the probability of getting:

   a) a 6   **b)** an even number   **c)** a number bigger than 4?   **d)** not a 12?

2 A standard 6-sided dice is thrown. What is the probability that it shows:

   a) a 2   **b)** an odd number   **c)** a 5 or 6   **d)** a 0

   e) a number less than 5   **g)** a number between 0 and 7?

3 All the letters from the word POSSIBILITIES are written on separate
   pieces of paper and put in a bag. One letter is taken out without looking.
   What is the probability that the letter will be:

   > Count how many letters there are in POSSIBILITIES.

   a) an S   **b)** an X   **c)** a B, L or T   **d)** Not an I?

4 A number is chosen from the integers 1 to 20 inclusive . What is the probability that the
   number will be

   a) 7   **b)** even   **c)** 23   **d)** less than 15?

   Show all your answers as a fraction, a decimal and a percentage.

5 A machine sells five different flavours of lollipop: cola, lime, lemon, raspberry, orange.
   The machine chooses the flavour for you. There are the same numbers of each flavour in
   the machine.

   Show all your answers as a fraction and a decimal.

   a) Nikki only likes lemon and orange. What is the probability of her getting a lollipop she likes?

   b) Fiona likes all of the flavours. What is the probability that she gets a flavour she likes?

   c) Ali does not like cola. What is the probability he gets a lollipop he likes?

   d) Draw a probability scale to show the probabilities of Nikki,
   Fiona and Ali getting a flavour they each like.

   > Look back at Example 2.

6 Copy and complete the spinner so that the probability of getting
   an odd number is $\frac{1}{2}$ and the probability of getting a 1 is $\frac{1}{3}$.

7 A bag contains three pairs of gloves: a red pair, a blue pair and
   a black pair, giving six gloves in total. A red glove is taken out.
   Another glove is taken out without looking.
   What is the probability that it is also red?

   > The first glove is not put
   > back, so work out how many
   > gloves are still in the bag.

8 Mandy has accidentally put two old batteries back into a packet that also contains six
   new ones. She picks out a battery.

   a) What is the probability that it will work?

   b) How many batteries should she take out to be certain that at least one will work?

Investigation

9 Design your own spinner. You could use either a circle or a
   regular polygon. Divide it up into labelled sections of various
   sizes. Try and make sure that the probabilities of it falling on
   each section are different.

   > A regular polygon is a
   > shape with all sides equal.

   > Look at the spinners in
   > Exercise 5.5 to help you.

Using algebra

◈ Know that algebra follows the same rules as arithmetic

Key words
term
expression
equivalent

When we use letters to stand in for unknown numbers, they follow the same rules as numbers. For example

$12 - 11 = 1$

$12x - 11x = 1x = x$ (We don't usually write the number 1 in front of a letter.)

Just as $3 + 3$ is two lots of 3 so $3 + 3 = 2 \times 3$,

$a + a$ is two lots of a so $a + a = 2 \times a = 2a$

(We don't need to include the multiplication sign between a number and a letter.)

We can also multiply two or more unknowns together.

$a \times b$ is written as ab

$a \times b \times c$ is written as abc

$2a \times 3b$ is written as $6ab$ because $2 \times a \times 3 \times b = 2 \times 3 \times a \times b = 6 \times a \times b = 6ab$

Example 1   Write these in a shorter form:

    a) $x + x + x + x$

    b) $5x + 3x$

    c) $5 \times 3 \times y \times z \times x$

a) $x + x + x + x = \mathbf{4x}$

b) $5x + 3x = x + x + x + x + x + x + x + x = \mathbf{8x}$

c) $5 \times 3 \times y \times z \times x = \mathbf{15xyz}$

This is 4 lots of x.

We always write the number first. We can write the letters in any order (just as $2 \times 3 = 3 \times 2$, $ab = ba$) but usually we write them in alphabetical order.

Example 2   Write an expression for the area of this rectangle.

Area of a rectangle = length × width

Area = $5a \times 7b$

    = $5 \times 7 \times a \times b$

    = $\mathbf{35ab}$

$5a$ and $7b$ are both **terms**.

This is called an **expression**.

Exercise 6.1

1 Write these in a shorter form:

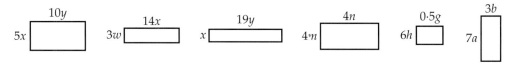

   a) $m + m + m + m + m$

   c) $x + x + x - x - x$

   e) $8w - 3w + 4w$

   g) $4a \times 8b$

   b) $y + y + y + y + y + y$

   d) $4h + 6h + 3h$

   f) $p - p + 2p + p$

   h) $3j \times k \times 4l$

> Remember, just as
> $2 + 2 + 2 = 3 \times 2$
> $n + n + n = 3 \times n = 3n$

> Remember k means $1k$.

2 Write expressions for the area of these rectangles:

$5x$ ▭ $10y$　　$3w$ ▭ $14x$　　x ▭ $19y$　　$4n$ ▭ $4n$　　$6h$ ▭ $0.5g$　　$7a$ ▭ $3b$

3 Complete this addition pyramid. The number in each brick is found by adding the two directly below it. Remember to simplify your answers as much as possible.

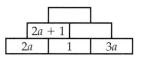

Pyramid bricks: $2a + 1$ | $2a$ | 1 | $3a$

4 **a)** Jenny has nine pet mice and Sanjay has seven pet mice. How many mice do they have altogether?

   b) Clare has x guinea pigs and June has three guinea pigs. How many guinea pigs do they have altogether?

   c) Tuin and Ann are making a kite. Tuin has $3x$ centimetres of string and Ann has $2x$ centimetres. They need $6x$ centimetres. Do they have enough? Explain your answer.

5 I choose a number, multiply it by 4 and add on 7. The answer is 43. What number did I choose? Check with a calculator.

6 **a)** Write down the pairs of cards that show equivalent expressions.

   b) Which two cards add together to give $6a$?

   c) Write a new card that added to K to gives the answer $10a - 3$.

$3ab$	$a + b$	$a \times 3$	$b + a$
A	B	C	D
$3a - a$	$2a$	$2a + 3a$	$a \times 3b$
E	F	G	H
$3a$	a	$5a$	$\frac{2a}{2}$
I	J	K	L

Investigation

7 Amy has a ribbon of length $8x + 4$. She wants to use it as a border round some rectangular, triangular and square boxes. Investigate the size and shape of boxes she could use, using whole numbers only. Here is an example:

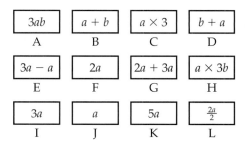

$4x + 2 + 4x + 2 = 8x + 4$

Collecting like terms

⊕ Understand which terms you can add together and which you cannot

$3a$ and $4a$ can be added together to get $7a$. These terms are called **like terms** because they contain the same letter. Like terms can be added together – this is called **collecting** like terms.

Instead of writing $2m + 3m + b + 2b$, we can write $5m + 3b$ or $3b + 5m$.
We cannot combine $5m$ and $3b$ in any simpler way than $5m + 3b$ or $3b + 5m$ because they are not like terms – they stand in for different **unknown** numbers.

Example 1   Simplify the following by collecting like terms:

    a) $m + m + m + n$
    b) $t + t - y - y + t$

a) $m + m + m + n = \mathbf{3m + n}$

b) $t + t - y - y + t = \mathbf{3t - 2y}$

There are three lots of t minus two lots of y.

Example 2   Simplify the following expressions by collecting like terms:

    a) $3a + 5b + 6a + 4b$
    b) $4m + 2z - 3m + z$

First look at the a terms:
$3a$ and $6a$.
So: $3a + 6a = 9a$
Now look at the b terms. You have $5b + 4b = 9b$

a) $3a + 5b + 6a + 4b = \mathbf{9a + 9b}$

b) $4m + 2z - 3m + z = \mathbf{m + 3z}$

First look at the m terms. $4m - 3m = 1m$ (which we usually write as m.)
Now look at the z terms.
$2z + z = 2z + 1z = 3z$

Exercise 6.2

1 Simplify the following expressions by collecting like terms:

    a) $y + y + y + x + x$
    b) $m + m + m + b + m$
    c) $x + x + y + m + y + m$
    d) $z + a + a + a$
    e) $p + r + p + p + p + r + r + p + r + p + p + r + p + p + r + p$

2 Simplify the following expressions by collecting like terms:

    a) $t + t - q + t - q - q$ **b)** $p + r - p + r + r - p$
    c) $x + y + y - x - y + x + y$ **d)** $b - t - t - t$
    e) $y + u + u + u + u + u - y + u - y$ **f)** $t + y - u - u + y - t$
    g) $x + y - x - y$

3 Write the following in longhand. For example $5m = m + m + m + m + m$
   a) $6y$
   b) $3z + 2y$
   c) $7a + 3b + 2c$
   d) $2s$

4 Simplify the following expressions:
   a) $3a + 2a$
   b) $4y + 5y$
   c) $5t + 20t$
   d) $2z + 5r + 4z$
   e) $3r + 2b + 5r + 4b$
   f) $8z + 5y + 7y + 3r + 4z$

5 Simplify the following expressions:
   a) $5y - 2y$
   b) $9m + 4r - 2m$
   c) $17r - 10r + 2t$
   d) $5y + 3u - 2y + 4u$
   e) $9x - 4x + 5t - 2t$
   f) $6t + 7y - t + 5y - 3t$

   > Look at one letter at a time.

6 Simplify the following expressions:
   a) $6 + 2y - 3 + 4y$
   b) $16 + t - 2s + 12$
   c) $3w - 6v + 4v - 100$
   d) $79t + 50 - 30t - 3$

7 Andrew buys m flowers for his teachers and n sweets.
   Patrick buys no flowers but twice as many sweets.
   India buys three times as many flowers but no sweets.
   Debbie buys twice as many of both flowers and sweets.
   Janice buys the same number of both flowers and sweets
   as Andrew.

   a) Write an expression for what each child buys,
   For example: Andrew $m + n$
   b) Write an expression for the total number of flowers
   and sweets bought by all the children.

   > Collect like terms.

8 Discuss with a partner how you think you could
   simplify the following:

   $2a + 3ab + 5b + 6a + 7b$

   > Remember that you can only add terms together if the letters are exactly the same.

9 A newsagent uses the following method to calculate the cost of photocopying, in pence:
   number of photocopies $\times 5$ + number of photocopies $\times 2$

   a) Replace the phrase 'number of photocopies' with the letter a and write out the
   expression.
   b) Simplify this expression.
   c) How would you describe to a sales assistant a simple way of calculating the cost
   of photocopying?

6.3 Substitution

⊕ Substitute values into expressions using algebra
⊕ Recognise that algebra follows the same rules as arithmetic

We use letters in algebra to represent numbers.
Substitution is replacing the letters with numbers.
Look at the expression: $2A + 3B + 4C$
If $A = 12$, $B = 10$ and $C = 7$, we can calculate the value of the **expression** above by replacing the letters with the numbers. (Remember $2A$ means $2 \times A$.)

$$2A + 3B + 4C = 2 \times 12 + 3 \times 10 + 4 \times 7$$
$$= 24 + 30 + 28$$
$$= 82$$

Remember the order of operations. We multiply before we add.

Example 1 Find the value of the following if $a = 1$, $b = 5$ and $c = 2$.
   a) $4a$ **b)** $3a + 2c$ **c)** $5b - 3a$

a) $4a = 4 \times a$
   $= 4 \times 1$
   $= 4$

b) $3a + 2c = 3 \times a + 2 \times c$
   $= 3 \times 1 + 2 \times 2$
   $= 3 + 4$
   $= 7$

Do the multiplication first

c) $5b - 3a = 5 \times b - 3 \times a$
   $= 5 \times 5 - 3 \times 1$
   $= 22$

Example 2 Simplify the following expressions and find their value when:
   $x = 100$, $y = 20$ and $z = 10$.
   a) $3x + 2y + 3x$ **b)** $4y + 5z - 3z + 3x + y$

a) $3x + 2y + 3x = 6x + 2y$

First simplify the expression.

$6x + 2y = 6 \times x + 2 \times y$
   $= 6 \times 100 + 2 \times 20$

Then substitute in the values.

   $= 600 + 40$
   $= 640$

b) $4y + 5z - 3z + 3x + y = 5y + 2z + 3x$
   $= 5 \times 20 + 2 \times 10 + 3 \times 100$
   $= 100 + 20 + 300$
   $= 420$

Exercise 6.3

1 Find the value of the following if $x = 3$, $y = 4$ and $z = 1$.
   a) $2x$ b) $7y$ c) $4z$ d) $x + y$ e) $x + z$
   f) $y + z$ g) $2y + 5z$ h) $3y - 2x$ i) $10z - 2y + 3z$

2 Simplify the following expressions.
   a) $2y + y$ b) $x + y + x + z + y$ c) $4x + 2y + 2x$
   d) $3x + 2z - z$ e) $4x + 5z - 3x + 5z$ f) $2x + 4y - x + 7z - 3z - 2y$

3 If $x = 10$, $y = 7$ and $z = 9$ find the value of the expressions in Q2.

> Use your simplified answers.

4 In a garage the cost of servicing a car is calculated like this:

   Cost in pounds $= 25 + p + 15h$

   p is the cost of parts, h is the number of hours spent.
   Four different cars are brought into the garage on one day. The mechanics note down in a table the cost of parts and the time spent on each car in the table below:

   a) What is the cost of the bill for the Renault owner?
   b) Which car cost more, the Morris Minor or the Toyota Celica?
   c) How much change does the BMW owner get from £500?

Car	Cost of parts	Hours
Toyota Celica	£105	3
Renault 5	£56.25	1
Morris Minor	£55.25	4
BMW	£300	3

5 Trevor has dropped his homework in a puddle and erased some of the information. His homework looks like this:
   Copy and complete Trevor's homework.

> **Question 1**
> If $m = 5$ and $z = $ [?] find the value of:
> $2m + 2z$
> $2m + 2z = 10 + $ [?] $ = 22$
>
> **Question 2**
> If $x = 5$, $z = $ [?] and $y = 10$ find the value of:
> $3x + 2z + 4y$
> $3x + 2z + 4y = 3$ [?] $ = 95$

6 For a mobile phone, the cost in pounds per month is: $12.99 + 0.10T + 0.25C$
   T is the number of text messages sent and C is the total minutes spent on calls.
   a) Janet sent 20 text messages and spent 12 minutes on calls. How much was her bill?
   b) James sent 400 text messages but didn't make any calls. How much was his bill?
   c) What is the cost of line rental per month?
   d) How much does one text message cost?
   e) How much does one minute of telephone calls cost?
   f) Debbie received a bill of £29.99. She knows she spent 30 minutes on the phone that month but how many text messages did she send?

Investigation

7 Find values that satisfy the following equation, if r, s and t are whole numbers.
   $2r + 4s - t = 46$
   For example, $2 \times 10 + 4 \times 8 - 6 = 46$
   $r = 10$, $s = 8$ and $t = 6$

> There are many possible combinations of values. You might choose to fix one value, for example $r = 1$, and find values of s and t.

Brackets and algebra

Key words
brackets
operation
unknown
expression
substitution

⊕ Understand the meaning of a bracket

⊕ Recognise that algebra follows the same rules as arithmetic

Brackets around numbers tell you that you must do the calculation in the brackets before you do anything else.

In the **expression** $3(15 - 5)$ you must calculate the part in brackets first: $15 - 5 = 10$

$3(15 - 5)$ means $3 \times (15 - 5)$, so next you multiply by 3: $3 \times 10 = 30$

In the same way:

$2(a + b)$ means you must add a and b before you multiply by 2. For example if $a = 3$ and $b = 4$ you must calculate $3 + 4$ before you multiply by 2.

Example 1 Calculate or simplify the following:

    a) $5(20 + 12)$ **b)** $3(5a + 7a)$

a) $20 + 12 = 32$

   $5(20 + 12) = 5 \times 32 = \mathbf{160}$

b) $5a + 7a = 12a$

   $3(5a + 7a) = 3 \times 12a = \mathbf{36a}$

First you must work out the calculation inside the bracket.

Remember the 5 outside the bracket means $\times 5$.

Example 2 If $x = 5$ and $y = 12$ find the value of the following:

    a) $6(x + y)$ **b)** $\dfrac{x + 19}{y}$

a) $6(x + y) = 6(5 + 12)$

          $= 6(17) = 6 \times 17 = \mathbf{102}$

b) $\dfrac{x + 19}{y} = \dfrac{5 + 19}{12}$

          $= \dfrac{24}{12} = \mathbf{2}$

First you must substitute the values in – remember **substitution** means replacing the letters with numbers.

Work out the calculation in brackets first.

We don't need brackets here since the long dividing sign tells us we must do the part on top first.

Exercise 6.4

1 Calculate or simplify the following:

    a) $(10 + 22) \times 4$ **b)** $6(6x - 2x)$ **c)** $(10 - 2) \div 4$

    d) $\dfrac{20b - 12b}{2}$ **e)** $7(90 - 81 + 2)$ **f)** $\dfrac{14 - 5 + 9}{3}$

    g) $4(20 + 5 - 15)$ **h)** $\dfrac{17m + 20m - m}{6}$

For parts **d, f** and **h** see Example 2 part **b**.

2 If $x = 5$, $y = 4$ and $z = 2$, calculate the value of the following:

a) $2(x + y)$ **b)** $5(x - y)$ **c)** $x(2 + z)$

d) $y(x - 3)$ **e)** $\dfrac{x + y}{3}$ **f)** $\dfrac{y - z}{2}$

g) $\dfrac{y + 30}{z}$ **h)** $\dfrac{y - 2}{z}$

3 If $p = 2$, $q = 6$ and $r = 10$, calculate the value of the following:

a) $2(r + q)$ **b)** $\dfrac{r - p}{4}$ **c)** $6(r - p) + 12$

d) $p(4 + q + r)$ **e)** $\dfrac{p + q + r}{9}$ **f)** $(p + r) \times (r - q)$

g) $\dfrac{r - p}{q - p}$ **h)** $6(p + q + r) - 10(r - q)$

4 Use a calculator correctly to evaluate:

a) $(3 + 5) \times 4 \div 2$

b) $7 - 3 \times 2 + 10$

c) $8 + 4 + 4 \times 7$

Check your answers.
The first one is done for you:
$(3 + 5) \times 4 \div 2 = 8 \times 4 \div 2 = 16$

5 Pair up the expressions that have equal value.

A $2 \times 3 + 1$ **F** $\dfrac{8 + 16}{4}$

B $2(5 + 5)$ **G** $\dfrac{m}{4}$

C $14 - 2 \times 3$ **H** $10 + (2 \times 5)$

D $(2m - m) \div 4$ **I** $2 \times (3 + 1)$

E $(3 \times 4) \div 2$ **J** 7

6 CDs normally cost £12.99 each. A music shop decides to reduce the cost of CDs by £2. You choose three CDs and the shop assistant calculates the cost as: $£12.99 - £2 \times 3$

a) If she works out this calculation following the order of operations, what is the cost of your three CDs?

b) How much should you have been charged?

c) How much have you been undercharged?

7 Part of Jim's and Chandra's homework is to simplify $a + 3a \times 5$. Jim says the answer is $20a$ and Chandra says it is $16a$.

a) Who is right? Explain how Jim and Chandra worked out their answers.

b) Check that your answer works when you substitute a number for a.

Expanding brackets

◈ Revise how to simplify expressions
◈ Learn how to multiply out brackets

To **simplify** expressions it is sometimes necessary to remove (or **expand**) the **brackets** .

The number outside the bracket multiplies **every value inside the bracket**.

For example: $2(7 + 5) = 2 \times 7 + 2 \times 5$
$$= 14 + 10$$
$$= 24$$

We could use the method from the last lesson instead:
$$2(7 + 5) = 2 \times 12$$
$$= 24$$

Example 1 By expanding the brackets, find the value of the following expression:
$$5(8 - 2 + 11)$$

$5(8 - 2 + 11) = 5 \times 8 - 5 \times 2 + 5 \times 11$
$$= 40 - 10 + 55$$
$$= 85$$

Check by working out.
$8 - 2 + 11 = 17$
$5 \times 17 = 85$ ✓

Example 2 Simplify the following expressions by expanding the brackets:

a) $2(x + 4)$ **b)** $10(8 - t)$

a) $2(x + 4) = 2 \times x + 2 \times 4$
$$= 2x + 8$$

b) $10(8 - t) = 10 \times 8 - 10 \times t$
$$= 80 - 10t$$

Example 3 Simplify the following expression:
$$3x - 2m + 4(x - 3) + 17$$

$4(x - 3) = 4 \times x - 4 \times 3 = 4x - 12$
So: $3x - 2m + 4(x - 3) + 17 = 3x - 2m + 4x - 12 + 17$
$$= 7x - 2m + 5$$

First expand the bracket.

Now collect together the like terms.

Exercise 6.5

1 Find the value of each of the following expressions by expanding the brackets:

a) $2(4 + 6)$ **b)** $3(8 + 2)$ **c)** $5(10 + 12)$ **d)** $11(9 + 6)$

e) $7(10 + 3)$ **f)** $4(9 - 6)$ **g)** $10(12 - 1)$ **h)** $8(6 - 5)$

i) $3(7 - 7)$ **j)** $10(14 - 3)$ **k)** $12(4 + 20)$

2 Calculate the following, then check your answer, using a different method:

> The two methods are:
> 1) to expand the brackets
> 2) to calculate the value in the bracket first.

   a) $7(4 - 2 + 3)$ **b)** $11(8 + 6 - 10)$ **c)** $3(20 - 7 - 12)$

   d) $10(23 + 41 - 3)$ **e)** $12(12 - 7 + 6)$ **f)** $2(20 + 14 + 12)$

3 Expand the brackets in the following expressions:

   a) $3(t + 5)$ **b)** $10(p + 7)$ **c)** $4(x + 6)$ **d)** $5(11 + m)$

   e) $12(12 + b)$ **f)** $30(4 + p)$ **g)** $3(x - 10)$ **h)** $8(t - 4)$

   i) $3(2x + 4)$ **j)** $10(3b + 2)$ **k)** $4(5p - 10)$ **l)** $7(4w - 12)$

   m) $6(3 + 6m)$ **n)** $2(13 - 4x)$ **o)** $20(1 + 10x)$ **p)** $100(8t - 15)$

4 Expand the brackets and then simplify the following expressions:

   a) $2(5 + 2c - 4)$ **b)** $4(8x + 3 - 4)$ **c)** $10(3 - 2n + 3n)$ **d)** $8(6m + 2q - 5 - q)$

   e) $7(3 + t + 2p - p)$ **f)** $6(4r - 2t + 10r)$ **g)** $11(12y - 2y + 40)$

5 Expand the brackets and then simplify the following expressions:

   a) $2 + 6m + 4(m + 3)$ **b)** $8(r - 5) + 12$ **c)** $11 + 2(r - 5) + 10r$

   d) $10(4 + 2r + q) - 7q$ **e)** $8 + 7(r - p) + 12p - 2q$

6 The cost of repairing a car is calculated like this:

     $\text{Cost} = 1.02(P + L)$

   P is the cost of parts and L is the cost of labour.

   a) Use two methods to work out the bill if the parts cost £50 and the labour costs £65.

   b) Which was the easiest way to calculate the bill?

7 Each expression in Column A has an equivalent one in Column B. Find the pairs that are equivalent:

Column A	Column B
a) $3(x + y)$	**i)** $6y + 12$
b) $2(3 - x)$	**ii)** $6 - 2x$
c) $3(x - 2y)$	**iii)** $6y + 6$
d) $3(2y + 2)$	**iv)** $3x + 3y$
e) $2(x - y)$	**v)** $2x - 2y$
f) $6(y + 2)$	**vi)** $3x - 6y$

Investigation

8 The following calculation is set for a maths homework.

   'Work out: $2x + 3(x - 5) - 2y + 10$ where $x = 5$ and $y = 2$.'

   Some of the incorrect answers given are below:

> *Federica:*
>
> $2x + 3(x - 5) - 2y + 10$
> $= 2 \times 5 + 3(5 - 5) - 2 \times 2 + 10$
> $= 10 + 0 - 2 \times 12 = 10 - 24$
> $= {}^-14$

> *India:*
>
> $2x + 3(x - 5) - 2y + 10$
> $= 2x + 3x - 5 - 2y + 10$
> $= 2 \times 5 + 3 \times 5 - 5 - 2 \times 2 + 10$
> $= 10 + 15 - 5 - 4 + 10$
> $= 26$

   a) Find the correct answer to the calculation.

   b) By looking at Federica and India's answers, find out what each of them did wrong and write down some advice you would give them.

Lines, angles and shapes

⊕ Know how to label lines, angles and shapes

⊕ Distinguish between and estimate acute, obtuse and reflex angles

⊕ Recognise and draw parallel and perpendicular lines using a ruler and set square

Key words
line segment
intersection
parallel
perpendicular
acute
obtuse
reflex
right angle

In maths there are agreed ways of labelling diagrams.
In this diagram the **line segments** AB and BC are labelled.

An angle can be described in three ways. This diagram shows angle ∠ABC or AB̂C or ∠B.

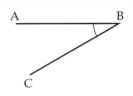

In a triangle we label the vertices clockwise in alphabetical order.

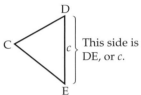

This side is DE, or *c*.

Parallel lines are straight lines which never ever meet or cross.

Perpendicular lines cross or meet each other at right angles (90°).
In this diagram DC is parallel to AB:

You can use a set square and ruler to draw parallel lines.
Draw AB. Move the set square along the ruler.
Draw CD.

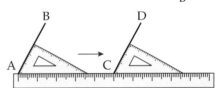

To draw perpendicular lines:
Draw EF. Place the set square onto the line and draw perpendicular line GH wherever it is required.

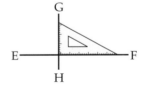

An **acute angle** is less than 90°. A **right angle** is exactly 90°. An **obtuse angle** is between 90° and 180°. A **reflex angle** is between 180° and 360°.

Example   Copy the diagram and mark:
AB = AG , GB parallel to FD,
∠GAB = 60° , ∠GBD = 120°.

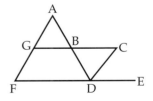

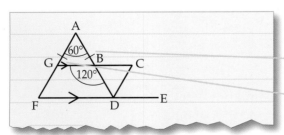

The '╱' symbol shows that AB = AG.

The '→' symbol shows that BG is parallel to FD.

Exercise 7.1

1 Which is which? Describe these angles correctly.

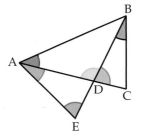

a) The angle coloured orange is _____.

b) The angle coloured blue is _____.

c) The angle coloured green is _____.

d) The angle coloured yellow is _____.

e) The angle coloured black is _____.

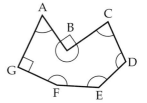

You could describe the red angle as ∠BAD or BÂD.

2 List all the marked angles in this diagram. For each one, state whether it is acute, a right angle, obtuse or reflex.

3 Which is which? Fill in the gaps.

a) _____ and _____ are parallel.

b) _____ and _____ are perpendicular to each other.

c) _____ is vertical.

d) _____ and _____ are horizontal.

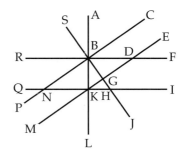

There may be more than one answer.

4 Draw these diagrams accurately.

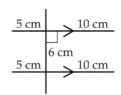

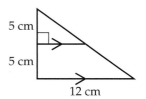

5 A rectangle PQRS has two shorter sides PQ and RS. PQ is 6 cm and QR is 10 cm long. Draw it accurately labelling the parallel and perpendicular lines. Measure the length of PR.

6 How many times between 6 am and 8 am are the hands on a clock at right angles? Explain how you worked it out.

Investigation

7 Below is a picture of a tangram. Use a set square and ruler to draw a tangram like this accurately. Cut out the pieces.
Using as many pieces as possible, investigate the shapes you can make, which have:

a) two parallel sides

b) at least one right angle

c) all acute angles

d) at least two obtuse angles.

Make up some similar challenges for a partner.

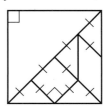

Angles

⊕ Measure angles correctly and draw acute, obtuse and reflex angles

⊕ Know the sum of angles at a point, on a straight line and in a triangle

⊕ Recognise vertically opposite angles and angles on a straight line

⊕ Use these properties to solve simple problems

An angle is a measure of turn and is measured using a **protractor**.

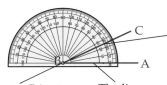

Read off the size of the angle in degrees here.
Angle AB̂C = 25°.

The vertex B is at the centre of the protractor.

The line segment BA is on the 0° line of the protractor.

Angles which meet at a point on a straight line add up to 180°.

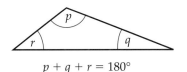

$a + b = 180°$

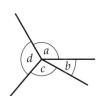

$a + b + c + d = 360°$

Angles which meet at a point add up to 360°.

The three angles of any triangle add up to 180°.

$p + q + r = 180°$

The two angles in a pair of **vertically opposite angles** are equal. (b and d are vertically opposite as they meet at a common vertex.)

$a = c \qquad b = d$

Example Find the size of the lettered angles. Give reasons for your answers.

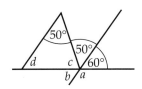

a is 120° because angles on a straight line add up to 180°.

b is 60° because it is vertically opposite an angle of 60°.

c is 70° because all the angles at a point add up to 360°.

d is 60° because the angles inside a triangle add up to 180°.

Exercise 7.2

1. Play with a partner. Take turns to draw an angle. Both of you write down an estimate for the size of the angle, then measure it. Whoever is the closer to the estimate wins one point. If you estimate exactly you get two points. Repeat five times to find the overall winner.

2. Arrange these lettered angles in order of size, smallest first.

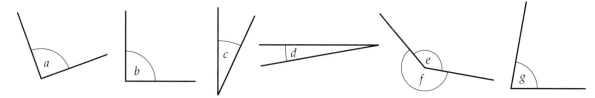

3. Draw angles of 40°, 65°, 87°, 103°, 15°, 210° and 355°. Label them clearly.

4. Calculate (don't measure) the lettered angles. Give reasons for your answers.

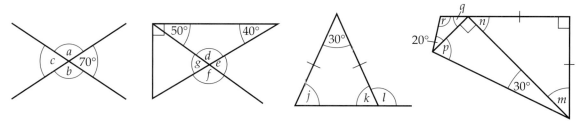

5. Draw the eight points of the compass accurately, using a protractor.
   Calculate (don't measure) the following turns, all in a **clockwise** direction:
   a) N to NW
   b) SE to NW
   c) NW to SE
   d) S to NE
   e) E to NW.

   Write down two turns which are:
   f) 90° clockwise
   g) 135° clockwise
   h) 225° clockwise
   i) 45° anticlockwise
   j) 45° clockwise.

6. Sketch a rectangle EFGH. Mark ∠GEF = 40°. Calculate the size of the other angles in the triangle EFG.

7. Sketch a quadrilateral ABCD. Mark in ∠CAB = 40°, ∠BCA = 45°, ∠BCD = 90° and ∠ADC = 60°. Calculate ∠ABC and ∠DAC.

> Remember, a quadrilateral is a shape with four sides.

Investigation

8. Draw a large triangle RST with no sides or angles the same. Mark the mid-point of TR as U, the mid-point of RS as V and the mid-point of ST as W. Join UVW to make another triangle. Mark the mid-points of the sides of UVW and join them. Repeat as many times as you can. Write down what you notice about:
   a) the lengths of the sides of the triangles
   b) the angles of the triangles
   c) the areas of the triangles.

Coordinates in all four quadrants

Key words
coordinates
origin
x-axis
y-axis
quadrant

⊕ Read and plot 2-D coordinates in all four quadrants

⊕ Find coordinates of points determined by geometric information

The **coordinates** of a point are written (**a, b**) where **a** is the distance across (left or right) and **b** is the distance up or down from the point (0, 0) which is called the **origin** . The *x*-**axis** is the horizontal axis and the *y*-**axis** is the vertical axis.

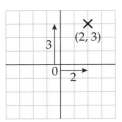 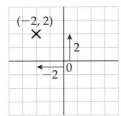 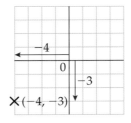 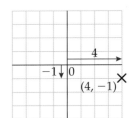

The coordinate grid is divided into four sections called **quadrants** .

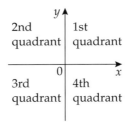

| 2nd quadrant | 1st quadrant |
| 3rd quadrant | 4th quadrant |

Example   Plot and name the points which could be the missing vertex of the parallelogram.

Join the three points. Parallelograms have two sets of parallel and equal sides. Draw a line from (4, 2) parallel to the one between (−2, 2) and (0, −1) and a horizontal one from (0, −1) and where they intersect could be the fourth point (6, −1).

Alternatively, draw a line from (−2, 2) parallel to the one between (4, 2) and (0, −1) and a line from (0, −1) parallel to the one between (4, 2) and (−2, 2). Where they intersect could also be the fourth point (−6, −1). A third possibility is the point (2, 5).

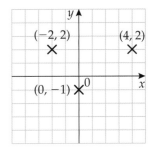

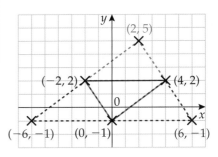

Exercise 7.3

1 Write down the coordinates of the missing vertex for each of these rectangles.

a)
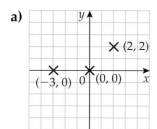
(−1, 4) (2, 4)
(2, −2)

b)
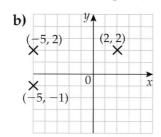
(−5, 2) (2, 2)
(−5, −1)

c)
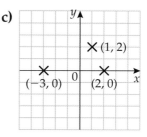
(1, 2)
(−3, 0) (2, 0)

2 Write down the coordinates of the point that could be the missing vertex from each of these parallelograms.

> There are 3 possible answers.
> Look back at the Example.

a)
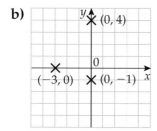
(2, 2)
(−3, 0) (0, 0)

b)
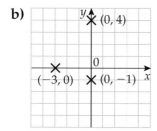
(0, 4)
(−3, 0) (0, −1)

c)
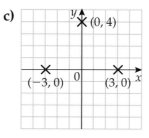
(0, 4)
(−3, 0) (3, 0)

3 Play with a partner. Label a grid −5 to 5 on both axes. Take it in turns to plot points, each using a different colour . The first person to place a point to complete a rectangle draws it in, gains a point, and has another go.

4 The points (3, 3) and (0, 0) are two vertices of a square. Plot these points on a 10 × 10 grid and then plot two more points to complete the square. How many different ways are there of completing the square?

5 On a 10 × 10 grid draw a rectangle which has a perimeter of 10 units and has one vertex at the origin and another at (0, −3).
  a) Write down the coordinates of the other vertices.
  b) What is the area of your rectangle?

6 AB is one side of a rectangle which has an area of 12 square units. Where could the other vertices be?

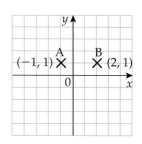
(−1, 1) A   B (2, 1)

7 An isosceles triangle has its base vertices at (−2, 0) and (2, 0). Where could its third vertex be? Explain how you can tell.

> An isosceles triangle has two equal sides and two equal angles.

8.1 Grouping data

⊕ Construct frequency tables for data

⊕ Find the range of a set of data and put data into equal groups

⊕ Find the modal class for a set of grouped data

If data has been measured – such as time or length – or has a large range (spread) then it is often grouped. These groups are called **class intervals** . The class interval with the highest frequency is the **modal class** or **modal group** .

Example 1 The number of lengths swum by pupils in a class for a sponsored swim were:

| 8 | 45 | 17 | 28 | 12 | 36 | 25 | 20 | 15 | 48 | 32 | 29 |
| 18 | 40 | 37 | 26 | 9 | 21 | 16 | 33 | 43 | 19 | 24 | 35 |

a) Use the class intervals 1–10, 11–20, 21–30, 31–40, 41+ to group the data.

b) Which class interval is the modal class?

a)

Number of lengths	1–10	11–20	21–30	31–40	41+
Tally	||	⊔⊔⊔ ||	⊔⊔⊔ |	⊔⊔⊔ |	|||
Frequency	2	7	6	6	3

We use 41+ to record 41 or more lengths.

b) The modal class is 11–20 lengths.

Example 2 The members of a rugby team counted how many sit-ups they could do without stopping. Their results were:

83	53	79	63	90
42	49	62	76	63
51	68	39	50	46

Sarah groups the data into two class intervals: 30–69 and 70+.
Tony uses nine class intervals: 30–39, 40–49 and so on, up to 100–109.

a) What are the disadvantages of the groups that Sarah and Tony use?

b) What is the range of the data?

c) How could the data be grouped more sensibly?

a) Sarah has not used enough class intervals. Most of the data will be recorded in the first class interval.

Tony would have about the right amount if he made an open last class interval as many of the last class intervals would have nothing in them.

b) The range of the data is $90 - 39 = 51$

c) Using six class intervals would be a sensible way to group the data:

30–39, 40–49, 50–59, 60–69, 70–79, 80+

As the range is 51, 5 groups of 10, plus one group of 80+ makes it easy to spot the pattern.

Exercise 8.1

1 Nathaniel counts the number of petals on daisies. Here are his results:

15 26 31 17 11 24 29 19 18 33 22
25 19 26 31 30 18 24 27

a) What is the range of the data?

b) Complete this frequency table for the data:

Number of petals	11–15	16–20	21–25	26–30	31–35
Tally					
Frequency					

2 Twelve pupils receive the following allowances each week:

£1.50 £2.50 £1.75 £3.50 £3 £1.75 £1 £6 £4.50 £5.50 £2 £2.75

a) What is the range of the data?

b) Complete this frequency table for the data:

Amount	Up to £1.50	£1.51–£3	£3.01–£4.50	£4.51–£6
Tally				
Frequency				

c) Which class interval is the modal class?

3 The ages last birthday of swimmers at a swimming pool were:

42 27 57 21 35 37 62 34 42 51 26 59
23 47 41 28 61 84 22 39 57 35 42

a) What is the range of the data?

b) Draw and complete a frequency table for the data using class intervals of 21–30, 31–40, 41–50, 51–60, 61+.

4 The number of hours twenty one teenagers spent watching TV per week were recorded as follows: 5 12 16   4 18 14 10   7 12 15 17
13   8 13 16   5 14 11   6 10 20

a) What is the range of the data?

b) Write down five equal class intervals that you could group the data into.

c) Draw and complete a frequency table for the data, using your five equal class intervals.

5 What is wrong with these class intervals?

a)
Amount spent on a pair of trainers (£s)				
0–20	20–40	40–60	60–80	80+

b)
Amount spent on a pair of trainers (£s)				
0–19	20–39	40–59	60–79	80+

6 Harry counts how many cars pass his school in a minute. He records his results over a 20 minute period: 6 13   9   8 15 12 19 11 21 15
12 14 20   8 11 16   5 12 19   9

a) What is the range of the data?

b) Construct a frequency table for the data, with equal class intervals.

Investigation

7 How long are words in the English language? Does the initial letter make a difference? Open a dictionary at any page. Record the length of each entry using equal class intervals of 1–3 letters, 4–6 letters and so on. Which class interval was the modal group?

⊕ Drawing pie charts

⊕ Interpreting pie charts

Pie charts show the fraction of the data in each group.

A **sector** is a 'slice' of a pie chart.

Example 1 The ages of fifty children in a playgroup are recorded in the table:
Show this data as a pie chart.

Age (years)	Frequency
2	5
3	15
4	13
5	17

Age (years)	Frequency	%
2	5	10
3	15	30
4	13	26
5	17	34

First find each frequency as a percentage. There are 50 children so each child will represent 2%.

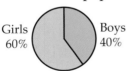

- ☐ 2 years
- ☐ 3 years
- ☐ 4 years
- ☐ 5 years

Each time you draw a new sector, turn the pie chart scale to 0%. There should be no gaps in the finished pie chart.

Example 2

Class 7A: 30 pupils

Girls 60%   Boys 40%

Class 7B: 20 pupils

Girls 40%   Boys 60%

a) Which class appears to contain the greatest number of boys?

b) Calculate how many boys are in each class to find out if your guess was right.

a) 7B appears to have more boys as its sector for boys is larger than 7A's.

b) 7A: 40% of 30 = 12.

7B: 60% of 20 = 12.

Both classes have the same number of boys.

Exercise 8.2

1 The table shows the percentage of households in Great Britain owning zero, one, or two or more cars.
Draw a pie chart to show this information.

Number of cars	Percentage
0	27
1	45
2 or more	28

2 The table shows the percentage coverage of each of the five oceans.
Draw a pie chart to represent this data.

Ocean	Percentage
Pacific	47
Atlantic	25
Indian	19
Southern	5
Arctic	4

3 Fifty people were asked what type of take-away meal they preferred:

Type of take-away	Frequency
Indian	12
Chinese	7
Fish and Chips	11
Burgers	15
Pizza	5

How many % would represent just one person? Look at Example 1.

Draw a pie chart to represent this data.

4 The table shows how many CDs were bought by pupils last week.

Number of CDs bought	Frequency
0	60
1	106
2	22
3	12

Find the total frequency. What percentage would represent one CD?

Draw a pie chart to show this information.

5 Sumi and Sam are drawing pie charts to show the number of boys and girls in their classes. Sam says "My chart shows that there are more girls in 7 Red than in 7 Blue". Explain why Sam may be wrong.

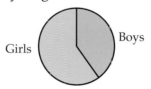

Sumi's pie chart showing boys & girls in class 7 Blue

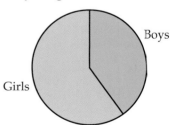

Sam's pie chart showing boys & girls in class 7 Red

6 **a)** From the pie charts, what can you say about the number of pupils in each class who walk to school?

b) There are twenty five pupils in 7R and twenty in 7B. How many pupils walk to school in each class?

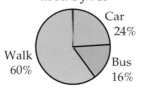

Type of transport to school used by 7R

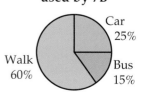

Type of transport to school used by 7B

Planning an experiment or survey

⊕ Suggest ways of finding data to answer a question

⊕ Decide what data you need and where to find it

We collect data in order to help us to answer particular questions or problems.
Data can be collected from **primary sources** (surveys and experiments) or secondary sources.

A **survey** : asking people questions

An **experiment** : measuring or counting to collect information

A **secondary source** : information from sources such as the Internet, a book or a CD-ROM.

Example 1   Which of the following data can be collected from:
i) a survey   ii) an experiment   iii) a secondary source?

a)   The number of *heads* showing when three coins are spun
b)   Which is the most popular newspaper among your classmates' parents?
c)   Which is the most popular newspaper in the United Kingdom?

a)   An experiment: the number of *heads* will be counted each time.

b)   A survey: classmates will be asked what newspaper their parents read.

c)   A secondary source: the Internet or a newspaper would have

information on how many copies were sold.

Example 2   Imogen is doing a survey to find the type of music pupils prefer at her school.
She asks ten of her best friends. Why might her survey not lead to her
gathering accurate information?

There are two main problems:

– She has only asked a small number of people.

– The people questioned were her friends and so are likely to share

similar tastes in music.

Exercise 8.3

1 For each of the following questions, decide whether doing a survey, an experiment, or
collecting data from a secondary source would be the best way of getting the data you
need.

a)   Are house prices in your area higher than those in a different part of the country?
b)   Do people with longer legs run faster?
c)   How many times each month does the average Year 7 pupil eat at a restaurant?
d)   Does a drawing pin always land with the point sticking up?
e)   What is the number of goals scored by the school football team in a season?
f)   What is the favourite TV soap of the pupils in your maths group?
g)   What is the number of peas in a pod?
h)   What is the most popular colour of car?

2 For part **b** of Q1, describe how you would go about collecting data.

> Think about what type of data to collect; how to collect the data; where to collect the data from; how much data to collect; and what units to use.

3 Juan is carrying out an experiment to test if a standard six-sided dice is fair. He throws the dice ten times and gets these results:

Number on dice	1	2	3	4	5	6
Frequency	2	1	4	0	2	1

> Look back at Example 2 for ideas.

Juan says that because he did not get any 4s his dice was not fair.
What was wrong with his experiment?

4 Explain why these surveys could lead to incorrect results:
   a) Asking 'What is your favourite sport?' outside a football ground
   b) Asking 'How many books do you read each week?' in the school library
   c) Asking 'Do you eat school dinners?' in the dinner hall
   d) Asking your friends 'Who is your favourite film star?'

5 Which units would be sensible to use if you were carrying out an experiment or survey on the following topics?
   a) 'Are Year 7 pupils shorter than Year 8 pupils?'
   b) 'How far do you live from school?'
   c) 'How long do you spend on homework each day?'
   d) 'Is there a connection between the age of a pupil and the size of his or her school-bag?'
   e) Are shoe size and handspan related?
   f) Is age connected to the amount of sleep children need?

Investigation

6 Plan one of the following experiments for the next lesson:
   a) How many 'times-table' questions can you answer in one minute?
   b) How many throws of a dice does it take until you get a 6?
   c) Does a drawing pin always land with the sharp point sticking up?
   d) How accurate are people's guesses when they estimate the number of beads in a clear glass jar?

For the experiment you have chosen decide:
   ● how many times you are going to carry it out
   ● who you are going to ask (**a** and **d** only)
   ● what equipment you need.
If you choose **a** you will need to decide **how** the questions will be asked.

Collecting data

⊕ Design a data collection sheet

⊕ Construct frequency tables for data, grouping data where appropriate

⊕ Collect and record data from an experiment

Once you have decided what problem you are going to investigate the next stage is to organise **how** you are going to collect the data. To do this you design a **data collection sheet** .

The data you will collect may or may not need to be grouped. You record grouped data in a **frequency table** .

Example 1   Design data collection sheets for the following:

a)   Is there a connection between height and handspan?

b)   How do teachers travel to school?

a)   You may want to know:

Name	Age (years)	Height (cm)	Handspan (cm)	Male or female?

b)   You may want to know:

Name of teacher	Transport used	Distance from school (km)	Time left home	Length of journey (minutes)

Example 2   Construct frequency tables for the following:

a)   The experiment 'How many lengths of a swimming pool can you swim in 30 minutes?'

b)   The survey 'How many books do you read in a month?'

Possible answers include:

a)

Lengths	0–19	20–39	40–59	60–79	80–99	100+
Frequency						

b)

Number of books	0–4	5–9	10–14	15–19	20+
Frequency					

Make sure your frequency tables have clear groups with no gaps or overlaps.

Exercise 8.4

1 Design data collection sheets for each of these experiments or surveys:

    a) Do countries with larger areas have bigger populations?

    b) Do all people with blue eyes have blonde hair?

    c) Do boys run faster than girls?

> Think of a way to test the running speed of boys and girls.

2 What is wrong with the following frequency tables? For each one, show how it can be improved.

    a) How often do you hire a video?

	Often	Sometimes	Never
Frequency			

    b) How many bags of crisps do you eat in a week?

Number of bags	0	1–3	4–8	More than 9
Frequency				

    c) How many pieces of fruit do you eat in a week?

Number of pieces	0–5	5–10	10–15	15–20	More than 20
Frequency					

3 Construct frequency tables for these experiments or surveys:

    a) The number of times that you get *tails* when spinning two coins at the same time

    b) The number you get when rolling a dice

    c) Answers to the question 'How many pets do you own?'

    d) Answers to the question 'What month of the year were you born?'

4 Construct frequency tables for **grouped** data collected for these experiments or surveys:

    a) The shoe sizes of Year 7 pupils

    b) The length of words (in letters) in a book

    c) 'How many packets of crisps do you eat in a month?'

    d) The age of people eating in a burger bar

    e) Parents' ages when their first child was born.

Investigations

5 Choose one of the experiments or surveys from Q2. Carry out the experiment or survey, collecting the results in the improved frequency table.

6 Design a data collection sheet for the experiment you chose in your last maths lesson. Decide if your experiment will produce data that needs to be put in a frequency table. When your teacher has checked your work, carry out your experiment. Record the results in your data collection sheet.

Representing data

⊕ Draw graphs and diagrams to represent data

Key words
axes
pie chart
bar chart
bar-line graph
pictogram

Different types of graphs can be used to represent the same information. When deciding which graph to use, choose one that shows the information clearly. For example, a pictogram may not be useful for representing information with large frequencies because of the number of symbols that you would need to draw.

Example 1   A survey to find the after-school clubs attended by a form group gives the following data:
Represent this data using:

a) a bar chart   b) a bar-line graph

c) a pictogram (use the symbol 👤 to represent 2 pupils).

Activity	Frequency
Football	6
Hockey	3
Music	7
Chess	4
Science	2

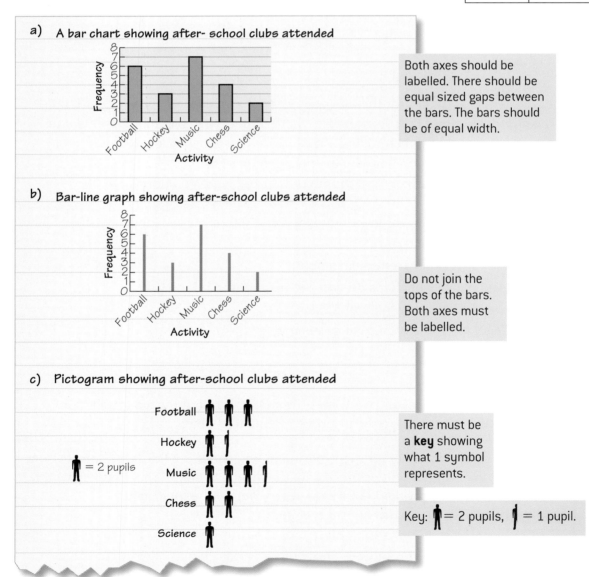

a)   A bar chart showing after- school clubs attended

Both axes should be labelled. There should be equal sized gaps between the bars. The bars should be of equal width.

b)   Bar-line graph showing after-school clubs attended

Do not join the tops of the bars. Both axes must be labelled.

c)   Pictogram showing after-school clubs attended

Football

Hockey

👤 = 2 pupils   Music

Chess

Science

There must be a **key** showing what 1 symbol represents.

Key: 👤 = 2 pupils, 👤 = 1 pupil.

Exercise 8.5

1 Fifty students were asked how many CDs they bought last month. Here are the results:

Number of CDs bought	Frequency
0	4
1	18
2	21
3	7

a) Draw a pictogram to represent this data, using the symbol ⊙ to represent a frequency of 2.

b) Draw another pictogram to represent this data, this time using the symbol ⊙ to represent a frequency of 4.

c) Draw a bar chart to represent this data.

How could the circle be split into four equal parts?
Remember to draw a key to show what each symbol represents.

2 This table shows the spread of ages of the population in the UK.

Age	Percentage
Under 16	20
16–44	40
45–64	22
65+	18

a) Draw pie chart to represent this data.

b) Say why you can't draw a bar chart to represent this data.

3 A survey to find the favourite crisp flavour of thirty children gives the following results:

Flavour	Frequency
Cheese & Onion	10
Plain	2
Salt & Vinegar	5
Chicken	9
Other	4

a) Draw a bar-line graph to show this information.

b) Draw a pictogram to show this information. Remember to include a key.

4 The populations of four European countries are:

Country	Population (millions)
France	59
Germany	83
Italy	57
United Kingdom	59

Decide which type of chart would be best to show this information and draw it.

5 Thirty pupils are asked how much money they have in their pockets. Show this information by drawing a bar chart or a bar-line graph.

Amount of money	Frequency
0–£0.99	12
£1–£1.99	7
£2–£2.99	4
£3–£3.99	2
£4–£4.99	3
£5–£5.99	2

6 For each of the questions below, write down whether you would draw a pictogram, bar chart or pie chart to show the data collected.

a) Answers to the question 'What is your favourite pizza topping?'

b) The percentage of left-handed people in your class.

c) The population of European capital cities.

d) The amount people spend on food each week.

Rounding

Key words
rounding
round up
round down
nearest ten
nearest tenth

⊕ Round a whole number to the nearest 10, 100 or 1000

⊕ Round a decimal number to the nearest whole number or nearest tenth

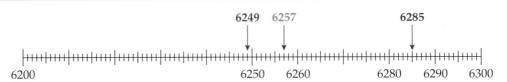

6257 lies between the tens 6250 and 6260 – the **nearest ten** is 6260.

6257 lies between the hundreds 6200 and 6300 – the **nearest hundred** is 6300.

6249 lies between the hundreds 6200 and 6300 – the **nearest hundred** is 6200.

6257 lies between the thousands 6000 and 7000 – the **nearest thousand** is 6000.

This is called **rounding** a number to its nearest ten, hundred or thousand.

6285 lies between the tens 6280 and 6290. It is exactly halfway between them. (6290 − 6285 = 5, 6285 − 6280 = 5)

When this happens we always **round up** , so we say the nearest ten is 6290.

7.28 lies between the tenths 7.2 and 7.3 – the nearest tenth is 7.3.

'**Rounding to the nearest tenth** ' is sometimes called '**rounding to one decimal place**'.

7.96 lies between the tenths 7.9 and 8.0 – the nearest tenth is 8.0.

We can also round to the nearest whole number.

7.28 lies between the whole numbers 7 and 8 – the nearest whole number is 7.

Example   Estimate the answer to this multiplication by rounding each number to the nearest whole number: 8.93 × 3.12

8.93 rounds to 9.   3.12 rounds to 3.

So, an estimate is 9 × 3 = **27**   (The calculator gives an exact
answer of 27.8616.)

Exercise 9.1

1 Below are the attendances at basketball matches last week:

a) Sharks: 4526

b) Dolphins: 3174

c) Porpoises: 5829

d) Panthers: 4371

e) Pumas: 2096

f) Marlins: 1508

g) Whales: 3971

h) Scorpions: 6009

i) Cheetahs: 8712

j) Tigers: 5379

Round each attendance to the nearest   **i)** 10,   **ii)** 100,   **iii)** 1000 people.

2 Round each price to **i)** the nearest pound **ii)** the nearest ten pence.

    a) £14.72   **b)** £15.09   **c)** £9.56   **d)** £6.49   **e)** £5.52

    f) £14.48   **g)** £25.95   **h)** £16.76   **i)** £0.88   **j)** £17.77

3 Use the digits 4, 7, 3 and 6 to make numbers with 2 decimal places between 1 and 10 such as 7.34 or 3.46.

You may only use each digit once in any number.

Find 3-digit numbers which, when rounded to the nearest tenth, round to the numbers below:

    a) 3.6   **b)** 6.3   **c)** 4.7   **d)** 7.3   **e)** 3.8 | 3.64 rounds to 3.6 |

    f) 4.4   **g)** 7.6   **h)** 6.5   **i)** 3.5   **j)** 4.8

    k) 7.4   **l)** 3.7   **m)** 6.7   **n)** 7.5   **o)** 4.6

4 Write an estimate of each calculation by first rounding each number to the nearest whole number:

    a) 7.3×4.9 **b)** 6.2×2.8 **c)** 3.17×8.91 **d)** 7.6×1.93

    e) $5.96 + 14.21$ **f)** $17.15 - 9.88$ **g)** $9.13 \div 2.91$ **h)** $7.86 \div 2.07$

Use a calculator to find the exact answers and compare them with your estimates.

5 Use the football statistics from a weekend newspaper. Record the attendance (the number of spectators) at each match, then round the numbers to the nearest:

    a) 10   **b)** 100   **c)** 1000.

6 The distance from A to B has been rounded to give 3000 miles. What is the maximum and minimum possible actual distance if the distance has been rounded:

    a) to the nearest 1000 miles   **b)** to the nearest 100 miles   **c)** to the nearest 10 miles?

7 Who am I?

    a) I am a number with 2 decimal places. My digits are 3, 4 and 6. I am half of 8.8 when rounded to one decimal place.

    b) I am a number with 2 decimal places. The sum of my digits is 19. If I am rounded to the nearest tenth, then subtracted from 10, the result is 3.3.

Investigation

8 Use four digit cards: 2, 5, 7, 8 and a counter for a decimal point.

Choose three cards and create different decimal numbers such as 57.8 or 2.57.

Round the numbers to the nearest whole number. For example:

    57.8 rounds to 58 and 2.57 rounds to 3.

Investigate how many different rounded numbers you can make.

| Work systematically. Start with numbers with 1 decimal place then with 2 decimal places and so on. |

Positive and negative numbers

⊕ Know how to put positive and negative numbers in order

⊕ Know how to add positive and negative numbers

The set of **positive** and **negative** whole numbers, including zero, are called **integers**.

To add two integers, use a number line to help you. Start on the line at the first number:
To add a positive number count right.
To add a negative number count left.

For example, to calculate ⁺3 + ⁻4, start at ⁺3, then count four places left to finish at ⁻1.

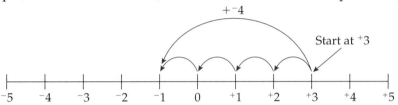

Example 1 Write the following numbers in order, smallest to largest:
⁻5, ⁺1, ⁻3, ⁺4, ⁺2

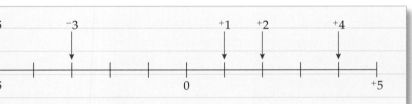

The order is: ⁻5, ⁻3, ⁺1, ⁺2, ⁺4

Mark the numbers on a number line.

Example 2 An addition pyramid has this as its bottom row.

| ⁻2 | ⁺3 | ⁻4 | ⁺4 | ⁻7 |

Complete the pyramid.

Complete each row in turn. The number in each brick is found by adding the two directly below it.

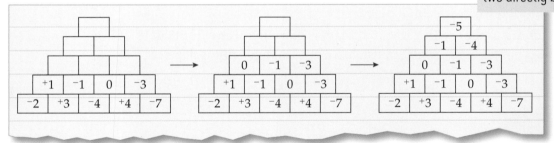

Exercise 9.2

1 Put the following temperatures in order, lowest to highest:
a) ⁻3 °C, ⁺2 °C, ⁻1 °C, ⁺4 °C, ⁺1 °C
b) ⁻5 °C, ⁻3 °C, ⁻6 °C, ⁺2 °C, 0 °C
c) 0 °C, ⁺4 °C, ⁺1 °C, ⁻3 °C, ⁺2 °C
d) ⁻6 °C, ⁺6 °C, ⁺3 °C, ⁻3 °C, ⁻1 °C
e) ⁺5 °C, ⁻1 °C, ⁺2 °C, ⁻6 °C, ⁺3 °C
f) 0 °C, ⁺2 °C, ⁻1 °C, ⁺1 °C, ⁻2 °C

2 Write each pair of numbers, with either a < or > sign between them:
a) ⁺2 and ⁺4
b) ⁺3 and ⁻5
c) ⁻3 and ⁺2
d) ⁺5 and ⁻1
e) ⁻1 and ⁺3
f) 0 and ⁻5
g) ⁺4 and 0
h) ⁻3 and ⁻5
i) ⁻6 and ⁻2

< means 'less than'
> means 'more than'

3 Which numbers are exactly halfway between each pair? Use a number line.
   a) −2 and −8 **b)** −3 and ⁺6.

4 This is the final Premier League Table for the season that ended in 2002. It shows the total number of goals scored by and against each team in the season. Complete the table by writing the 'goal difference' for each team as an integer. The goal difference is found by subtracting the goals against from the goals for.

	Arsenal	Liverpool	Man Utd	Newcastle	Leeds	Chelsea	West Ham	Aston Villa	Tottenham	Blackburn	Southampton	Middlesbro	Fulham	Charlton	Everton	Bolton	Sunderland	Ipswich	Derby	Leicester
Goals for	79	67	87	74	53	66	48	46	49	55	46	35	36	38	45	44	29	41	33	30
Goals against	36	30	45	52	37	38	57	47	53	51	54	47	44	49	57	62	51	64	63	64
Goal difference	+43	+37	+42	+22																

5 Complete the following additions:
   a) ⁺3 + ⁻2 **b)** ⁻5 + ⁺4 **c)** ⁻6 + ⁻3
   d) ⁺4 + ⁺2 **e)** ⁺5 + ⁻7 **f)** ⁺1.5 + ⁻0.5
   g) ⁺6 + ⁻3 **h)** ⁻14 + ⁺8 **i)** ⁻12 + 0 + ⁺6

6 Complete these addition pyramids.
   The number in each brick is found by adding the two directly below it.

   a) 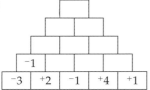 **b)**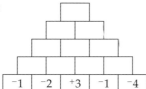

7 A game for two players. Use four dice, two red and two blue.
   The numbers on the red dice are positive, the numbers on the blue dice are negative.
   Take turns to roll the four dice and write the four integers with the correct sign. For example, '4' on a red dice is ⁺4. '3' on a blue dice is ⁻3. Add all four integers together. Write down your score. Repeat for ten additions each. The winner is the player with the highest total score from the ten rounds.
   How many different scores do you have between you? What are the minimum and maximum possible scores?

8 Complete these magic squares. In a magic square the rows, columns and diagonals all add to the same total.

   a)
⁺2	⁻5	
⁻2	⁺3	⁻4

   ⁻2 + ⁺3 + ⁻4 = ⁻3. So every row, column and diagonal in this square has a total of ⁻3.

   b)
0		⁻2
	⁻5	
⁻4		⁻6

Investigation

9 Use one set of integer cards ⁻5 to ⁺5, including zero.
   Investigate different additions that can be made using three cards. For example: ⁻2 + ⁻1 = ⁻3
   Investigate different additions that can be made using four cards.

   Be systematic. For example: keep one number fixed on the right and explore different possibilities for the cards on the left.

Subtracting integers

⊕ Know how to subtract positive and negative numbers

Key words
positive number
negative number
integer

Subtracting a **positive number** is the same as **adding** a **negative number** .
Subtracting a **negative** number is the same as **adding** a **positive** number. You can use a number line to show this.

To subtract one **integer** from another, convert the subtraction into an addition of its inverse. For example, for $^-3 - ^-5$, first convert it into $^-3 + ^+5$ because the inverse of $^-5$ is $^+5$. On the number line, start at $^-3$ and move 5 places to the right to finish at $^+2$.

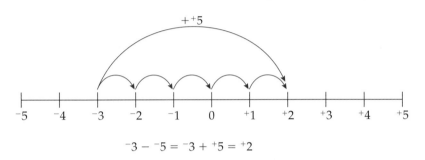

$$^-3 - ^-5 = ^-3 + ^+5 = ^+2$$

Example   Find the result of the following subtractions:

   a) $^-3 - ^+1$ **b)** $^+4 - ^-2$

   a) $^-3 - ^+1$ is the same as $^-3 + ^-1 = ^-4$

   b) $^+4 - ^-2$ is the same as $^+4 + ^+2 = ^+6$

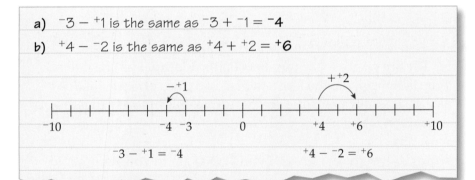

To add a negative number, count left. To subtract a negative number, count right.

Exercise 9.3 ....

1 Find ☐ in each of the following:

   a) $^+3 - ^-1 = ^+3 + \square$ **b)** $^+4 - ^+2 = ^+4 + \square$

   c) $^-76 - ^+1 = ^-76 + \square$ **d)** $^-1091 - ^-768 = ^-1091 + \square$

2 Find the result of the following subtractions:

   a) $^+6 - ^+3$ **b)** $^+2 - ^-1$

   c) $^-3 - ^+2$ **d)** $^-5 - ^-4$

   e) $^+27 - ^+15$ **f)** $^+103 - ^-6$

   g) $^-28 - ^+52$ **h)** $^-1 - ^-6$

   i) $^+1.5 - ^-2.5$ **j)** $^+16 - ^-17$

3. Complete this table to show the outputs for different inputs in a subtraction machine:

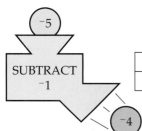

Subtract ⁻1 machine

Input	+2	+1	-5	+7	0	+1	-3	+1.5	$-\frac{1}{2}$	$+\frac{1}{2}$
Output	+3	+2								

Now complete the tables for the following two machines:

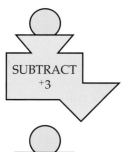

Subtract ⁺3 machine

Input	+2	+1	-5	+7	0	+1	-3	+1.5	$-\frac{1}{2}$	$+\frac{1}{2}$
Output	⁻1	⁻2								

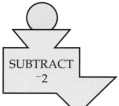

Subtract ⁻2 machine

Input	+2	+1	-5	+7	0	+1	-3	+1.5	$-\frac{1}{2}$	$+\frac{1}{2}$
Output	+4	+3								

4. Complete the following subtraction tables by subtracting the second number from the first number:

a)

2nd number				
	+3	**-2**	**+5**	**-1**	**+1**

1st number. ⁻2 − ⁺3

1st number	+3	-2	+5	-1	+1
-2	-5				-3
+4		+6			
+3					
-1					
+1		-4			

b)

1st number	+2	-4	-3	$+3\frac{1}{2}$
+2				$-1\frac{1}{2}$
+3			+6	
-5		-1		
$+\frac{1}{2}$				

5. A game for two players.
Use two cubes.
Write ⁻2, ⁻1, 0, ⁺1, ⁺2, ⁺3 on one cube, and ⁻3, ⁻2, ⁻1, 0, ⁺1, ⁺2 on the other.

Take it in turns to roll the dice, and subtract the number on the red dice from the number on the blue dice. The player with the highest answer wins the round.

Repeat for ten throws each. The winner is the player who wins the most rounds.

6. Who am I?
   a) When I am subtracted from ⁺4, the result is half of ⁻2.
   b) When I am subtracted from ⁻5, the result is double ⁺3.

Multiplying

Key words
multiply
multiplication
estimate
grid method
standard method

⊕ Multiply a three-digit number by a two-digit number using a standard written method

⊕ Estimate the result of a multiplication by rounding

⊕ Check the result by comparing it with the estimate

Multiplication can be calculated using mental or written methods.

Written methods of multiplying a three-digit number by a two-digit number can include:

a) a **grid method**   **b)** a **standard method**

Whichever method you use:

- **Estimate** the answer by rounding, then multiplying the rounded numbers
- complete the multiplication
- compare the result with the estimate to check if it is sensible.

Example 1   Use a grid method to calculate 423×28.

An estimate is $400 \times 30 = 12\,000$.

	400	20	3
20			
8			

	400	20	3	
20	8000	400	60	8 4 6 0
8	3200	160	24	3 3 8 4
				1 1 8 4 4

Check: 11 844 is close to 12 000. ✓

Draw a 2 × 3 grid, writing the parts of the numbers alongside.

Multiply each part of the grid, then combine the parts in each row.

Add these together. Check the answer against the estimate.

Example 2   Use a standard method to calculate 326×29.

An estimate is $300 \times 30 = 9000$.

```
      3 2 6
        2 9
      6 5 2 0    (326 × 20)
      2 9 3 4    (326 × 9)
      9 4 5 4
```

Check: 9454 is close to 9000. ✓

Remember to check the answer against the estimate.

Exercise 9.4

1 Copy these grids, then do the multiplications using the grid method.
Start by making an estimate.

326 × 45

	300	20	6
40			
5			

178 × 26

	100	70	8
20			
6			

486 × 38

	400	80	6
30			
8			

313 × 19

	300	10	3
10			
9			

2 Calculate the total cost of each school trip:

a) Theatre: 186 pupils at £27 each

b) London: 117 pupils at £45 each

c) France: 47 pupils at £285 each

d) Skiing: 25 pupils at £516 each

e) Sailing   32 pupils at £179 each

f) Camping: 113 pupils at £38 each

3 Find the missing digits in the following calculations:

a) 527 × 28 = 1 4 ☐ 5 6

b) 36 × 227 = 8 1 ☐ 2

c) 286 × 45 = 1 2 ☐ 7 0

d) 31 × 309 = 9 ☐ 7 9

e) 118 × 45 = 5 ☐ ☐ 0

f) 53 × 316 = 1 ☐ 7 ☐ 8

g) 54 × 186 = 1 ☐ ☐ 4 4

h) 253 × 78 = 1 ☐ 7 ☐ 4

4 A playing field measures 135 m by 63 m. The field is to be sprinkled with fertiliser. One bag of fertiliser is enough for 100 m² of field. How many bags are needed?

5 Flyaway Travel Company sold 18 holidays to Majorca yesterday at £478 each. How much money did they receive in total for the Majorcan holidays?

Investigations

6 Use the four consecutive digit cards: 3, 4, 5, 6.
Create two 2-digit numbers, using each digit only once.
Multiply them together.
Investigate which two numbers give the largest possible answer, and which give the smallest possible answer.
Repeat the activity for a different set of five consecutive digits.
Can you see a pattern?

7 Start with 25 000.
Investigate different pairs of 3-digit and 2-digit numbers which have a product close to 25 000. Each pair must contain five different digits.
How many can you find within 1000 of 25 000?
Can you find any within 100 of 25 000?

Multiplying decimals

⊕ Multiply a number with 2 decimal places by a 1-digit number, using a standard written method

⊕ Estimate the result of decimal multiplication by rounding

⊕ Check the result by comparing it with the estimate

Multiplications can be calculated using mental or written methods.

Every method should start with an **estimate** .
- Estimate the answer by rounding, then multiplying the rounded numbers
- complete the multiplication
- compare the result with the estimate to check if it is sensible.

When using a **standard method** to multiply numbers with 2 decimal places by a 1-digit number:
- Change the decimal number into a 3-digit whole number by multiplying by 100
- Calculate the 3-digit number multipled by the 1-digit number
- Divide the answer by 100.

Example 1   Use a grid method to calculate 4.23×8.

An estimate is $4 \times 8 = 32$

	4	.2	.03
8			

Draw a 1 × 3 grid, writing the parts of the numbers alongside it.

	4	.2	.03	
8	32	1.6	.24	→ **33.84**

Check: 33.84 is close to 32. ✓

Multiply each part of the grid then combine the parts in each row. Finally, add them together. Check your answer against the estimate.

Example 2   Use a standard method to calculate 3.26×9.

An estimate is $3 \times 9 = 27$

$3.26 \times 10 = 326$

$326 \times 9 = 2934$

$2934 \div 100 = 29.34$

Check: 29.34 is close to 27. ✓

Change 3.26 into a 3-digit number by multiplying by 100.

Divide the answer by 100.

Check your answer against the estimate.

Exercise 9.5

1 Copy these grids, then use a grid method to do the multiplications.

Start by making an estimate.

a) 3.26×4

	3	.2	.06
4			

b) 5.83×7

	5	.8	.03
7			

c) 9.15×6

d) 4.78×9

2 Use a standard written method to do these multiplications:

a) 5.28×3 b) 7.15×6 c) 4.92×8 d) 6.17×9

e) 8×3.74 f) 9×6.08 g) 7×5.69 h) 4×7.38

3 Calculate the total cost of each set of clothes:

a) Gloves: 8 pairs at £2.78 per pair

b) Scarves: 6 at £3.26 each

c) Caps: 5 at £6.46 each

d) Socks: 7 pairs at £1.88 per pair

e) T-shirts 4 at £8.69 each

f) Ties: 8 at £7.28

g) Tops: 7 at £9.45 each

4 Find the missing digit in the following calculations:

a) $4.23 \times 7 = 2\ \square\ .\ 6\ \ 1$ b) $8.16 \times 5 = 4\ \square\ .\ 8\ \ 0$

c) $8 \times 1.73 = 1\ 3\ .\ \square\ 4$ d) $5.29 \times 6 = \square\ 1\ .\ \square\ 4$

e) $7 \times 4.76 = 3\ \square\ .\ 3\ \ 2$ f) $9 \times 3.81 = \square\ 4\ .\ \square\ 9$

g) $8.69 \times 3 = 2\ \square\ .\ 0\ \square$ h) $9.76 \times 4 = \square\ 9\ .\ \square\ 4$

5 Use a set of 1 – 9 digit cards and a counter as a decimal point.

Your first target is 28.

Shuffle the digit cards and deal out four of them. Use these four cards to create a 3-digit number with 2 decimal places and a 1-digit whole number.

Choose numbers that multiply together to give an answer close to the target.

Score points equivalent to the difference.

Record your calculations, scoring points accordingly.

Replace the cards and repeat for each of these targets: 18, 31, 23, 11.5.

What is your total score?

Can you score less than 15?

6 Gary is building a fence. He has eight pieces of fencing, each 1.65 m long. How many more pieces will he need to build a fence 20 metres long?

7 Jane calculates that to drive to work and back she uses 1.32 litres of petrol. She doesn't work at weekends, or on Wednesdays. How much petrol does she use per week for work?

> A **product** is the answer when you multiply numbers together. The product of 2×3 is 6.

Investigation

8 Your aim is to get an answer as close as possible to 160.

Choose five different digits to create a 2-digit whole number and a number with 2 decimal places that have a product close to 160.

How many numbers can you find within 10 of 160?

Write down any numbers that you find within 2 of 160.

Reading scales

- Read a position on a scale
- Mark a position on a scale

To read a **scale** accurately:

a) work out the **range** or distance between the main **divisions** on the scale

b) work out the range or distance between the small divisions (or **subdivisions**) on the scale

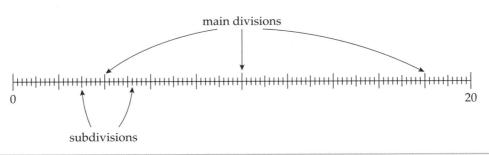

Example   What are the positions of the pointers on this line:

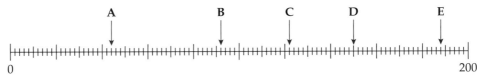

| The range between main divisions is 20. |
| The range between subdivisions is 2. |
| A is 44, B is 92, C is 122, D is 150, E is 188. |

Exercise 9.6

1 Write the position of the pointers on each measuring instrument:

> Remember to write the unit of measurement.

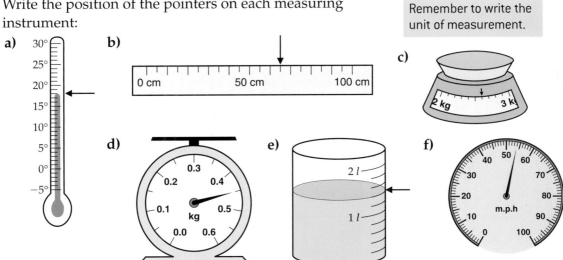

2 Copy the diagrams in Q1 and draw pointers in the following positions:

    a) 10°   **b)** 25 cm   **c)** 2.1 kg

    d) 0.25 kg   **e)** 0.5 ℓ   **f)** 65 m.p.h.

3 Write the positions of A to E on each of these scales:

  a)   **b)**   **c)**

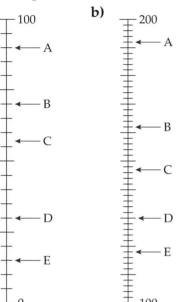

4 Write the position of the pointers if the ends of the line are marked:

    a) 0 and 100   **b)** 0 and 1000   **c)** 0 and 20

    d) 3 and 4   **e)** 50 and 60   **f)** ⁻5 and ⁺5

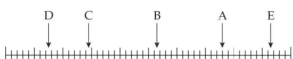

5 Draw a twenty-point scale, and label the end points 5 and 6. Draw pointers to show these positions: A: $5\frac{1}{2}$, B: 5.2, C: 5.65.

6 Draw a fifty-point scale, and label the end points 20 and 30. Draw pointers to show these positions: A: 23, B: 28.6, C: $26\frac{1}{2}$.

7 Draw a hundred-point scale, and label the end points 9 and 10. Draw pointers to show these positions: A: $9\frac{6}{10}$, B: 9.9, C: $9\frac{34}{100}$, D: 9.77, E: 9.07.

Investigation

8 Find as many different scales as you can at home. Draw a picture of each, and record the range between the main divisions and any subdivisions.

Measuring length

⊕ Convert between metric units of length

⊕ Begin to know rough metric equivalents of common imperial measures

---

Metric units of length are: **kilometre (km)**, **metre (m)**, **centimetre (cm)** and **millimetre (mm)**.

km			m		cm	mm	

1 km = 1000 m
1 m = 100 cm
1 m = 1000 mm
1 cm = 10 mm

To convert kilometres to metres, multiply by a 1000. To convert metres to kilometres, divide by a 1000. Use a place-value table as shown above to help.

Imperial units of length are: **miles**, **yards**, **feet**, **inches**.
In the UK, in most contexts, imperial units were replaced by metric units in 1971.

5 miles is approximately 8 km.
1 mile is approximately $1\frac{2}{3}$ km or 1.6 km.
3 feet = 1 yard
12 inches = 1 foot
1 m is approximately 3 feet 3 inches or 1 yard 3 inches.

Example 1 Put the following in order, smallest first:

45 cm   0.035 m   25.5 cm   480 mm   0.5 m

45 cm   3.5 cm   25.5 cm   48 cm   50 cm

The order is: 0.035 m, 25.5 cm, 45 cm, 480 mm, 0.5 m.

Choose a common unit, such as cm, and convert each measure into cm. Use a place value table to help you.

Example 2 Convert the following measurements:

a) 6 km to metres   b) 4.3m to centimetres

a) 6 km = 6 × 1000 m = **6000 m**

b) 4.3 m = 4.3 × 100 cm = **430 cm**

Remember there are 100 cm in 1 m, so multiply by 100.

Exercise 9.7

1 Write the following lengths in millimetres:

a) 1 cm   b) 3 cm   c) $1\frac{1}{2}$ cm   d) 1 m   e) $\frac{1}{2}$ m

f) 3.2 cm   g) 1.1 m   h) 4.3 cm   i) 1 km   j) 0.4 cm

Multiply cm by 10 to get mm, multiply m by 1000 to get mm.

2 Write the following lengths in centimetres:

a) 30 mm   b) 15 mm   c) 1 m   d) $\frac{1}{2}$ m   e) 0.3 m

f) 1.2 m   g) 730 mm   h) 5.1 m   i) 46 mm   j) 0.45 m

3 Write the following lengths in metres:

a) 100 cm   b) 2000 mm   c) 1 km   d) 250 cm   e) $\frac{1}{2}$ km

f) 3500 mm   g) 1.2 km   h) 2500 cm   i) 0.3 km   j) 4.5 cm

4 Write the following lengths in kilometres:

   a) 1000 m   **b)** 3000 m   **c)** 1500 m   **d)** 2700 m

   e) 1 000 000 mm   **f)** 1 000 000 cm   **g)** 45.5 m

5 Write each distance approximately in kilometres:

   a) Carbury to Midtown: 5 miles

   b) Sunsea to Darrington: 50 miles

   c) Smithborne to Penfield: 90 miles

   d) Belston to St Tawes: 500 miles.

6 Write these distances, flown by birds in a day, approximately in miles:

   a) starling: 16 km   **b)** duck: 80 km

   c) crow: 4 km   **d)** goose: 160 km.

7 Put the following in order, smallest to largest:

   a) 35 cm   0.025 m   1.7 cm   330 mm   0.2 m

   b) 150 cm   2.3 m   35.5 cm   1600 mm   0.9 m

   c) 0.15 km   1.8 m   160 cm   2500 mm   1.1 km

   d) 0.02 m   25 mm   12.5 cm   1.5 mm   2.4 cm

8 A pupil paced the length and width of a rectangular station platform. She found it was 9 paces wide by 235 paces long. Each of her paces is 75 cm. What is the approximate length and width of the platform in metres?

9 Home-Dec Estate Agents work out distances from houses for sale to local services:

	Distance from school	Distance from doctors	Distance from post office	Distance from park	Distance from shops
1 Short Lane	1.5 km	580 m	2.63 km	1.25 km	908 km
7 High Grove	0.89 km	0.36 km	0.8 km	1.73 km	740 km
15 Long Street	1.26 km	450 m	1.9 km	1.9 km	0.8 km
23 Upper Hill	2.5 km	1.62 km	0.75 km	1.5 km	806 m

Home-Dec Estate Agents collect details about the needs of their buyers.

- Mrs Alter collects her pension weekly, so wants to live close to the post office.
- Mr Bee has a dog that he exercises twice a day. He wants to live close to the park.
- Mr Cog has a bad hip and wants to live within 500 m of the doctors.
- Dr Dent has four children and no car so would prefer to be within 1 km of the school.

Can you match each house to a different buyer, taking account of each buyer's needs?

Measuring mass and capacity

⊕ Convert between metric units of mass and capacity

⊕ Begin to know rough metric equivalents of common imperial measures

Key words

capacity	mass
litre	gram
centilitre	kilogram
millilitre	pound
pint	ounce
gallon	

Capacity is a measure of the amount a container will hold.

Metric units of capacity are: **litre (ℓ)** , **centilitre (cl)** **millilitre (ml)** .

		l		cl	ml

$1\ \ell = 100$ cl
$1\ \ell = 1000$ ml
1 cl $= 10$ ml

To convert litres to millilitres, multiply by 1000.

Metric units of **mass** are **kilograms** and **grams** .

Remember 1 kg = 1000 g

Imperial units of capacity are **gallons** and **pints** .

1 litre is approximately $1\frac{3}{4}$ pints.   8 pints = 1 gallon
550 ml is approximately 1 pint.

Imperial units of mass are **pounds (lb)** and **ounces (oz)** .

1 kg is approximately 2.2 lb   16 ounces = 1 pound (lb)
4 oz is approximately 100 g

Example 1   Put the following in order, smallest first:

a)   3.3 ℓ   320 cl $3\frac{1}{2}$ ℓ   345 cl   3400 ml

a)   3300 ml   3200 ml   3500 ml   3450 ml   3400 ml

The order is: 320 cl, 3.3 ℓ, 3400 ml, 345 cl, $3\frac{1}{2}$ ℓ

Chooses a common unit, such as ml, and convert each measure to that unit. Use a place value table to help you.

Example 2   Convert 2.5 litres to   a) cl   b) ml

a)   2.5 ℓ = 2.5 × 100 cl = **250 cl**

b)   2.5 ℓ = 2.5 × 1000 ml = **2500 ml**

1 ℓ = 100 cl so multiply by 100.
1 ℓ = 100 ml so multiply by 1000.

Exercise 9.8

① Write these capacities in the units shown:
a)   3 ℓ in centilitres
b)   2.6 ℓ in centilitres
c)   350 ml in centilitres
d)   2.4 ℓ in millilitres
e)   35 cl in millilitres
f)   1.75 ℓ in millilitres
g)   500 ml in litres
h)   150 cl in litres
i)   65.5 cl in litres.

② Write these masses in grams:
a) $\frac{1}{4}$ kg
b)   7.5 kg
c)   0.65 kg

3 Put these in order, smallest to largest:

a) $3.5\,\ell$ 250 cl   3300 ml   325 cl $\frac{1}{2}\,\ell$

b) $0.6\,\ell$ 600 cl   65 cl   7000 ml   750 ml

c) $1\frac{1}{2}\,\ell$ 140 cl   770 ml $\frac{3}{4}\,\ell$ 1300 ml

d) 3.6 kg   1500 g $\frac{1}{2}$ kg   800 g $\frac{7}{8}$ kg

4 Write these masses approximately in the units shown:
a) 500 g in pounds
b) 2 kg 500 g in pounds
c) 150 lb in kilograms
d) 48 ounces in kilograms

5 Write these capacities approximately in the units shown:
a) 500 cl in pints
b) $5\,\ell$ in pints
c) 1 gallon in litres
d) 10 pints in litres

6 Look at the labels of different food packets, tins, bottles and cans to find the mass or capacity of the contents. Record each measure in both metric and imperial units. Record the measures in two tables: one for capacity, and one for mass:

Mass		
Item	**Metric**	**Imperial**
Low fat spread	$\frac{1}{2}$ kg	1 lb

Capacity		
Item	**Metric**	**Imperial**
Cranberry Juice	1 litre	$1\frac{3}{4}$ pints

7 Which is heavier – a kilogram of potatoes or a kilogram of feathers?

8 A bag of 30 oranges of equal mass weighs 3.6 kg when full. After 11 oranges have been eaten, what is the mass of the bag?

9 A full bucket holds 3.3 litres. A full jug holds 200 ml. How many full jugs of water are needed to fill the bucket?

10 Some of the ingredients for two recipes include:

Lasagne
$\frac{1}{2}$ lb of lasagne verdi
3 oz of butter
2 oz plain flour
$1\frac{1}{2}$ pints milk
$\frac{1}{4}$ pint single cream

Fisherman's pie
$1\frac{1}{2}$ lb white fish
4 oz butter
1 pint milk
2 oz plain flour
4 oz peeled prawns
2 lb potatoes

Convert each measure to approximate metric units (grams and millilitres).

11

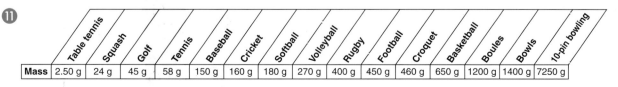

	Table tennis	Squash	Golf	Tennis	Baseball	Cricket	Softball	Volleyball	Rugby	Football	Croquet	Basketball	Boules	Bowls	10-pin bowling
Mass	2.50 g	24 g	45 g	58 g	150 g	160 g	180 g	270 g	400 g	450 g	460 g	650 g	1200 g	1400 g	7250 g

The table shows the mass of different balls used in sport.
You are asked to fetch 2 kg of each type of ball. How many of each ball will you collect?

Special numbers

⊕ Be able to find the multiples and factors of any number

⊕ Recognise square, prime and triangular numbers

Key words
multiples
factors
square numbers
prime numbers
triangular numbers

Multiples of a number are that number multiplied by any other whole number. Multiples of 3 are 3, 6, 9, 12, 15 … (you could go on writing down multiples of 3 forever.)

Factors of a number are numbers that will divide exactly into that number. Factors of 20 are 1, 2, 4, 5, 10 and 20 (every number has a fixed number of factors.)

Square numbers are the result when a number is multiplied by itself. For example, 1, 4, 9 and 16 are all square numbers.

1	2	3	4
1 $\boxed{1}$	2 $\boxed{4}$	3 $\boxed{9}$	4 $\boxed{16}$

Prime numbers are numbers which have exactly two factors, 1 and the number itself. For example 2, 3, 5, 7 and 11 are prime numbers.

Example 1   Find the factors and the first five multiples of the following numbers:

        a) 24   **b)** 9

a)   The factors of 24 are: 1, 2, 3, 4, 6, 8, 12, 24

    Multiples: $1 \times 24 = 24$ $2 \times 24 = 48$

                 $3 \times 24 = 72$ $4 \times 24 = 96$

                 $5 \times 24 = 120$

    The first five multiples of 24 are: 24, 48, 72, 96, 120

> Work out the factors by finding all the pairs of numbers which multiply to give 24.
> For example:
> $1 \times 24 = 24$
> so 1 and 24 are factors

b)   The factors of 9 are: 1, 3, 9

    Multiples: $1 \times 9 = 9$ $2 \times 9 = 18$

                 $3 \times 9 = 27$ $4 \times 9 = 36$

                 $5 \times 9 = 45$

    The first five multiples of 9 are: 9, 18, 27, 36, 45

> Factors:
> $1 \times 9 = 9$ so 1 and 9 are factors
> $3 \times 3 = 9$ so 3 is a factor
> Here we get a repeated pair of factors: 3 and 3. This is because 9 is a **square number**.

Example 2   1, 3, 7, 16, 21, 40, 100

        From this list of numbers, write down:

        a) A prime number   **b)** A multiple of 4

        c) A factor of 21   **d)** A square number

> There may be more than one answer to each question.

a) 3 or 7   (both 3 and 7 have exactly two factors, themselves and 1)

b) 16, 40 and 100 $(4 \times 4 = 16, 10 \times 4 = 40$ and $25 \times 4 = 100)$

c) 1, 3, 7 and 21 $(1 \times 21 = 21$ and $3 \times 7 = 21)$

d) 1, 16 and 100 $(1 \times 1 = 1, 4 \times 4 = 16, 10 \times 10 = 100)$

1. Write down the first five multiples of the following numbers:
   a) 4
   b) 10
   c) 12
   d) 7
   e) 25
   f) 15
   g) 13
   h) 100

2. List the factors of the following numbers:
   a) 8
   b) 15
   c) 36
   d) 44
   e) 25
   f) 100
   g) 17
   h) 56

3. Find numbers which satisfy the following statements:
   a) A prime number which is a factor of 17
   b) A number whose factors include 3 and 9
   c) A number whose multiples include 24 and 60
   d) A number which has only two factors
   e) A prime number which is even
   f) A number with only one factor
   g) A square number between 20 and 50.

   > There may be more than one answer to each question.

4. Triangular numbers can be illustrated by drawing triangles of dots:

Picture				
Number of dots	1	3	6	10

   a) Draw diagrams to help you find the next two triangular numbers.
   b) Without drawing a diagram, find the seventh triangular number.

5. Each of the sets of numbers in the following questions are multiples of 1 and of another number. Find that number.
   a) 8, 20, 28, 36, 400
   b) 7, 28, 56, 91, 105
   c) 11, 33, 44, 110, 209
   d) 9, 36, 54, 108, 117

   > There may be more than one answer to each question.

6. 1, 2, 9, 10, 19, 20, 29, 30, 37

   From the list of numbers above, find:
   a) A triangular number
   b) A square number
   c) An odd prime number
   d) A factor of 12
   e) A multiple of 5.

   Investigation

   7. List all the numbers below 50 that have an odd number of factors. Can you spot a pattern?

⊕ Generate a sequence given a general term

Key words
sequence
term
general term
*n*th term
consecutive terms

A **sequence** of numbers can be described by a first term and a term-to-term rule.

For example, the first term is 4 and the term-to-term rule is add 3, the sequence would be: 4, 7, 10, 13 …

Another way of describing a sequence is by giving a rule that connects the term number and the term. We call this the **general term** (or the ***n*th term**).

For example, the *n*th term of a sequence is $2n + 1$.

It is often easier to draw a table to help find the first few terms of a sequence. In each column we substitute the term number for *n* to find each term.

Term number (*n*)	1	2	3	5	10
Sequence	$2 \times 1 + 1 = 3$	$2 \times 2 + 1 = 5$	$2 \times 3 + 1 = 7$	$2 \times 5 + 1 = 11$	$2 \times 10 + 1 = 21$

Example 1   Find the first five terms of a sequence whose general term is $n + 4$:

Term number (*n*)	1	2	3	4	5
Sequence	5	6	7	8	9

In each case substitute the term number into the general term.

Example 2   The *n*th term of sequence is $3n + 5$.

    a) Find the sixteenth term.

    b) Find the twentieth term.

    c) Find the term number if the value of the term in the sequence is 17.

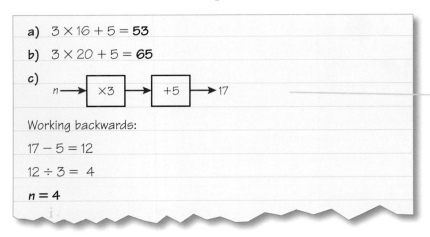

a) $3 \times 16 + 5 = \mathbf{53}$

b) $3 \times 20 + 5 = \mathbf{65}$

c)

$n \rightarrow \boxed{\times 3} \rightarrow \boxed{+5} \rightarrow 17$

Working backwards:

$17 - 5 = 12$

$12 \div 3 = 4$

$n = 4$

Draw a function machine to help you find the term number. You need to do the inverse of each operation.

Exercise 10.2

1 Find the first five terms of the sequence if the nth term is:

a) $n + 5$ b) $4n$ c) $5n - 2$ d) $4n + 8$ e) n

2 Find the 25th term of the sequences above.

3 Find the seventeenth term of a sequence whose general term is $4n + 5$.

4 A sequence is generated by the formula $3n - 5$.

a) Find the thirteenth term.   b) Find the 100th term.

c) Find the term number which has value 10.   d) Find the term number which has value 190.

5 The number of bricks needed to build houses depends on how many there are in a row. To calculate the number of bricks needed, you multiply the number of houses by 2000 and add 1000.

a) Copy and complete the table below:

Number of houses	1	2	3	4	5
Number of bricks					

Look at how you calculated the terms.

b) What is the general term of this sequence?

6 a) Describe the sequences in Q1 by giving the first term and the term-to-term rule.

b) What do you notice about the term-to-term rule and the number in front of the n in the general rule?

Write your answers in the form: 1st term = 6, rule is 'add 1'.

7 For every egg used in a cake mix you make 12 cakes.

a) If you used 3 eggs, how many cakes would you make?

b) If you used n eggs, how many cakes would you make?

c) If you made 120 cakes, how many eggs did you use?

Investigations

8 a) Write down the first five terms of the sequence whose general term is $2n$.

b) What is the difference between consecutive terms?

c) Write down the first five terms of the sequence whose general term is $2n + 5$.

Consecutive terms are terms that are next to each other.

d) What is the difference between consecutive terms?

e) What do you notice about the differences between consecutive terms compared to the general term?

9 Write down the first five terms of the following sequences and describe what you notice about the difference between consecutive terms for each one:

a) $3n + 5$, $3n - 2$, $3n$

b) $4n - 4$, $4n$, $4n + 3$

c) $10n$, $10n + 100$, $10n - 5$

d) Can you suggest a rule for finding the difference between consecutive terms if you know the nth term of a sequence?

Finding the general term

⊕ Find the general term of a sequence

Key words
general term
nth term
consecutive terms

To find the **general term** of a sequence, look at the difference between **consecutive terms** .

If the difference between consecutive terms is always the same, then the **general term** for the sequence will include that difference multiplied by n.

In the sequence: 1, 5, 9, 13, 17, … the difference between terms is always 4. So the **general term** will include $4n$.
But the first term is 1, not 4.
To get from 4 to 1 we subtract 3. The **general term** of the sequence is therefore $4n - 3$.
Check that this works for the sequence:

$$4 \times 1 - 3 = 1 \qquad 4 \times 2 - 3 = 5 \qquad 4 \times 3 - 3 = 9$$

Example 1 Find the general term of this sequence: 3, 5, 7, 9, 11 …

Term number	1	2	3	4	5
Sequence	3	5	7	9	11

Differences   2   2   2   2   2

First look at the difference between the terms in the sequence. The difference is 2 so you know the general term will include $2n$.

The general term will include $2n$:

Term number	1	2	3	4	5
$2n$	2	4	6	8	10
Sequence	3	5	7	9	11

The general term is: $2n + 1$

How do you get from the sequence you've found to the sequence you want? Add 1.

Example 2 Find the general term of this sequence and give a reason for your answer:

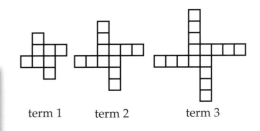

term 1   term 2   term 3

Term number	1	2	3
Number of squares	8	12	16

Differences   4   4

Look at the difference between terms.

←n 4 The general term is $4n + 4$ because there are 4 squares in the centre and then n squares on each arm.

$n + 1$ There are 4 arms and each arm contains $n + 1$ squares. 4 lots of $n + 1$ is equal to $4n + 4$ so the general term is $4n + 4$.

There are different reasons you could give.

Exercise 10.3

1 Copy and complete the following table and find a general term for each sequence:

Term number	1	2	3	4	5	6
a)	2	4	6			
b)	3	6	9			
c)	10	20	30			
d)	0.5	1	1.5			

2 Find the general term for the following sequences:

a)

Term number	1	2	3	4
Sequence	2	5	8	11

b)

Term number	1	2	3	4
Sequence	£10	£18	£26	£34

c) 0, 10, 20, 30, 40 …

d) 1cm, 6cm, 11cm, 16cm…

3 Find the general term for the following sequences:

Term number	1	2	3	4
a)	3	5	7	9
b)	9	19	29	39
c)	5	8	11	14
d)	3	8	13	18

> Copy each sequence separately and look at the difference between terms.

4 Find the ninth and tenth terms of these sequences without working out all the terms in between:

a) 4, 8, 12, 16 …

b) 0.5, 1, 1.5, 2 …

c) 11, 12, 13, 14 …

d) ⁻4, ⁻3, ⁻2, ⁻1 …

> First find the general term and then substitute the values of 9 and 10 into your general term.

5 A seamstress makes curtains. If the width of the window is 1 m, she needs 2.5 m of fabric. If the width of the window is 2 m she needs 4.5 m and if it's 3 m she needs 6.5 m.

a) Find a general term which will calculate the amount of material needed for a window of width n metres.

b) How much fabric will she need for curtains for a window that is 9 m wide?

c) How much fabric will she need for curtains for a window that is 1.5 m wide?

6 To make one beach-hut out of matchsticks we use six matchsticks. To make two beach-huts we use eleven matchsticks.

a) Copy and complete this table:

Number of beach-huts	1	2	3	4	5
Number of matchsticks					

b) Find a general term that connects the number of beach-huts to the number of matchsticks you use.

c) Give a reason for your answer to part **b**.

Plot a straight-line graph given an equation

Key words
straight-line graph
y-axis
x-axis
plot
equation

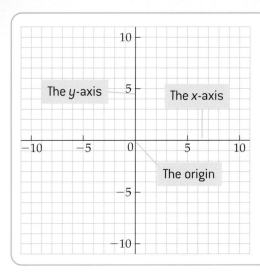

The four sections of a **graph** are called **quadrants**.

When you draw a graph:
- Make sure that you mark the scales accurately and label the *x*- and *y*-axes
- **Always** use a ruler
- **Plot** your points accurately with a sharp pencil
- Remember that a line is of infinite length so it should stretch across the grid.

Example 1   Plot the graph of the **equation** $y = x + 4$.

x	0	4	−5	−1
y				

First, draw up a table to show the *x* and *y* values. Next choose some values of *x*. (You can choose any value of *x* you like but remember that you will need to plot these points. For each *x*-value, calculate the *y*-value.)

$y = x + 4$:   when $x = 0$, $y = 0 + 4 = 4$

$y = x + 4$:   when $x = 4$, $y = 4 + 4 = 8$

$y = x + 4$:   when $x = -5$, $y = -5 + 4 = -1$

$y = x + 4$:   when $x = -1$, $y = -1 + 4 = 3$

The table now looks like this:

x	0	4	−5	−1
y	4	8	−1	3

Next draw an appropriate pair of axes.

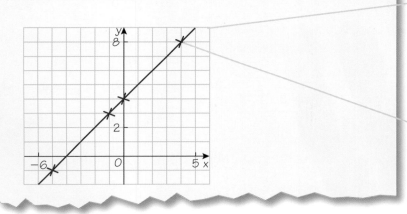

Next **plot** the points and join them with a straight line. The **straight-line graph** looks like this.

Exercise 10.4

1 On graph paper, draw a pair of axes labelled from -10 to 10.
Copy and complete the tables below and then draw the straight-line graphs:

a) $y = x$

x	-4	0	5	
y				-3

b) $y = x + 2$

x	-5	-1	0	
y				4

c) $y = x - 5$

x	-1			10
y		-3	2	

2 **a)** On a suitable pair of axes, plot the following coordinates:
$$x = -5, y = -4 \qquad x = 7, y = 8 \qquad x = 1, y = 2$$

b) Draw a straight line through the points.

c) From looking at your graph, copy and complete the following table reading the x- and y-values from your graph:

x	-3		2.5	
y		0		10

3 **a)** On a pair of axes labelled from -10 to 10 plot the following coordinates and join them with a straight line:
$$(-1, -3) \quad (2, 6) \quad \left(\tfrac{1}{2}, 1\tfrac{1}{2}\right)$$

b) Does the line go through the origin?

4 **a)** On graph paper draw a pair of axes labelled from 0 to 15.
By drawing up tables of values, plot the following graphs:
i) $y = 2x$ **ii)** $y = 3x$ **iii)** $y = 4x$

> Remember $2x$ means $2 \times x$.

b) Describe what happens to the graphs as the number in front of the x increases.

5 **a)** On graph paper draw a pair of axes labelled from -5 to 5.
By drawing up tables of values, plot the following graphs:
i) $y = x$ **ii)** $y = \tfrac{1}{2}x$ **iii)** $y = \tfrac{1}{4}x$

b) Describe what happens to the graphs as the number in front of the x decreases.

Investigation

6 Some equations of straight-line graphs look like this:
$$y = x + \square$$
Investigate what happens to the graphs when you replace $\square$ with different numbers.

Properties of graphs

◈ Recognise graphs and their equations

Equations of straight-line graphs always look something like: $y = 2x + 3$

The number in front of the x tells you the **gradient** of the graph. It is a measure of steepness.

If the line goes **up** from left to right, the gradient is **positive**. If the line goes **down** from left to right, the gradient is **negative**.

The number that you add on '+3' tells you where the graph crosses the y-axis. It is the **y-intercept** .

Example   Draw the graph of $y = 2x + 3$ for values of x between -2 and 12.

a)   Where does the graph cross the y-axis?

b)   Is the gradient of the graph positive or negative?

x	0	1	2	3	4
y	3	5	7	9	11

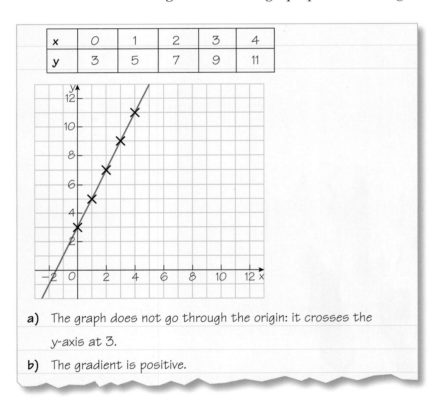

First draw up a table of x- and y-values.

a)   The graph does not go through the origin: it crosses the y-axis at 3.

b)   The gradient is positive.

Exercise 10.5

1 Draw the following graphs and decide whether or not they pass through the origin. (You may use a graph sketching package.)

a) $y = 2x$ b) $y = x + 5$ c) $y = -x$

d) $y = x - 10$ e) $y = 6x$ f) $y = 12x$

2 What do you notice about the equations of the graphs in Q1 that pass through the origin?

3 Draw the following graphs and say whether their gradient is positive or negative:

a) $y = x$ b) $y = -x + 1$ c) $y = 5x$ d) $y = \frac{1}{2}x$ e) $y = 12 - x$

4 What do you notice about the equations of the graphs in Q**3** with negative gradients?

5 Without drawing the graphs, copy and complete the table below:

Graph	Is the gradient positive or negative?	Where does the graph cross the *y*-axis?
$y = 5x - 4$		
$y = -x + 4$		
$y = -x - 26$		
$y = -x$		
$y = 100x$		
$y = \frac{1}{2}x + 3$		

6 Match the graphs to the equations of the lines given below:

a) $y = 2x$ b) $y = -x + 6$ c) $y = -x - 6$ d) $y = 10x$ e) $y = 2x - 1$

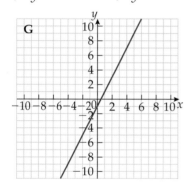
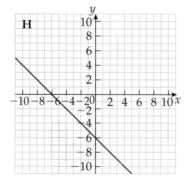
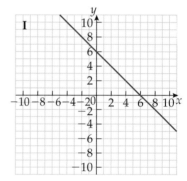

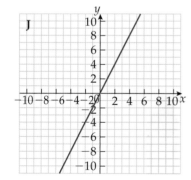
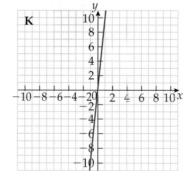

7 Draw the following pairs of graphs on the same pair of axes (you may use a graph sketching package):

a) $y = x, y = x + 3$ b) $y = 2x, y = 2x - 5$ c) $y = 3x, y = 3x - 10$

d) What do you notice about all the pairs of lines? e) Why do you think this is?

8 Draw the following pairs of graphs on the same pair of axes (you may use a graph sketching package):

a) $y = x + 3, y = 3 + x$ b) $y = 2x + 4, y = 4 + 2x$ c) $y = \frac{1}{2}x + 10, y = 10 + \frac{1}{2}x$

d) What do you notice about the pairs of lines? e) Why do you think this is?

Special graphs

⊕ Draw graphs of the form $y = a$ and $x = a$, where a is
   a number

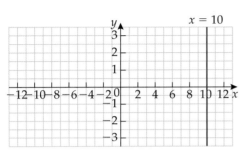

For the graph $x = 10$, whatever the **y-coordinate**,
the **x-coordinate** is always 10.

All graphs of the form $x = a$ (where a is a number)
are **parallel** to the **y-axis**.

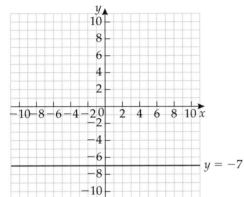

For the graph $y = -7$, whatever the x-coordinate,
the y-coordinate is always ⁻7.

All graphs of the form $y = a$ (where a is a number)
are **parallel** to the **x-axis**.

Example 1 Draw the graph of $y = 2$.

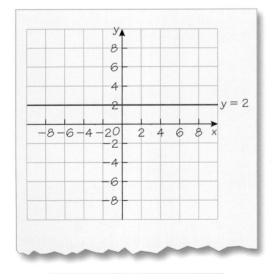

Whatever the x-coordinate,
the y-coordinate is always 2.

Example 2 Draw the graph of $x = -4$.

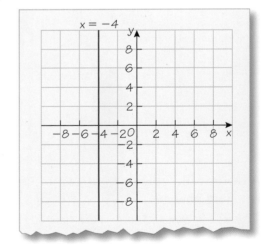

The x-coordinate is always -4.

Exercise 10.6

1 On graph paper draw a pair of axes labelled from -5 to 5.
Draw the following graphs:

a) $x = 2$ **b)** $y = 3$ **c)** $y = -4$ **d)** $y = 0$ **e)** $x = 0$ **f)** $y = -1.5$

2 What is the equation of   **a)** the x-axis   **b)** the y-axis?

3 Write down the equations of the lines which pass through the following pairs of coordinates.

a) $(1, 7)$, $(1, -4)$ **b)** $(2, 3)$, $(4, 3)$ **c)** $(0, 1)$, $(0, 0)$

d) $(-2, 1)$, $(-2, 21)$ **e)** $(-5, 6)$, $(3, 6)$

> You could plot the points and draw a line through them to help you find the equations.

4 a) Write down which of the following lines are symmetrical about the x-axis?
For example, $x = -4$ is symmetrical about the x-axis:

$y = 7$ $y = x$ $y = -3$ $y = x + 2$

$x = 7$ $y = 4$ $x = -1$

b) Write down the equations of the lines which are symmetrical about the y-axis.

c) In general, which lines are symmetrical about the x-axis?

d) In general, which lines are symmetrical about the y-axis?

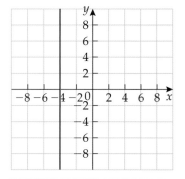

> If you replaced the x-axis with a mirror, would you still see the same line?

5 Match the equations of the lines with their graphs.

a) $y = x$ **b)** $x = 5$ **c)** $y = -x$ **d)** $y = -6$ **e)** $y = x + 4$ **f)** $x = -1.5$

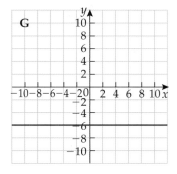 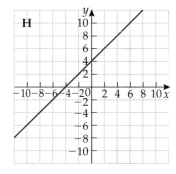 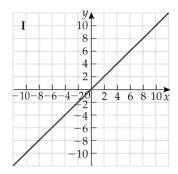

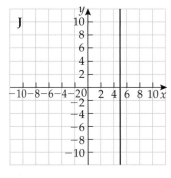 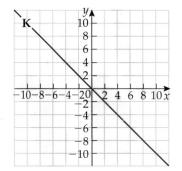 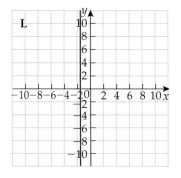

Investigation

6 Draw a pair of axes from -10 to 10. Construct a geometric picture by drawing straight lines. Write an equation for each of the lines you draw.

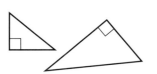

11.1 Triangles

⊕ Know the names of different triangles

⊕ Be able to describe the angle, side and symmetry properties of different triangles

Key words
equilateral
isosceles
right angled
scalene
symmetrical

 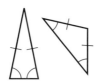 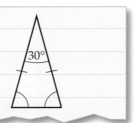 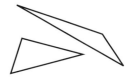

Right-angled triangle. One angle of 90°.   Isosceles triangle. Two equal sides and two equal angles.   Equilateral triangle. Three equal sides and three equal angles.   Scalene triangle. No equal sides and no equal angles.

Example   One angle in an isosceles triangle is 30°. What are the other two? Explain your answer.

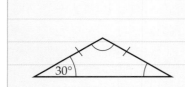

If the equal angles are 30° then the remaining angle must be 180° − 30° − 30° = **120°** because the angles in a triangle add up to 180°.

If the other angle is 30° the equal angles must be $\frac{1}{2}(180° - 30°) = \mathbf{75°}$.

An isosceles triangle must have two equal angles, and the angles of a triangle add up to 180°. Either the two equal angles will be 30° or the other angle will be 30°.

Exercise 11.1

1 Which of these are:

   a) right-angled triangles

   b) isosceles triangles

   c) equilateral triangles

   d) scalene triangles

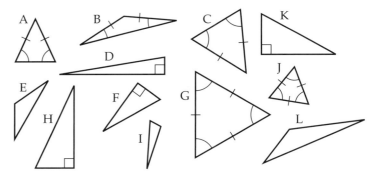

2 Which of these are:

   a) right-angled triangles

   b) isosceles triangles

   c) equilateral triangles

   d) scalene triangles

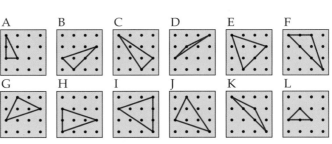

3 True or false? Explain your answers.

    a) A triangle can be both scalene and right-angled.

    b) A triangle can be both isosceles and right-angled.

    c) A triangle can be both right-angled and equilateral.

    d) A triangle can be both scalene and isosceles.

4 On squared paper plot three possible vertices of an isosceles triangle that has a right angle at the origin and shorter sides of length 4 units.

5 Find the sizes of the missing angles:

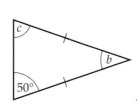 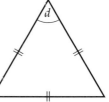 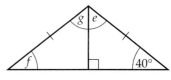

6 Which is which?

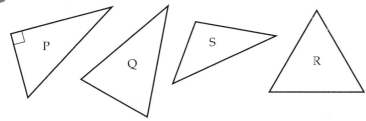

Triangle _____ has no equal sides and one 90° angle.

Triangle _____ has two angles of sixty degrees.

Triangle _____ has one side of 3 cm, one of 2 cm and one of 30 mm.

Triangle _____ has one angle of 45° and one of 35°.

7 Use square dotty paper. How many isosceles triangles of different shapes and sizes can be drawn on a 3 × 3 square grid?

8 Use triangular dotty paper. How many triangles of different shapes and sizes can be drawn on a 3 × 3 triangular grid?

Investigation

9 How many different types of triangles can you make with a loop of string 12 cm long? Use whole number sides, and write down the length of the sides of each triangle and the type of triangle it is. How will you know when you have found all the possible triangles?

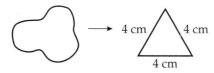

11.2 Quadrilaterals

- ⊕ Know the names of the different quadrilaterals
- ⊕ Describe the angle, side and symmetry properties of different quadrilaterals

Key words
parallelogram
rhombus
kite
arrowhead
trapezium

A quadrilateral is a 4-sided shape. These are examples of quadrilaterals:

Square:
all angles 90°, all sides equal, opposite sides parallel.

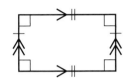

Rectangle:
all angles 90°, 2 pairs of opposite parallel sides.

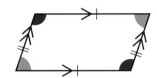

Parallelogram:
opposite angles equal, 2 pairs of opposite parallel sides.

Rhombus:
a parallelogram with equal sides.

Kite:
2 pairs of adjacent equal sides, 1 pair of opposite equal angles.

Arrowhead:
a concave kite.

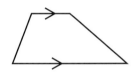

Trapezium:
one pair of opposite parallel sides.

Example 1 Find the following values for this rectangle: ∠DAB, ∠BCD, ∠DBC, ∠ADB, ∠ABD, AB, AD.

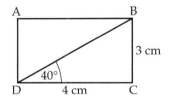

∠DAB = ∠BCD = 90°	(all angles in a rectangle are 90°)
∠DBC = 50°	(angles in a triangle sum to 180°)
∠ADB = 50°	(angles in a right angle sum to 90°)
∠ABD = 40°	(angles in a right angle sum to 90°)
AB = DC = 4 cm	(opposite sides equal)
AD = BC = 3 cm	(opposite sides equal)

Exercise 11.2

1 Match Shapes 1–8 to the shapes in the explanation box.

Step	Yes	No
1) All sides equal?	Go to step 2.	Go to step 3.
2) All angles 90°?	It is Shape 1.	It is Shape 2.
3) All angles 90°?	It is Shape 3.	Go to step 4.
4) Opposite angles equal?	It is Shape 4.	Go to step 5.
5) Adjacent sides equal?	Go to step 6.	Go to step 7.
6) Any reflex angles?	It is Shape 5.	It is Shape 6.
7) Any parallel sides?	It is Shape 7.	It is an irregular quadrilateral.

A reflex angle is one that is more than 180°.

2 Find the following values for these quadrilaterals:
  a) ∠CDA, AD, CD.
  b) ∠DEF, ∠EFG, DG, GF.
  c) ∠HML, ∠MLI, ∠JIL, ∠IJK, ∠JKL, ∠KLI, ML, HM, IL, IJ, JK, KL.

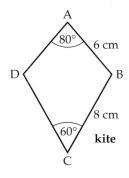

kite

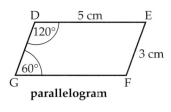

parallelogram

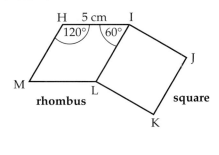

rhombus

square

3 Find the size of the lettered angles, giving reasons for your answers.

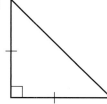 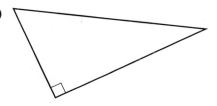 

4 Twenty questions. Play with a partner. Take turns to think of a quadrilateral and write it down. The other person has to ask questions such as 'does it have any parallel sides?' Record how many questions it takes to guess correctly. The winner is the one who has guessed the most shapes after twenty questions.

5 Each of these shapes is half of another. What could the whole shape be? Draw sketches and record your working.

  a)

  b)

  c)

Investigation

6 Fold a piece of paper once and make two straight cuts across the fold. Try to predict what shape the hole will be. Repeat several times and record your results.
Investigate what other shapes you can make by folding and cutting in different ways. Record your discoveries.

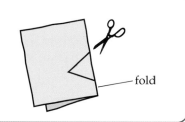

fold

Drawing accurately

◈ Draw and measure lines to the nearest mm, and acute, obtuse and
reflex angles to the nearest degree, using a ruler and protractor

Key words
protractor
acute
obtuse
reflex
vertex

Before drawing an angle, you need to know:
● roughly what size it is and what it will look like
● where the vertex is going to be.

Example   Draw DE 2.3 cm, EF 2.5 cm and ∠DEF 120°.

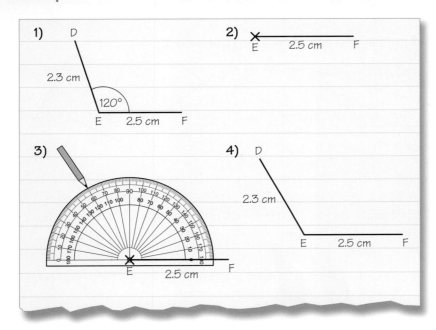

1) First sketch your angle
   and label it.
2) Draw EF accurately and
   make a mark at the
   vertex.

3) Place the protractor
   accurately and make a
   mark at 120° using
   the scale that goes
   anti-clockwise.
4) Take the protractor away
   and join the mark to the
   vertex, making DE 2.3 cm.

Exercise 11.3

1 Sketch then draw the following angles:
∠ABC = 80°   ∠FGH = 123°   ∠MNP = 32°   ∠XYZ = 15°   ∠KLM = 170°.

2 Sketch then draw the following:
a) AB = 3 cm, BC = 6 cm ∠ABC = 70°
b) DE = 3.1 cm, DC = 6.3 cm ∠CDE = 66°
c) GH = 52 mm, HJ = 16 mm ∠GHJ = 35°
d) MN = 4.4 cm, NP = 6.6 cm ∠MNP = 160°.

3 To finish in the same place, what other turn could you make instead of:
a) 320° clockwise   **b)** 320° anticlockwise
c) 20° clockwise   **d)** 50° anticlockwise
e) 270° clockwise   **f)** 155° clockwise?

Remember a complete
turn is 360°.

4 Measure the lines and angles in these shapes.

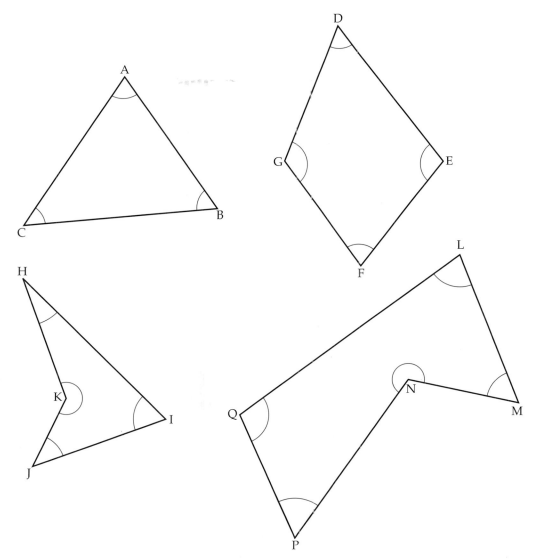

5 Sketch then draw these angles:
   a) $\angle ABC = 190°$ **b)** $\angle MNP = 232°$ **c)** $\angle XYZ = 315°$ **d)** $\angle KLM = 270°$.

6 Sketch then draw the following:
   a) $AB = 3\,cm$, $BC = 6\,cm$ $\angle ABC = 170°$ **b)** $DE = 3.1\,cm$, $DC = 6.3\,cm$ $\angle CDE = 266°$
   c) $GH = 52\,mm$, $HJ = 16\,mm$ $\angle GHJ = 335°$ **d)** $MN = 4.4\,cm$, $NP = 6.6\,cm$ $\angle MNP = 260°$.

Investigation

7 Draw a large circle and mark every 10°.

Number the marks from 0 to 35. Using a coloured pencil start
at point 0 and join it to point 9, then join point 9 to point 18
then point 18 to point 27 and point 27 to point 0. What shape
have you made? Repeat making up your own rules. Can you
draw a rectangle? What is your rule? Can you draw a hexagon?
What is your rule? Investigate some more shapes and rules.

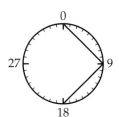

Drawing shapes

◈ Be able to construct triangles using a ruler and protractor

To draw a triangle accurately we need information about its sides and angles. The least information we need to be sure the triangle we are drawing is the only one of its kind is: **either** the lengths of two sides and the angle between them (**SAS**) **or** two angles and the line that joins them (**ASA**).

Example 1   Draw a triangle ABC with sides AB = 4 cm and AC = 2.4 cm and ∠BAC = 40°.

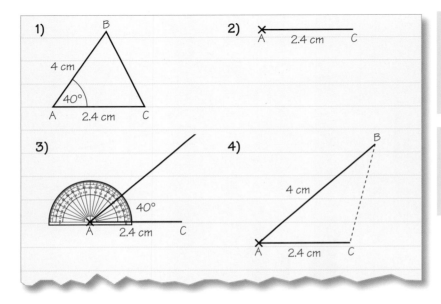

1) Draw a sketch first and mark on all the measurements.
2) Draw a base line AC of 2.4 cm. Mark a vertex for the angle at A.

3) Draw an angle of 40° with a long line.
4) Mark a second line AB of 4 cm. Complete the triangle by joining BC.

Example 2   Draw triangle CDE where CD = 2.6 cm, ∠ECD = 45° and ∠EDC = 30°.

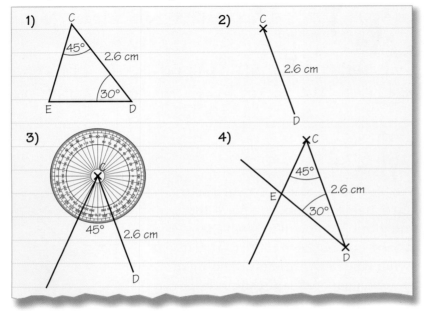

1) Draw a sketch first and mark on all the measurements.
2) Draw a base line CD of 2.6 cm. Mark a vertex for the angle at C.

3) Draw an angle of 45° with a long line.
4) Mark a vertex for an angle at D. Draw an angle of 30° and continue the line until it intersects with CE. The triangle is complete.

Exercise 11.4 .... Drawing shapes ....

1 Draw triangle ABC where AB = 5 cm, AC = 6 cm and ∠CAB = 60°.
Measure ∠BCA.

2 Draw triangle DEF where DE = 52 mm, EF = 61 mm and ∠DEF = 160°.
Measure ∠EDF.

3 Draw triangle JKL where JK = 5cm, ∠JKL = 86° and ∠LJK = 22°.
Measure LK.

4 Draw triangle PQR where PQ = 5cm, ∠PQR = 100° and ∠RPQ = 20°.
Measure RQ.

5 Draw the shapes sketched below accurately. Measure the angle with the star in each one and write it down.

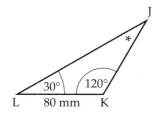

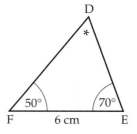

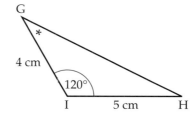

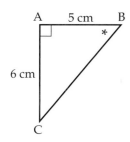

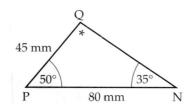

6 Draw rectangle ABCD where AB = 6 cm, BC = 10 cm.
Measure AC.

Investigation

7 All the pupils in a class are asked to draw a quadrilateral with sides 5 cm, 6 cm, 7 cm and 8 cm.
Will they all be the same? How do you know?
All the pupils in a class are asked to draw a quadrilateral with angles 90°, 110°, 70° and 90°.
Will they all be the same? How do you know?
What is the least information you need to be given about a quadrilateral in order to draw it accurately?

Visualising 2-D shapes

⊕ Be able to visualise and sketch 2-D shapes in different orientations

Dynamic geometry programs such as LOGO use two different types of directions:

movement in a **straight line** such as forward 5 units.

turning movements with a **direction** such as right 60°.

Example 1 Write the instructions for drawing a rectangle with two sides of 5 units and two sides of 10 units.

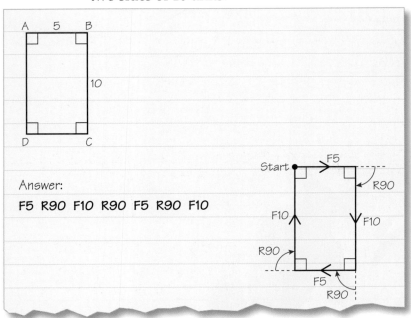

Answer:

F5 R90 F10 R90 F5 R90 F10

Sketch your rectangle first. Mark on everything you know and where you are going to start drawing.

Give a separate instruction for each straight line and each turn.

Example 2 Draw a right-angled isosceles triangle.

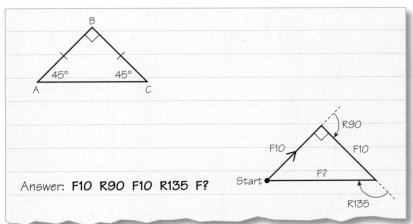

Answer: **F10 R90 F10 R135 F?**

Sketch your triangle first. You aren't given any lengths so you can make the sides whatever you wish. But AB = AC because it is an isosceles triangle.

Decide where to begin your drawing. Here we are starting at A. CA will have to be as long as it needs to be to meet up at A.

Exercise 11.5

1 Write the instructions for drawing:

    a)   a rectangle with sides 6 and 8 units

    b)   an isosceles triangle with two equal angles of 50°

    c)   a right-angled triangle with an angle of 60°

    d)   a parallelogram with two angles of 100° and two angles of 80°

    e)   a kite with two equal angles of 120°, one angle of 80° and one angle of 40°.

> You can choose any size you wish for all sides except in part **a**. Sketch out the shapes first and write in the information you will need to use. Then decide on the best place to start.

    If you have the use of a computer, check to see whether your instructions work.

2 Work in pairs.
Decide on a shape you wish to draw and then sketch it. Give instructions to your partner so that they can draw the shape.
Compare your shapes, then swap roles with your partner.

3 Here are the instructions for a drawing robot to trace out a trapezium:

    F10 L60 F10 L60 F20 L120 F10 L60

    a)   One of the instructions is wrong. Which one is it?

    b)   What should the instruction be?

4 Look at your answers to Q**1**. What shapes would you get if you reversed the order of the instructions?

Investigation

5 Use a dynamic geometry program to draw a triangle with a base of 10 units and base angles of 50 and 70 degrees.
Explore what happens as you change the length of the base. Record your results.

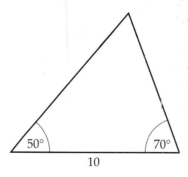

Percentages

- ⊕ Convert a fraction to an equivalent percentage
- ⊕ Convert a decimal to an equivalent percentage

To convert a fraction to a **percentage**, find an **equivalent** fraction with a denominator of 100. The numerator will be the percentage.

For example, $\frac{3}{5} = \frac{60}{100}$, so $\frac{3}{5}$ is **equivalent** to 60%.

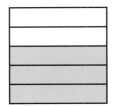 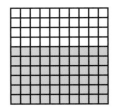

The equivalence can be seen on a 10 by 10 square. Colour $\frac{3}{5}$ of the 100 squares.

Start by colouring $\frac{1}{5}$, then repeat this two more times to give $\frac{3}{5}$.

To convert a decimal to an equivalent percentage, simply write it as a number of **hundredths**. This is the equivalent percentage. For example, $0.42 = \frac{42}{100} = 42\%$

Notice that $0.421 = 42.1$ hundredths, or 42.1%.

Example 1 Convert $\frac{19}{25}$ into an equivalent percentage.

$$\frac{19}{25} = \frac{?}{100}$$

$$\frac{19}{25} = \frac{76}{100} = \mathbf{76\%}$$

First, convert to a fraction with 100 as the denominator. The denominator of the left-hand fraction has been multiplied by 4 to give the denominator of the right-hand fraction, so multiply the left-hand numerator by 4 as well.

Example 2 Convert **a)** 0.39 and **b)** 1.396 to percentages.

a) $0.39 = \frac{39}{100} = \mathbf{39\%}$

b) 1.396 is 1 whole and 39.6 hundredths = **139.6%**

1 whole is 100% and 39.6 hundredths is 39.6%.

Exercise 12.1

1 a) What is the percentage of each grid that is shaded?

i)   **ii)**   **iii)**

iv)   **v)**   **vi)**

b) What percentage of each grid is unshaded?

2 Convert each fraction to an equivalent percentage:

a) $\frac{3}{10}$ b) $\frac{2}{5}$ c) $\frac{3}{4}$ d) $1\frac{1}{4}$ e) $\frac{11}{20}$

f) $\frac{23}{20}$ g) $\frac{17}{25}$ h) $\frac{34}{50}$ i) $\frac{84}{200}$ j) $\frac{63}{200}$

3 Write each decimal as an equivalent percentage:

a) 0.35   b) 0.6   c) 0.47   d) 0.50   e) 0.71

f) 1.36   g) 0.09   h) 1.07   i) 0.01   j) 0.155

4 For each list, predict the order by writing the letters A to E, smallest to largest. Next convert each fraction or decimal to an equivalent percentage. Write out the correct order. Compare the result with your prediction:

a) A: $\frac{3}{5}$ B: 0.7   C: $\frac{3}{4}$ D: 0.81   E: $\frac{73}{100}$

b) A: $\frac{1}{2}$ B: 0.42   C: $\frac{2}{5}$ D: $\frac{11}{20}$ E: $\frac{23}{50}$

c) A: $\frac{7}{20}$ B: $\frac{3}{10}$ C: $\frac{11}{25}$ D: 0.29   E: $\frac{27}{50}$

d) A: $\frac{3}{20}$ B: 0.12   C: $\frac{13}{100}$ D: $\frac{7}{50}$ E: 0.1

e) A: $1\frac{4}{5}$ B: 1.78   C: $1\frac{3}{4}$ D: 1.82   E: $\frac{92}{50}$

5 Draw this number line.

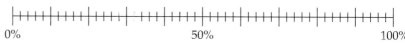

0%   50%   100%

Write these fractions as equivalent percentages, and mark them with a pointer on the line.

$\frac{1}{2}, \frac{3}{5}, \frac{7}{10}, \frac{3}{4}, \frac{13}{20}, \frac{63}{100}, \frac{18}{50}, \frac{2}{3}$

Put the fractions in order, smallest to largest.

6 Look at the first chapter of a book. Explore what percentage of the first 300 letters are vowels, and what percentage are consonants.

7 If $\frac{17}{20}$ of the pupils in a year group passed a science exam, what percentage failed it?

8 In a quiz game, contestants had to choose between answers A, B, C or D. Of all the contestants, $\frac{3}{10}$ chose A, $\frac{1}{4}$ chose B, $\frac{2}{5}$ chose C, and the remainder chose D. What percentage chose D?

9 Who am I?

a) I am a fraction with a denominator of 20. My equivalent percentage lies between 60% and 70%.

b) I am a fraction with a numerator of 7. I am more than 0.25 and less than 30%.

Investigation

10 Find fractions with percentage equivalents between 30% and 50%. The percentage must be a whole number.
The denominators must be even and less than 30.

Work systematically. For example start searching for fractions with a denominator of 2, then 3, then 4, and so on.

Working with percentages

⊕ Calculate percentages of numbers, quantities and measures

⊕ Check an answer by seeing if it is about the right size

We can find a **percentage** of an amount in different ways:

a) Without using a calculator, find some useful percentages, for example 50%, 10%, 1%, and use combinations of these.

For example: to find 21%, double 10% and add 1%;
to find 63%, find 50% then 10%, and then 3 times 1%. See Example 1.

b) Using a calculator, and the % key.

For example: to find 21% of 450, press 4 5 0 × 2 1 % =

c) Using a calculator, and changing the percentage to a decimal.

For example: to find 21% of 450, press 4 5 0 × . 2 1 =

Example   Find 67% of £1300.

50% of £1300 = £650 ($\frac{1}{2}$ of £1300)
10% of £1300 = £130 ($\frac{1}{10}$ of £1300)
5% of £1300 = £65 (half of 10%)
1% of £1300 = £13 ($\frac{1}{100}$ of £1300)
So, 67% of £1300 = £650 + £130 + £65 + 2 × £13 = **£871**

Find 50%, 10%, 5% and 2%, then add them together to make 67% of £1300.

67% = 50% + 10% + 5% + 2%
2% = 2 × 1%

Exercise 12.2

1 Calculate the following amounts:

a) 10% of £140

b) 20% of £75

c) 50% of 170 kg

d) 60% of 85 m

e) 25% of 240 g

f) 75% of 6 m

g) 90% of £1200

h) 40% of £600

i) 30% of 40 kg

j) 15% of 80 kg

Check your answers using a calculator.

2 Calculate the following amounts:

a) 11% of 70 km

b) 21% of 160 m

c) 15% of 32 g

d) 12% of 45 kg

e) 51% of £170

f) 53% of £1200

g) 111% of 2500 litres

h) 89% of 900 g

i) 26% of 1400 km

j) 18% of £300

Check your answers using a calculator.

3 Calculate the number of votes for each player in the 'Player of the Month' competition:

a) January: 11 000 votes

Clogger 21%   Fowler 51%   Trippet 28%

b) February: 12 500 votes

Diver 32%   Fell 43%   Conn 25%

4 Copy and complete the percentage chart.

	£3000	£240	£650	£12 500
10%				
21%				
79%				
52%				
131%				

Check your answers using a calculator.

5 Prices are reduced in a sale. Calculate the sale price of each item.

a) Coat: £150   10% off   b) Skirt: £24   20% off

c) Jacket: £60   25% off   d) Trousers: £32   15% off

e) Jeans: £45   11% off

6 Use a set of 40 – 99 number cards. Choose a percentage, for example 22%. Shuffle the cards and deal out five numbers. For each number, find 22% of it by:

a) finding 20% and 2% and then combining them

b) using the percentage key on the calculator

c) changing the percentage to a decimal (0.22), and using multiplication on the calculator.

Repeat for a different set of cards and a different percentage.

7 The population of Newtown Market was 14 000 in the year 2000. It has since increased by 12%. What is its population now?

> To find the increase in population, find 12% of the population in 2000.

8 The Palace Theatre has 1600 seats. Last Wednesday evening, 86% of the seats were filled. How many empty seats were there?

Investigation

9 Choose an amount of money, for example £270. Investigate different percentages of amounts that match it, for example:

10% of £2700;   5% of £5400;   15% of £8100.

Investigate for different amounts of money. Can you find more than five expressions for each?

12.3 Proportion

⊕ Describe a proportion as a percentage, a fraction or a decimal

⊕ Solve problems involving proportions

Key words
percentage
proportion
decimal
fraction

A proportion is a part of a whole.
It can be expressed as a fraction, a decimal,
or a percentage.

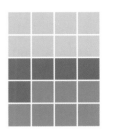

In this grid:
the proportion of yellow squares is $\frac{8}{20}$, or 0.40 or 40%
the proportion of red squares is $\frac{5}{20}$ or 0.25, or 25%
the proportion of blue square is $\frac{7}{20}$, or 0.35, or 35%

Example 1   Which of these proportions is greater: 9 out of 20 or 23 out of 50?

9 out of 20 = $\frac{9}{20}$ = $\frac{45}{100}$ = 45%

23 out of 50 = $\frac{23}{50}$ = $\frac{46}{100}$ = 46%

So 23 out of 50 is greater

Write each proportion as a
fraction, decimal or
percentage to compare
them.

Example 2   If 500g of mince is needed to make a bolognese for 4 people, how
much mince is needed to make a bolognese for 5 people?

500g for 4 people

(÷4) 125g for 1 person

(×5) 625 g for 5 people

To find out how much you
need for 1 person, divide
by 4.

Then multiply by 5 for 5 people.
Check that the answer is sensible.

Exercise 12.3

1 For each grid, write as a fraction:
   (a) The proportion of squares which are red.
   (b) The proportion of squares which are blue.
   (c) The proportion which are yellow.
   (d) Write each proportion as a percentage.

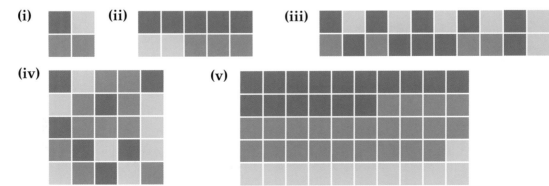

(i)   (ii)   (iii)

(iv)   (v)

2 Draw these grids and colour them in the following proportions:

(a) 2×5 grid: red $\frac{2}{5}$, yellow $\frac{3}{5}$

Find 10% and 5% of 20.

(b) 4×5 grid: blue 35%, red 65%

(c) 5×10 grid: blue 18%, red 54%, yellow 28%

3 Which of these proportions is greater?

(a) 40 out of 160 or 30 out of 150

(b) 20 out of 30 or 70 out of 100

(c) 3 out of 10 or 16 out of 50

(d) 19 out of 100 or 37 out of 50

(e) 16 out of 25 or 5 out of 8

4 Look at the recipe on the right.

(a) What proportion of the **mass of fruit** is:
(i) raspberries; (ii) redcurrants; (iii) blackcurrants?

(b) How much of the following will you need to make a summer pudding for 10 people:
(i) blackcurrants (ii) caster sugar (iii) raspberries?

(c) How much of the following will you need to make a summer pudding for 4 people:
(i) raspberries, (ii) redcurrants, (iii) blackcurrants?

(d) How much of the following will you need for enough summer pudding for 35 people:
(i) caster sugar (ii) blackcurrants (iii) raspberries
(iv) slices of bread?

> **Recipe for summer pudding**
> serves 5 people
>
> 450 g raspberries
> 200 g redcurrants
> 100 g blackcurrants
> 150 g caster sugar
> 8 slices bread

5 Sunset orange paint is made from banana yellow and ruby red colours.
If 1 litre of orange contains 300ml of red,

1 litre = 1000ml

(a) how much ruby red is needed to make (i) 5 litres of orange (ii) 1.5 litres of orange?

(b) how much orange paint has been made if you used 1.4 litres of yellow?

6 £1 is worth 2.5 Australian dollars.

(a) How many dollars will you get for £50?

(b) How much is 1 Australian dollar worth in £?

7 Four ice lollies cost £1.60.

(a) What is the cost of 10 ice lollies?

(b) What change will you have from a £10 note if you bought 7 ice lollies?

Investigation

8 Use a TV guide. Choose a channel, e.g. BBC1.
Investigate the proportion of the total TV time for the day which is devoted to films.
Do the same for another type of programme, e.g. sport. Repeat for a different TV channel.
Compare the two.

◈ Recognises a ratio, and write it using ratio symbols

◈ Simplify a ratio by cancelling

◈ Solve problems about ratio and proportion

A **proportion** compares one part with the whole.

A **ratio** is a way of comparing one part with another part.

To compare the amount of jam to the amount of marmalade, we use the shorthand 3 : 1. *'A ratio of three to one'*. (Three times as many jars of jam as jars of marmalade).

Alternatively,

To compare the amount of marmalade to the amount of jam, we use the shorthand 1 : 3. *'A ratio of one to three'*. (One third as many jars of marmalade as jars of jam.)

Ratios can be **simplified** (by cancelling, as with fractions).
A ratio of 4 : 8, for example, simplifies to 1 : 2. ————— Compare $\frac{4}{8} = \frac{1}{2}$.

Example

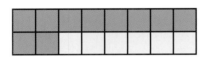

For this grid, write:

a) the proportion of red squares   **b)** the proportion of yellow squares

c) the ratio of red to yellow squares   **d)** the ratio of yellow to red squares.

The proportions are:

a) $\frac{10}{16} = \frac{5}{8}$ **b)** $\frac{6}{16} = \frac{3}{8}$

The ratios are:

c) $10 : 6 = 5 : 3$ **d)** $6 : 10 = 3 : 5$

Exercise 12.4

1 For each grid, write:

a) the proportion of red squares   **b)** the proportion of yellow squares

c) the ratio of red to yellow squares   **d)** the ratio of yellow to red squares.

i)   **ii)**    **iii)**   **iv)**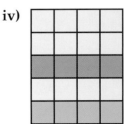

2 Copy each grid. Colour the squares red and yellow to match these ratios:

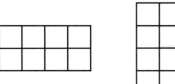 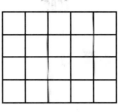 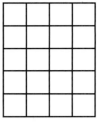

1:3   1:2   4:1   7:3

3 Simplify the following ratios:

a) 6 : 2   **b)** 4 : 20   **c)** 25 : 10   **d)** 12 : 8   **e)** 140 : 210

f) 12 : 120   **g)** 2 : 18   **h)** 16 : 16   **i)** 75 : 35   **j)** 125 : 225

4 Copy this chart to show the hours in a day from midnight through to midnight:

	12	1	2	3	4	5	6	7	8	9	10	11	12
a.m.													
p.m.													

Write 'S' for sleeping in each box to indicate your sleeping hours for an ordinary weekday.

> Use approximations to the nearest hour.

Write 'Sc' for hours you normally spend in school.

Write abbreviations for the other hours, for example 'H' for homework, 'O' for 'out', 'TV' for watching television, and so on.

a) Write the ratio of hours spent sleeping to hours spent awake.

b) Choose five other ratios to describe your day, for example the ratio of homework to time spent in school.

5 In a café $\frac{3}{7}$ of the people are female.
Write the ratio of females to males in the café.

6 In a class 6 out of 30 pupils travel to school by car.
Write the ratio, in its simplest form, of those who come by car to those who don't.

> First, find how many don't travel by car.

7 The school team won 15 and lost 5 of their Home matches, and won 7 and lost 13 of their Away matches. Write the ratio of:

a) home matches lost to home matches won

b) away matches won to away matches lost

c) total matches won to total matches lost.

> Remember to simplify the ratios.

Investigation

9 Investigate the ratio of the number of prime numbers to the number of non-prime numbers in:

> Look back to lesson 10.1 for a reminder about prime numbers.

a) the numbers 1 to 50 inclusive

b) the numbers 1 to 100 inclusive.

More ratio

Key words
ratio
proportion

⊕ Divide an amount into two parts in a given ratio
⊕ Check a result by working the problem backwards

To divide an amount in a given **ratio** , there are four stages:
For example, to divide £15 in the ratio 2 : 3.
a) Find the total number of small parts. Two small parts and three small parts is a total of five small parts.
b) Work out how much each small part is worth. £15 divided by 5 is £3.
c) Multiply each part of the ratio by this amount 2 × £3 = £6; 3 × £3 = £9.
d) Check the two parts are in the given ratio, and that the total is correct:
(£6 : £9 = 2 : 3 and £6 + £9 = £15)

Example 1 Divide 1200 ml in the ratio 3 : 7.

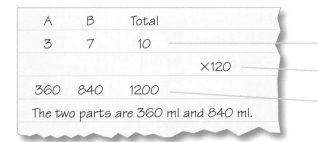

A	B	Total
3	7	10
		×120
360	840	1200

The two parts are 360 ml and 840 ml.

Total of the two parts is 10

Each part is worth 1200 ml ÷ 10 ml

Check that 360 : 840 reduces to 3 : 7

Exercise 12.5

1 Divide £24 in the following ratios:
  a) 1 : 2   **b)** 3 : 5   **c)** 3 : 1   **d)** 7 : 5   **e)** 1 : 7   **f)** 19 : 5

2 Sally and Jeevan have earned £36 cleaning cars. They divide it up according to how much work they have each done. How much will they each receive if they decide to divide it in the following ratios:
  a) 5 : 1   **b)** 4 : 5   **c)** 1 : 3   **d)** 11 : 1   **e)** 5 : 13   **f)** 1 : 1

3 Start with a 4 × 6 grid.
The squares can be either shaded or unshaded.
Investigate different possible ratios for shading the grid.
Here are two examples:

  1 : 3 (6 shaded, 18 unshaded)   3 : 5 (9 shaded, 15 unshaded)

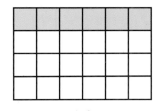

1 : 3

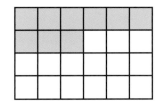

3 : 5

4 Cocktail recipes:
'Pack-a-punch'; 800 ml using blackcurrant juice and lemonade in the ratio 3 : 5.
'Orange Sunrise': 500 ml using orange juice and ginger beer in the ratio 2 : 3.
'Pink Fizz': 750 ml using nectarine juice and tonic water in the ratio 1 : 2.

a) How much nectarine juice is needed to make these amounts of 'Pink Fizz'?
   i) 750 ml   ii) 300 ml
b) How much blackcurrant juice is needed to make these amounts of 'Pack-a-punch'?
   i) 1600 ml   ii) 2 l
c) How much orange juice is needed to make these amounts of 'Orange Sunrise'?
   i) 750 ml   ii) $1\frac{1}{2}$ l
d) How much tonic water is needed to make these amounts of 'Pink Fizz'?
   i) 600 ml   ii) 1800 ml
e) How much lemonade is needed to make these amounts of 'Pack-a-punch'?
   i) 400 ml   ii) 2 l
f) How much ginger beer is needed to make these amounts of 'Orange Sunrise'?
   i) 750 ml   ii) 1250 ml

5 A recipe for lemon curd uses caster sugar and butter in the ratio of 3 : 2.

   a) How much butter is needed if 150 g of caster sugar is used?

   b) How much caster sugar is needed if 150 g of butter is used?

6 A class has 27 pupils, and the ratio of boys to girls is 4 : 5.
  How many girls are there?

7 The ratio of males to females at a concert is 7 : 8.
  There are 1200 females at the concert. How many people are there at the concert
  altogether?

Investigation

8 Choose a ratio such as 3 : 4. Investigate ways of making two amounts of money in this
  ratio, using the fewest possible coins.
  For example:

total of 7p	1p, 2p and 2p, 2p	4 coins needed
total of 14p	5p, 1p and 5p, 2p, 1p	5 coins needed
total of 21p	5p, 2p, 2p and 10p, 1p, 1p	6 coins needed

Investigate the ratio 2 : 3, then choose some of your own ratios to investigate.

⊕ Understand how simplification can help you when you need to substitute values into an expression

To find the value of an **expression** using algebra such as $6(x + y)$ when $x = 2$ and $y = 1$, work out the bracket first, then multiply by the number outside the bracket.

$$6(x + y) = 6(2 + 1)$$
$$= 6 \times 3$$
$$= 18$$

For more complicated expressions, it often helps to first **expand the brackets** and then collect the like terms together.

For example, if $x = 2$ and $y = 5$ find:

$$22 + y + 4(x + y) - 13 - x$$

Substituting $x = 2$ and $y = 5$ into the expression:

$$22 + 5 + 4(2 + 5) - 13 - 2 = 22 + 5 + 4 \times 7 - 13 - 2$$
$$= 22 + 5 + 28 - 13 - 2$$
$$= 40$$

This looks very complicated and it is very easy to make mistakes.

Simplify the expression first:

$$22 + y + 4(x + y) - 13 - x = 22 + y + 4x + 4y - 13 - x$$
$$= 3x + 5y + 9$$

Now substitute the values in:

$$3x + 5y + 9 = 3 \times 2 + 5 \times 5 + 9$$
$$= 6 + 25 + 9$$
$$= 40$$

Before substituting values into an expression, make sure you simplify it as much as possible.

Example 1 Substitute $a = 5$, $b = 4$, $c = -1$ to find the value of:

a) $3(a + 2b)$ **b)** $5(2a - b + 3c)$

a) $3(a + 2b) = 3(5 + 2 \times 4)$
$$= 3(5 + 8)$$
$$= 3 \times 13$$
$$= 39$$

b) $5(2a - b + 3c) = 5(10 - 4 - 3)$
$$= 5 \times 3$$
$$= 15$$

Example 2 Find the value of $2x + 3(2x + y + 4) + 2y$ when $x = 2$ and $y = 1$.

$$2x + 3(2x + y + 4) + 2y = 2x + 6x + 3y + 12 + 2y$$
$$= 8x + 5y + 12$$
$$= 8 \times 2 + 5 \times 1 + 12$$
$$= 16 + 5 + 12$$
$$= 33$$

First simplify the algebraic expression by multiplying out the brackets.

Now substitute the values you are given for x and y into the expression.

Exercise 13.1

1 Substitute $x = 4$, $y = 10$ and $z = 5$ into the following expressions to calculate their value:

a) $2(x + 5)$ b) $4(2 + y)$ c) $3(z - 2)$ d) $4(x + y)$

e) $7(x + z)$ f) $10(y - z)$ g) $4(2x - 5)$ h) $11(3y + 4)$

i) $10(y - 2x)$ j) $9(2x + 2z)$ k) $12(x + y + z)$ l) $5(y + z - x)$

2 Find the value of each of the following expressions using algebra:
when $x = 10$, $y = 25$ and $z = 1$:

a) $3x + 2(x - 5)$ b) $4z - 12 + 3(z + 4)$ c) $18 + 6z + 3(4 + 2z)$

d) $3(2x + 5) - 2x$ e) $3(4y - 12) + 50$ f) $35 + 7(z - x) + 12x$

3 Find the value of each of the following expressions using algebra:

a) $3(x + 5) - x + y$ $x = 100$, $y = 25$ b) $4x + 2(y + x) - 30$ $x = 25$, $y = 75$

c) $2(3x - 4) + 12 - 5x$ $x = 30$ d) $5(2x + 2y) - 3x + 4y$ $x = 150$, $y = 10$

4 To calculate the amount anyone can borrow from SouthKey Bank, bankers use a formula:

Loan = 2 (Income − £10,000)

a) Mr Amis' income is £35,000 per year. What amount can he borrow from the bank?
b) Expand the brackets in the formula.
c) Describe in words the amount SouthKey Bank will lend you.

5 An expression using algebra is written on the whiteboard:

$$2x + 5(x - 10) + 20y - 4x + 5 + 3(y + 15) - 3x$$

The teacher asks the class what the value of this expression will be when $x = 2$ and $y = 50$.
Some pupils suggest the following answers:

Anish: 112
Victoria: 1150
Kathleen: 234

Simplify the expression and explain briefly without doing any calculations who is correct and why the other two must be wrong.

6 Try expanding the brackets in the following expressions. Then substitute in values such as $x = 1$ to see if your expanded expression is the same.

a) $x(x + 10)$ b) $2x(3x + 5)$

⊕ Solve simple equations

Key words
equation
solve
equals
inverse operations
balancing

An **equation** is when two things are equal. An **equals** sign means that both sides are the same.

For example, $x + 4 = 8$

To **solve** equations, we can use inverse operations as we did in lesson 1.6 or we can balance the equation by doing the same thing to each side.

Example   Solve the equation $x - 4 = 10$.

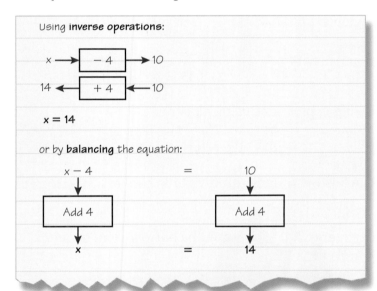

To remove -4 we must add 4.

Exercise 13.2

1 Solve each of the following equations:

a) $x + 7 = 50$ b) $x + 5 = 12$

c) $x + 6 = 14$ d) $x + 10 = 22$

e) $x + 100 = 250$ f) $x - 2 = 8$

g) $x - 12 = 7$ h) $x - 35 = 70$

i) $x - 4 = 13$ j) $x - 81 = 100$

2 Solve each of the following equations:

a) $3 + x = 5$ b) $4 + x = 20$ c) $7 + x = 12$

d) $24 + x = 120$ e) $324 + x = 500$

3 Solve each of the following equations:

a) $10 = x + 5$
b) $24 = x + 9$
c) $100 = x + 33$
d) $55 = 29 + x$
e) $72 = 34 + x$
f) $105 = x - 12$
g) $79 = x - 21$
h) $18 = x - 101$

> It doesn't matter which side of the equals sign the unknown is found on.

4 Check your answers to Q3 by substituting your value for x back into the original equation.

> For example, $x + 5 = 11$
> $x = 11 - 5$ (subtract 5 from both sides)
> $x = 6$
>
> Check: $x + 5 = 11$
> $6 + 5 = 11$ ✓

5 Simplify the following equations and then solve them:

a) $2x + 4x - 5 + 2x - 12 - 7x = 10$
b) $5t - 10t - 26 + 6t = 2x + 3 - 2x$
c) $7y - 7y = 5x + 12 - 4x$

> Work out how many x's and how many numbers you have on each side of the equation.

6 Lord Savelottes is mad about money! He keeps it all locked up in his safe.

The combination on his safe each day is the solution to an equation. He forms the equations by writing:

$x -$ month number $=$ date

For example, on the 5th July which is the 5th day of the 7th month, the equation he uses is:

$x - 7 = 5$

a) What is the combination on the 20th January?
b) What is the combination on the 5th July?
c) List all the different combinations he uses in January. Can you spot a pattern?
d) Investigate the combinations for the other months.
e) Which combinations does he use only once?
f) What dates are these for?

⊕ Solve equations involving multiples of x

We can **solve** **equations** such as $5x + 3 = 18$ which involve more than one step.

We always do the same thing to both sides of the equation so that it stays balanced.

Example 1 Solve the equation $3x - 4 = 14$.

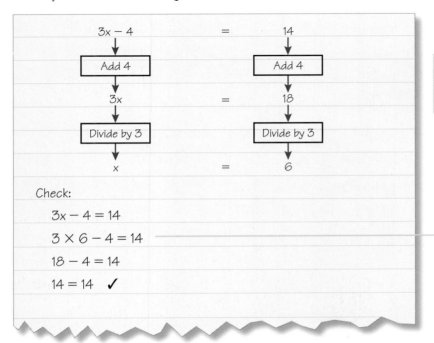

To solve this equation add 4 to each side then divide each side by 3.

Check:

$3x - 4 = 14$

$3 \times 6 - 4 = 14$ ———— Substitute $x = 6$.

$18 - 4 = 14$

$14 = 14$ ✓

Exercise 13.3

1 Solve each of the following equations. Make sure you check all your answers:

a) $2x + 3 = 11$ b) $3x + 5 = 14$

c) $5x + 9 = 19$ d) $2x + 21 = 45$

e) $10x + 122 = 192$ f) $2x - 2 = 18$

g) $3x - 5 = 25$ h) $6x - 35 = 1$

i) $10x - 20 = 30$ j) $12x - 64 = 8$

2 Solve each of the following equations. Make sure you check all your answers.

a) $3 + 4x = 11$ b) $4 + 2x = 18$ c) $10 + 5x = 60$

d) $18 + 7x = 67$ e) $351 + 11x = 362$

3 Solve each of the following equations:

a) $53 = 6x + 5$
b) $24 = 4x + 8$
c) $81 = 8x + 9$
d) $105 = 6 + 11x$
e) $99 = 39 + 5x$
f) $6 = 6x - 30$
g) $235 = 12x - 5$
h) $73 = 2x - 77$

> Remember, it doesn't matter which side of the equals sign the unknown is found on.

4 Solve each of the following equations. Make sure you check all your answers.

a) $5(x + 5) = 30$
b) $4(x + 8) = 48$
c) $3(x + 5) = 21$
d) $7(x + 12) = 105$
e) $10(x + 6) = 180$
f) $20(x + 3) = 80$

> Multiply out the brackets first.

5 Five bags of flour weigh 20 kg.

a) Write out an equation using x to stand in for a bag of flour.

b) Solve the equation to find the mass of each bag of flour.

6 Two CDs and one single cost £18. The single costs £1.98.

a) Form an equation from this information using x to stand in for the cost of one CD.

b) Solve the equation to find the cost of one CD.

7 By solving the equations in the clues, copy and complete the crossword below:

Across:

1 $x + 120 = 200$

2 $y + 95 = 400$

4 The number of days in the year.

6 I choose a number, subtract 60 and get 1995. What number did I choose?

7 I multiply this number by 11 and get 121.

8 $3x + 1 = 37$

9 $\dfrac{m}{3} = 111$

10 $1.5x = 46.5$

12 I choose a number, add 7 and get 21. What number did I choose?

14 Double 70

15 $15\,000 - x = 8000$

16 $2x + 5 = 107$

Down:

1 I choose a number, divide it by 2 and get 401. What number did I choose?

2 $\dfrac{r}{7} = 5$

3 I add 40 to this number and get 551.

4 $2x + 10 = 80$

5 $10a = 650$.

7 To get this number, you add 10 000 and 2000, then add 300, then add 50, then subtract 5.

9 $3x - 1000 = 20$

11 I am 5 more than 96.

12 If I divide 34 by this number, I get 2.

⊕ Form and solve equations representing real life situations

Algebra is used all the time in everyday life. For example, we use it to:
- calculate bills
- work out areas
- convert from one unit to another, such as from kilometres to miles.

If you do something to one side of an equation, you must do **exactly** the same thing to the other side.

Example 1 Find the size of the angles in the triangle:

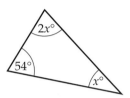

$$x + 2x + 54 = 180$$
$$3x + 54 = 180$$
$$3x = 180 - 54$$
$$3x = 126$$
$$x = \frac{126}{3}$$
$$x = 42$$

The two missing angles are **42°** and $2 \times 42° = $ **84°**.

The angles in a triangle add up to 180°.

Check that the angles add up to 180°.
$54 + 42 + 84 = 180$ ✓

Example 2 The perimeter of a rectangle is 52m. If the width is 8m what is the length?

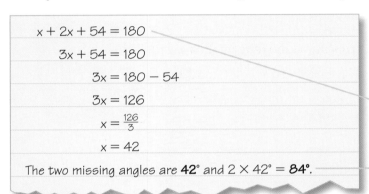

$$A + A + 8 + 8 = 52$$
$$2A + 16 = 52$$
$$2A = 52 - 16$$
$$2A = 36$$
$$A = 18 \text{ metres}$$

First draw a diagram and label the unknown numbers with letters.

The perimeter of a shape is the distance all the way round it.

Exercise 13.4

1 Write down equations and then solve them to find the unknown angles in the following triangles:

a)

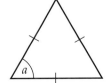

b)

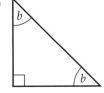

c)

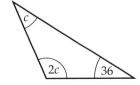

2 The area covered by a rectangular pond is 200 m²:
What is the width if the length is

Remember:
area = length × width

    a) 20 m   **b)** 50 m   **c)** 100 m   **d)** 200 m?

3 The cost of this shopping bill is £5.25.

If the pack of yoghurts costs £1.20 and a loaf of bread costs 50p, what was the cost of one carton of milk?

2 loaves of bread,

5 cartons of milk,

1 pack of yoghurts.

4 The perimeter of a swimming pool is 80 m.
    a) If the width is 10 m, what is the length?
    b) If the length is 25 m, what is the width?
    c) If the swimming pool is square, what is the length of each side?

5 In Class 7A, the heights of five people were measured and the mean was found to be 1.5 m. Four people's heights were: 1.65 m, 1.45 m, 1.6 m, 1.4 m.
What was the height of the fifth person?

Look back at lesson 5.2:
The mean for help.

6 The perimeter of a square is 30 cm.
    a) Draw a diagram using x to stand in for the length of a side of the square.
    b) Write down an equation that connects x to the perimeter.
    c) Calculate the length of one side of the square.
    d) What is the area of the square?

7 The area of the red rectangle is twice the area of the blue rectangle. If the height of the whole shape is 10 cm and the width of the blue rectangle is 2 cm:
    a) What is the area of the red rectangle?
    b) What is the width of the red rectangle?
    c) What is the width of the whole shape?

8 The total area of carpet needed for the dining room and kitchen in a house is 24 m². If the dining room is square with sides of length 3 m, and the kitchen is a rectangle with two sides of length 5 m, what is the width of the kitchen?

Investigation

9 **a)** The surface area of a cuboid is 88 cm². The length of the cuboid is 6 cm and the height is 2 cm. What is its width?

Draw a net of a cuboid and label the sides.

    b) Investigate what other widths and heights a cuboid could have if its surface area is 88 cm² and its length is 6 cm.

Reflection

⊕ Know how to describe a reflection

⊕ Recognise where a shape will be after reflection

Key words
equivalent points
perpendicular bisector
mirror line
reflection

The image A′B′C′ is a **reflection** of the object ABC.
A and A′, B and B′, C and C′ are **equivalent points** . Equivalent points are the same distance from the **mirror line** .
The mirror line cuts the line joining equivalent points at right angles: it is the **perpendicular bisector** of this line.

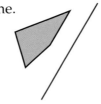

Example 1 Reflect this shape in the mirror line.

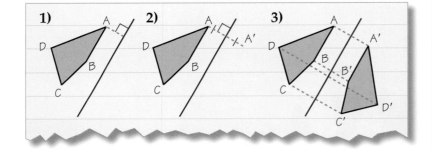

1) Label the vertices. Draw straight line from A to cut the mirror line at 90°.
2) Measure the distance. Continue the line behind the mirror and measure the same distance and mark A′.
3) Repeat with the other vertices, and join up the points.

Example 2 Reflect this shape in both mirror lines.

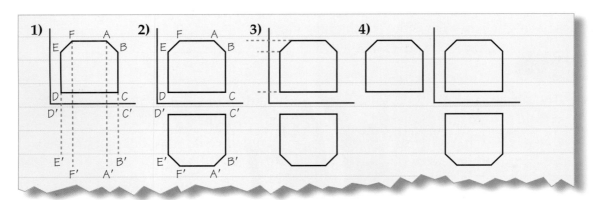

Exercise 14.1 ....

1 Copy each diagram and reflect the shapes in the mirror lines.

a)

b)

c)
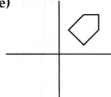

d)

e)

f)
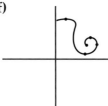

2 Copy each diagram and reflect the shapes in the mirror lines:

a)

b)

c)

d)

e)
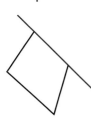

f)
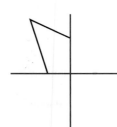

g)
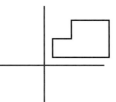

3 This diagram shows two mirrors at 60° to each other. Copy it on to triangular paper and draw in the reflected images as they would appear.

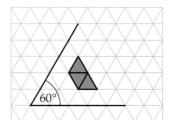

4 Try writing your name back to front so that you can read it in a mirror placed at the end of the word.

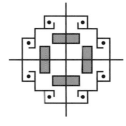

What would you have to do differently if you wanted to read your name in a mirror placed above the word? Is this the same as writing your name upside down?

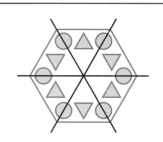

Investigation

5 Rangoli patterns are drawn as decorations during the festival of Divali. Here are two examples. Make up one of your own using either square or triangular dotty paper.

Reflection symmetry

⊕ **Recognise and explore reflection symmetry**

Key words
symmetrical
line of symmetry
reflection symmetry

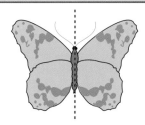

A **line of symmetry** exists where one half of a shape reflects on to the other.
Shapes which are **symmetrical** about a line have **reflection symmetry** .
Regular polygons have the same number of lines of symmetry as sides.

| Equilateral Triangle | Square | Regular Pentagon | Regular Hexagon | Regular Octagon |

Example 1   How many lines of symmetry does this shape have?

The shape has four lines of symmetry.

Each of the eight sections is a mirror

image of the section next to it.

Draw in all the lines of symmetry.

Exercise 14.2 ....

1 How many lines of symmetry does each shape have? Sketch them into your book.

a)

b)

c)

d)

e)

f)

2 Each of these shapes is half of a symmetrical shape. Draw the complete shape.

There may be more than one possible answer.

 A
 B
 C
 D
 E

3 a) Draw a quadrilateral with one line of symmetry and name it.

b) Draw a triangle with one line of symmetry and name it.

c) Draw a quadrilateral with two lines of symmetry and name it.

d) Draw a quadrilateral with four lines of symmetry and name it.

> Look back at Unit 11 for help with naming shapes.

4 Play with a partner. Take it in turns to write a three letter word in capital letters. Score one point for each *letter* in your word that has one line of symmetry, two points for those that have two etc. You get a bonus point if the whole word has a horizontal line of symmetry, for example: or a vertical line of symmetry, for example: TOT .

5 Add on one more square to make a shape with reflection symmetry.

a) How many different solutions are there? Add on one extra square at a time.

b) How many squares would you need to make a shape with four lines of symmetry? Illustrate your answer.

6 Is it possible:

a) to draw a triangle with only two lines of symmetry? Explain your answer.

b) to draw a quadrilateral with only three lines of symmetry? Explain your answer.

c) to draw a hexagon with one, two, three, four, five or six lines of symmetry? Explain your answers.

Investigations

7 Fold a piece of paper twice. By making cuts at the folded corner and opening out the cut piece, make:

a) any octagon

b) a regular octagon

c) any hexagon.

d) a regular hexagon.

e) What other regular polygons can you make when folding the paper twice? Which are impossible to make? Explain your answer.

> Your folds don't always have to be at right angles.

8

Hubcaps on cars always have symmetry, although not all of them have reflection symmetry. Here are some examples. Investigate others, using either real examples or pictures on the web or from magazines. What is the greatest number of lines of symmetry you can find on a hubcap?

Rotation

⊕ Know how to describe a rotation

⊕ Be able to draw the rotation of a shape about a point

Key words
rotate
rotation
centre of rotation
clockwise
anticlockwise

- We describe a **rotation** by stating the angle of degrees through which a shape has moved, and where the **centre of rotation** is.
  This shape has turned 60° anticlockwise about the star.
- The centre of rotation can be inside, outside or on the shape, and is the only point that does not move during a rotation.
- If a direction is not stated, it is assumed to be **anticlockwise** .
- This cat has rotated 60° **clockwise** . To return it to the starting position, it must be rotated either through a further 300° clockwise, or 60° anticlockwise.

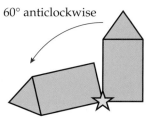

60° anticlockwise

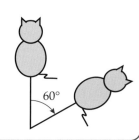

Example 1 Rotate this shape through half a turn (180°) about the centre of rotation shown.

centre of rotation

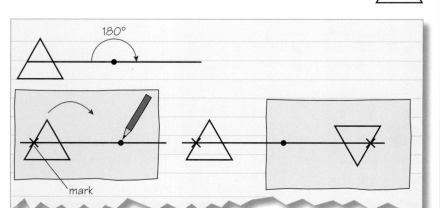

We need to draw a line from the shape to the centre of rotation first, and measure an angle of 180°. Next, place a piece of tracing paper over the shape and trace it. Put a pencil or other point over the centre of rotation so that the tracing paper doesn't slip, and rotate the shape through 180°. If you put a small mark at the starting position you will be able to line it up at the end.

Example 2 Rotate this shape through a quarter of a turn (90°) clockwise about the centre of rotation.

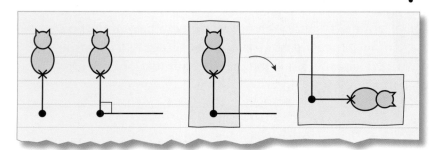

Join one part of the shape to the centre of rotation first and draw an angle of 90°. Put a pencil or other point over the centre of rotation so that the tracing paper doesn't slip, trace the shape and rotate the image through 90°. If you put a small mark at the starting position you will be able to line it up at the end.

Exercise 14.3

1 Copy these shapes and the centres of rotation. Use tracing paper to rotate them through 180°.

a)   b)  c)   d)

> Don't forget that if no direction is given, it is **anticlockwise**.

2 Copy these shapes and the centres of rotation. Use tracing paper to rotate them through 90°.

a)  b) 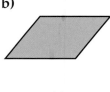 c)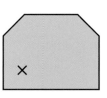

3 Copy this shape and use tracing paper to rotate it through each sixth of a whole rotation through 360°.

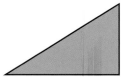

> First work out how much is a sixth of a whole rotation.

4 Use tracing paper to work out which is the centre of rotation for each pair of shapes.

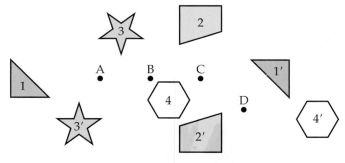

5 a) Describe the rotations necessary to get from the object to the image for each of the shapes in Q4. The object is marked with a number such as 1. The image is marked with a number and a dash such as 1′.

   b) Describe the two possible inverse rotations to get back to the object from the image.

Investigation

6 Draw a pencil circle and mark the centre and every 90° around the circumference. Cut out an irregular shape and draw around it as shown. Rotate it through 90° and draw around it; repeat with each quarter of a turn. Colour the shapes in the pattern that are the same. Try rotating it through other angles.

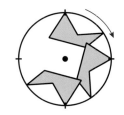

Rotation symmetry

⊕ **Know which 2-D shapes have rotational symmetry and describe it**

Key words
rotation
centre of rotation
order of rotation
symmetry

- The **order of rotation symmetry** is the number of ways a shape can map onto itself in a complete 360° turn. In this child's jigsaw the rectangle has rotation symmetry of order two because in a complete turn it maps onto itself twice. In the jigsaw there are shapes that have rotation symmetry of orders one, two, three, four, five and infinity (∞).

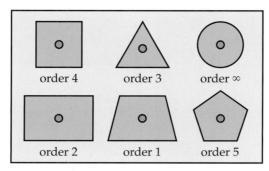

order 4   order 3   order ∞

order 2   order 1   order 5

- The square, equilateral triangle and pentagon in the jigsaw are regular shapes because they have equal sides and equal angles. Regular polygons have the same order of rotation symmetry as number of sides.

Example 1 What is the order of rotation symmetry of this shape?

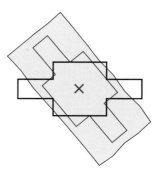

There are two ways in which it can map onto itself in a complete turn. It has rotation symmetry of order **two**.

Trace it and rotate the tracing to see how many times it fits.

Example 2 What is the order of rotation symmetry of this shape?

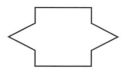

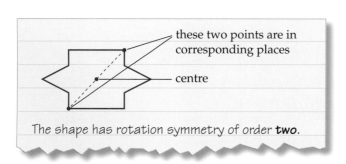

these two points are in corresponding places

centre

The shape has rotation symmetry of order **two**.

Look for a set of corresponding points. Join the points to the centre and check that the sections are identical. There are two ways in which this shape can map onto itself.

Exercise 14.4

1 What is the order of rotation symmetry of each of these shapes?

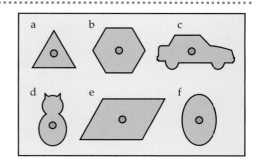

2 What is the order of rotation symmetry of each of the letters in this word?

MATHEMATICS

3 Add another triangle to each shape so that it has rotation symmetry of order three. Is there more than one way you can do this?

a)   b) 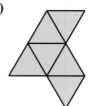 c)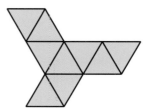

4 This word has rotation symmetry of order two: **OXO**
Can you find any more words like this? What are the things you have to check for?

5 A tile shop is advertising some of the variations in tiling borders which could be made with their tiles. Which illustration is the odd one out and why?

a)  b)

c)  d)

e)  f)

Investigations

6 Print out some of the characters from Wingdings or one of the other symbol fonts.
For example: ☐ ●➤ ✳ ✿ ✑.   Find three characters which:
a) have rotation symmetry of order one and no line symmetry
b) have rotation symmetry of order two and no line symmetry
c) have rotation symmetry of order one and one line of symmetry
d) have rotation symmetry of order one and two lines of symmetry.

7 Draw a circle of radius 5 cm. Mark every 45° on the circumference and join the marks to the middle. Fill in the segments to give a design with rotation symmetry of order eight, but no lines of symmetry.

Translation

⊕ Know how to describe a translation

⊕ Be able to draw the translation of a shape

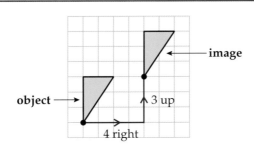

This type of sliding movement is called a **translation** . To describe a translation we have to give both the **direction** and the **distance**. We usually give the movement across first. This **object** has moved four right and three up. We can tell by choosing one point on the **object**, looking at the corresponding point on the **image** and counting how far it has moved. The rest of the shape will have moved in the same way.

To move it back again, we move it the same distance in the opposite direction (4 left and 3 down). This is called the **inverse** of the translation.

Example Translate this object three squares to the left and one square up.

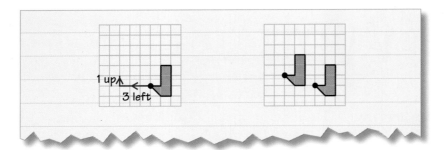

Choose a point on the object and count along three squares to the left and one square up. Mark the new point and use it to help you draw in the rest of the image. You may want to check by working out where more than one point moves to.

Exercise 14.5 ·····

① Draw these shapes on squared paper and translate them as instructed.

a)

2 right, 1 up.

b)

2 left, 2 down.

c)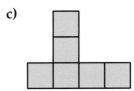

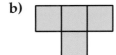

5 right, 1 up, 2 left, 1 down.

2 a) Describe the translation to move from each object to its corresponding image:

    i) 1 to 2   **ii)** 2 to 3   **iii)** 3 to 4   **iv)** 4 to 5

    v) 5 to 1   **vi)** 3 to 2   **vii)** 2 to 6.

b) Which two translations are the same?

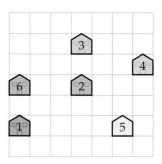

3 Here are parts of three wrapping paper patterns, made from tessellations. For each design, describe the translation of the object to each of the lettered images.

a) 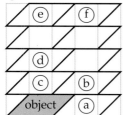   **b)** 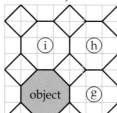   **c)**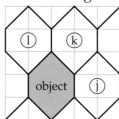

> A tessellation is a tiling pattern with no gaps.

4 Can you fill in the large shape by translating the small shape? (You are not allowed to reflect or rotate the small shape.) Describe the translations that are necessary.

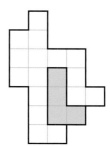

5 Knight and the chessboard.

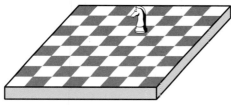

> A knight moves two squares across and one square forward, or one across and two forward. Knights can also move backwards.

Can you visit each square on the chessboard by moving the knight? Record your solution and ask someone else to check it.

6 Use a dynamic geometry package to design a tessellation that uses only translation.

Transformations and coordinates

◈ Use a coordinate grid to plot transformations

- Reflection, rotation and translation are all **transformations** .

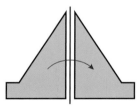 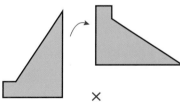 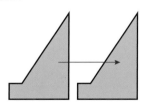

Reflection produces
an image of a shape
in a mirror line

Rotation turns a shape
through an angle about
a centre of rotation

A translation moves a
shape up, down or across

- A transformation moves a shape to a new position, from the **object** to the **image** .
- The shape and size stay the same when an object is reflected, rotated or translated.

Example 1 Find:
the shapes which are reflections of each other,
the shapes which are translations of each other,
the shapes which are rotations of each other.

A and C, B and C, are reflections.

A, B and E are all translations of each other.

D is a rotation of C.

It is the only one to have been turned around a
point so that it is orientated differently.

A is reflected in a mirror line to
make C, B is reflected in a mirror
line to make C.

A, B and E are the same shape
moved up, down or across.

Example 2 Give the new coordinate of Q after these translations:

a) reflection in the line $x = 2$

b) rotation of 180° about (1, 2).

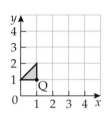

a) The new position is at Q′ (3,1).

b) The new position is at Q″ (1,3).

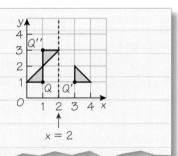

Exercise 14.6

1 Which is which?

    a) Find: **i)** the shapes which are reflections of each other

             ii) the shapes which are translations of each other

             iii) the shapes which are rotations of each other.

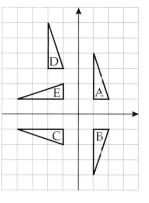

    b) Copy and complete the sentences which describe the
transformations above.

        i)   From _____ to/_____ is a reflection in the x-axis.

        ii) From _____ to _____ is a translation three left and two up.

        iii) From _____ to _____ is an anticlockwise rotation about (0,0)
through an angle of 90°.

2 Give the new coordinate of P after these transformations:

    a) translation two right, one down

    b) rotation 90° clockwise about (1,1)

    c) reflection in the line $x = 1$.

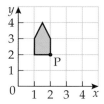

3 Reflect a shape in the x-axis and then in the y-axis. What transformation is needed to
return it to the starting position?

4 Rotate a shape about the point (0,0) through 90° anticlockwise and draw in the image.
Then rotate the image another 90° anticlockwise about the same point again. What
transformation would you need to return to the starting position?

5 Translate a shape four right and two up and draw the image . Then translate it three left
and five down. What transformation is needed to return it to the starting position?

6 Copy the grid. Across the top row transform the tile by
rotating it through 90° clockwise about the bottom right
corner of the tile. Repeat for each new tile that is formed
until the top row is filled. To fill the second row, transform
the tile by reflecting it in the dotted line. Repeat for each tile
in the top row. Write down what you notice.

Investigation

7

Here is a tessellation designed by the Dutch
graphic artist Maurits Escher (1898–1972).
Investigate some of his other ones.
Find examples of tessellations that include
rotation, reflection and translation.

15.1 The three averages

⊕ Revise the three different averages and the range
⊕ Compare the mean, median and mode of a set of data

For a set of data:

The **median** is the **middle** value once the data is in order.

The **mode** is the value that has the **highest frequency**.

The **mean** is the sum of the data divided by the total number of items in the data set.

The **range** is the highest value minus the lowest value.

Example   In a survey, 100 people were asked how many holidays they had taken last year. The table shows the results.

Number of holidays	Frequency
0	41
1	34
2	25

a) Find the range, mode, median and mean number of holidays taken.
b) One of the averages calculated in part **a** shows that 'on average people in the survey took no holidays last year'. Is this a good way to describe the data? Explain your answer.

a) Range = 2 − 0 = 2

Mode = 0 holidays per year

Median = 1 holiday per year

50 is half way. 41 took no holidays, so 50 lies in the '1 holiday' category.

Number of holidays	Frequency	Number of holidays × frequency
0	41	0
1	34	34
2	25	50
Total	100	84

Mean = $\frac{84}{100}$ = 0.84 holidays per year

b) No, it is not a good way to describe the data as 59% of people took at least 1 holiday. It would be better to use the median or mean.

Exercise 15.1

1 A brand of match states on the box that it contains 'on average' 50 matches per box. The contents of twenty boxes are counted as follows:

45   48   51   50   46   48   51   50   44   49
47   46   52   45   50   50   48   45   49   46

   a) Make a frequency table for the data.
   b) Find the mean, median and mode of the data.
   c) Which of the three averages has been used to describe the 'average contents'?
   d) Do you think this is a fair description of the number of matches in a box? Explain your answer.

2 The table below shows the number of days it rains each month in Mexico.

Month	J	F	M	A	M	J	J	A	S	O	N	D
No. of days of rain	0	0	1	1	2	6	7	7	6	2	0	0

   a) Calculate the mean, median and mode for this data.
   b) Which average is most typical of the rainfall in Mexico?

3 A school shop records the sizes of the hockey boots it sells.

   6   4   2   3   6   2   3   5   2   6   3   6   2   6   5   3

   a) Find each of the three averages and the range for this data.
   b) Should the shop always stock the whole range of sizes? Explain your answer.

4 The table below shows the average cost of a detached house in England by region.

Region	North East	North West	Yorkshire & the Humber	East Midlands	West Midlands	East	London	South East	South West
Average price (£'000)	130	150	140	140	170	190	410	280	190

   a) Find the mean, median and mode of the data.
   b) Calculate the three averages again without including London in the data set.
   c) Which of the averages is affected most by the very high cost of houses in London?

5 **a)** Which of the three averages has a value that must appear in the data set?
   b) Which of the three averages can have more than one value?
   c) Which of the three averages may not be a number?
   d) Which of the three averages can be affected by one very high or very low value?

Investigation

6 Look through newspapers and magazines for references to the word 'average'. Decide which average you think would have been used in each case and make a list of your results.

Comparing data

⊕ Use the range and one of the three averages to compare two sets of data

> Averages help us to describe a set of data. We can look at the **range** and averages together to compare two sets of data.

Example   Jah can choose between two different bus routes when he travels to school. He catches each bus for ten days, recording how many minutes he has to wait each time before a bus arrives.

Route 1	3	12	2	1	2	14	2	1	3	15
Route 2	9	3	7	1	9	4	6	2	9	5

a) Find the range and the mean, mode and median length of time he has to wait for each bus route.

b) Which bus should Jah catch so that 'on average' he has the shortest waiting time? Explain your choice.

a)

	Range	Mean	Mode	Median
Route 1	14	5.5	2	2.5
Route 2	8	5.5	9	5.5

The mean time is the same for both routes, so the total length of time Jah waits over the ten days is:
$5.5 \times 10 = 55$ minutes.

b) The mean time for each route is the same. Route 1 has the lowest mode and median. Jah should catch a bus on Route 1 if he wants to have a shorter waiting time most often. However, Route 1 has a bigger range so there will be times when he will have to wait for a very long time!

Exercise 15.2

1 The number of goals scored in the football matches between Manchester United and Arsenal from 1998–2002 are below:

Manchester United	0	1	0	6	0	1	2	2	0	1	0
Arsenal	1	3	4	1	1	1	1	1	0	1	3

a) Find the mode, median and mean number of goals for each of the two teams.

b) **Using your answers only**, what do you think would be a likely outcome if the two teams play each other in another match? Explain your answer.

2 The average number of holidays taken in 1975 and 1995 by people over the age of 18 in Great Britain is shown below together with the range.

	Range	Mean	Mode	Median
1975	3	0.79	0	1
1995	3	0.87	0	1

Did people take more holidays in 1995 than in 1975? Explain your answer.

3 The table below gives the average number of letters in each of the first 100 words in two books.

	Range	Mean	Mode	Median
Book 1	11	4.3	3	4
Book 2	9	4.1	3	3

One book is an adult's book; the other book is a children's book.
Is Book 1 or Book 2 the children's book? Give reasons for your answer.

4 The table below shows the number of goals scored by two different girls in five hockey matches.

	Britney	Christina
Match 1	0	10
Match 2	7	1
Match 3	0	7
Match 4	15	2
Match 5	8	10

a) Calculate the mean, mode, median and range for the number of goals scored by each girl.

b) Only one of the two girls can be chosen for the next match. Which girl would you choose?

c) Use the mean, mode, median and range to explain your answer.

5 The table below shows the average and range of the amount of rainfall in inches per month in Great Britain and in Guatemala in Central America.

	Mode	Median	Mean	Range
Great Britain	2	3	2.4	1
Guatemala	0	3.5	4.3	11

a) The mean for Guatemala is higher than the mean for Great Britain. What does this tell you about the total rainfall there?

b) The range for Great Britain is smaller than the range for Guatemala. Explain what this shows.

c) If you were advertising holidays to Guatemala, which average would you use and why?

Investigation

6 Are girls faster than boys at threading a needle?
Time how long it takes boys and girls to thread a needle.
Find the range and the three averages of the data you collect to help you to decide.

Understanding graphs

⊕ **Interpret diagrams and graphs**

Key words
interpret
proportion

Diagrams and graphs can be an excellent way of showing information, but sometimes not all the information we need to know is given.

Pie charts show the **proportion** (or fraction of) the data in each category.

Example 1 25 young people were asked what activity they preferred to do in the evening. Find the frequency of each activity.

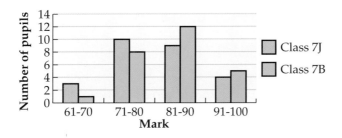

Youth club — Cinema
Play sport — Disco

☐ Cinema   32%
☐ Disco   8%
☐ Play sport 24%
☐ Youth club 36%

Cinema = $\frac{32}{100} \times 25 = $ **8 people**

Disco = $\frac{8}{100} \times 25 = $ **2 people**

Play sport = $\frac{24}{100} \times 25 = $ **6 people**

Youth club = $\frac{36}{100} \times 25 = $ **9 people**

32% is the same as $\frac{32}{100}$

Check that
8 + 2 + 6 + 9 = **25 people**.

Example 2 This chart shows the marks of two different classes: 7J and 7B in a test. Describe the differences between the marks in the two classes.

Number of pupils

14
12
10
8
6
4
2
0

61-70   71-80   81-90   91-100
Mark

☐ Class 7J
☐ Class 7B

The differences between the marks that the pupils in the two classes obtained are not great.

Class 7B scored more highly than Class 7J. More pupils in Class 7B got marks above 81 than did in Class 7J. The greatest number of pupils in Class 7B scored between 81 and 90 whereas the greatest number of pupils in Class 7J scored between 71 and 80.

Look at the differences between the heights of the bars.

Look at the highest bar for each class.

Exercise 15.3

1 The pie chart shows the favourite bread type of 50 people. How many people preferred:

a) brown bread   b) white bread   c) granary bread?

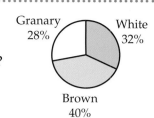

Granary 28%   White 32%   Brown 40%

2

Amount of money spent on sweets by Class 7A and 7B

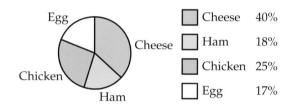

Class 7A and 7B both have 29 pupils in them. Write two sentences to compare the amounts of money the classes spend on sweets.

> Look at Example 2 to help you.

3 The pie chart shows the type of sandwich bought by 200 people.

a) How many people bought each type of sandwich?

b) How many more people bought Cheese rather than Egg?

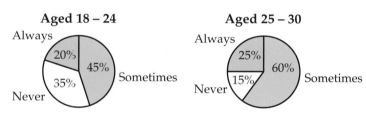

Cheese   40%
Ham   18%
Chicken   25%
Egg   17%

4 The pie charts show how often two different age groups recycle newspaper.

a) Explain why we cannot compare the number of people aged 18–24 who recycle newspaper with those aged 25–30.

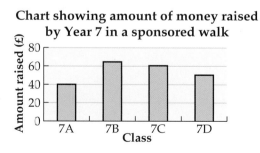

Aged 18 – 24

Always 20%   Sometimes 45%   Never 35%

Aged 25 – 30

Always 25%   Sometimes 60%   Never 15%

b) Which age group has the largest proportion that recycles newspapers?

5 a) Does this Chart show that more people took part in the sponsored walk in Class 7B than any other class? Explain your answer.

b) How much more money did 7B raise than 7A?

c) How much was raised altogether?

Chart showing amount of money raised by Year 7 in a sponsored walk

Designing a questionnaire

⊕ Write and use a questionnaire

> A **questionnaire** is similar to a survey, but often asks for opinions not facts.
> Questions should:
> ● be short and quick to answer ● be to the point ● use tick boxes, if possible.

Example 1 Nikki has written a questionnaire to find out information about the school library. Her teacher's comments are in the green box. Show how the questionnaire could be improved.

1) Age:

2) Do you read a lot of books?
(tick 1 box)

Less than average ☐

Average ☐

More than average ☐

3) What is your favourite type of book?

4) Why do you visit the library?

5) We need more computers in the library, don't we?

Yes ☐ No ☐

6) How many times a week do you go to the library?

0-2 ☐ 2-4 ☐ 5-7 ☐

Q1: Does the age of the person give you enough information about them?

Q2: 'a lot' and 'average' could mean anything.

Q3: You could have too many answers here to make sense of.

Q5: This question might make people agree because of the way it is worded.

Q6: Which box would you tick if you go twice a week or more than 7 times a week?

1) Age: 2) Boy/Girl:

3) How many books do you read each week? (tick 1 box)
1 ☐ 2 ☐ 3 ☐ 4 ☐ 5+ ☐

4) What is your favourite type of book?
Romance ☐ Science fiction ☐ Non-fiction ☐
Funny stories ☐ Adventure ☐ Other ☐

5) Why do you usually visit the library?
Borrow books ☐
Use computers ☐ Other ☐

6) Are there enough computers in the library?
Yes ☐ No ☐ Don't know ☐

7) How many times a week do you go to the library?
0-2 ☐ 3-5 ☐ 6-8 ☐ 9+ ☐

Include 'Boy/Girl', as there might be a difference in their answers.

Be more exact by using tick boxes.

Give a choice. Remember the 'other' box.

Improve the wording of the question. Include a box for those who perhaps never use computers.

Use 6–8 and 9+ boxes and make sure the class intervals don't overlap.

Example 2 Nikki uses her new questionnaire. She asks her two best friends, eight other people in her class and ten people in the library. Why might her results be inaccurate?

Her best friends and the people in her class are probably all the same age. Nikki should ask people from different years.

It is likely that the people she asks in the library visit the library often. She needs to include the views of other people: perhaps those playing football outside or people in the dining room.

Exercise 15.4

1 For each of the questionnaires below, design tick boxes to use to record the answers:

a)

How many videos/DVDs do you hire in a week?
Where do you hire them from?
What type of video/DVD do you hire?

b)

What sports do you play regularly?
How many times each week do you play sports?
Do you play for a team?

c)

How much spending money do you get each week?
How much do you spend on clothes?
Do you buy your own clothes?
Where do you buy your clothes?

2 Why might the information gathered in these situations be unreliable:

a) asking if people are vegetarian outside a butcher's shop

b) asking people at a bus stop how they travel to work

c) asking people outside a fast-food shop about their eating habits

d) asking the question 'Why are girls better at tennis than boys?'

e) asking the question 'We need more water fountains at school, don't we?'

3 Ian has written a questionnaire about going to the cinema.

a) Show how his questionnaire could be improved.

How often do you go to the cinema?
Less than average ☐   average ☐   more than average ☐
What type of film do you watch?
Do you always go with your friends?
If you do not go to the cinema, why not?

b) Should he stand outside the cinema to ask his questions? Explain your answer.

4 Noah has written a questionnaire to find out information about parents' evenings at his school. Show how his questionnaire could be improved.

Age:
How many children do you have at this school?
How long should appointments be?
There should be free tea and coffee, shouldn't there?

Investigation

5 Design a questionnaire to find out information about a topic that interests you.
For example, use questions like:
'Where do you buy clothes, and why?' or 'What sports do you play, and why?'

Writing reports

◈ Write a report about information collected using questionnaires and illustrate it

When you write a **report** about data you have collected, you should include any **statistics** you know. These statistics may include the mean, median, mode and the range of the data. You should also try to illustrate your report by drawing graphs and charts for the data.

Example 1 Here are some of the graphs and charts that Nikki drew using the answers to her questionnaire about her school library:

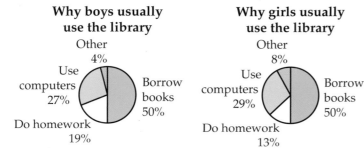

Why boys usually use the library
- Other 4%
- Use computers 27%
- Borrow books 50%
- Do homework 19%

Why girls usually use the library
- Other 8%
- Use computers 29%
- Borrow books 50%
- Do homework 13%

How often they use the library per week	Boys	Girls
0–2	1	0
3–5	7	7
6–8	10	10
9+	8	7

Use the diagrams to say if each of the following is true or false.

1) Nikki asked a total of 50 pupils.
2) She asked the same number of boys as girls.
3) The same number of girls as boys borrow books from the library.
4) The mode of the type of book preferred by boys is funny stories. For girls, it is non-fiction.

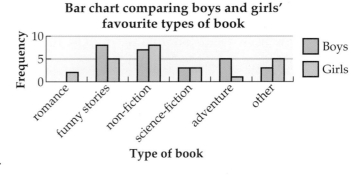

Bar chart comparing boys and girls' favourite types of book

Frequency — Type of book: romance, funny stories, non-fiction, science-fiction, adventure, other — Boys / Girls

1) True, she did ask 50 pupils.
2) False, she asked 26 boys and 24 girls.
3) False. It is the percentages, not the frequencies that are the same. A different number of boys and girls were asked.
4) True.

Example 2 Use the statements that were true and any other information to write a report to go with the diagrams and charts.

Nikki asked 24 girls and 26 boys.

On average, they visited the library 6–8 times per week.

The same percentage of boys as girls used the library to borrow books.

The most popular type of books for girls were non-fiction ones and for boys were ones with funny stories.

Exercise 15.5

1 **a)** Which of the following statements are true?

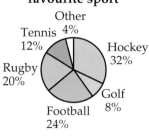

Pie chart showing favourite sport

Other 4%
Tennis 12%
Hockey 32%
Rugby 20%
Golf 8%
Football 24%

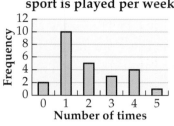

Bar chart showing number of times sport is played per week

i) 24 people were questioned.
ii) Hockey was the favourite sport.
iii) One person did not play sport.
iv) The modal number of times sport was played was once a week.
v) One person preferred a different type of sport.
vi) 92% of people played sport at least once a week.

b) If a statement in part **a** was false, write a correct version.

c) Use this information to write a report.

2 Here is some information from a questionnaire about hiring films:

Number of films hired each week	Frequency
0	2
1	5
2	10
3	2
4	1

Where films are usually hired from	Frequency
Library	3
Big chain	11
Local shop	4
Other	2

a) Draw two different diagrams to show this information.

b) Calculate the mean, median and modal number of films hired each week.

c) What percentage of pupils hired at least one film per week?

d) Use all of this information to write a short report.

3 A teacher is asked to write a report about the number of times pupils in his class were late during the previous week. Here is the information he collected:

Number of times late	Frequency
0	17
1	6
2	8
3	1

Reason	Number of girls	Number of boys
Overslept	1	4
Bus late	4	4
Other reason	2	0
Not late	8	9

a) Draw two different types of diagram for this data.

b) Find a suitable average for each set of data.

c) Use this information to write a report.

4 The following table shows the percentage of people who regularly recycle waste, arranged by age group. Use this information to write a report and draw a diagram to show the results.

Action \ Age	18–24	25–44	45–64	65+
Glass taken to a bottle bank	44%	44%	51%	57%
Paper taken to a paper bank	47%	46%	57%	63%

Possible outcomes

⊕ Find all the possible outcomes

⊕ Find the probabilities of these outcomes

If a card is chosen at **random**, every card has the same chance of being chosen. When choosing a coin from a purse at random, there are many possible **outcomes**.

For example: is it copper or silver? Is it a 10p coin? Is it a pound coin? Is it worth more than 5p? Each of these different outcomes will have different probabilities.

Example 1 If the letters in the word REVERSE are written on counters which are put into a bag, and then a counter is picked out at random, there are four possible outcomes: R E, V and S.

a) What is the probability that the counter chosen at random shows an R? An E? A V?

b) If a letter is chosen at random, what is the probability that it is a vowel? A consonant?

> Random means that each counter has the same chance of being chosen.

a) The probability of an $R = \frac{2}{7}$; of an $E = \frac{3}{7}$ and of an $S = \frac{1}{7}$.

b) The probability of a vowel $= \frac{3}{7}$ and of a consonant $= \frac{4}{7}$.

Example 2 Helen spins a three-sided spinner and throws a dice.

a) List all the possible outcomes.

b) What is the probability of:
  i)   a blue on the spinner and a 6 on the dice
  ii) the spinner landing on red
  iii) a blue on the spinner and a 3 OR 4 on the dice?

> There are 18 outcomes in total.

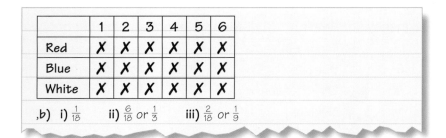

	1	2	3	4	5	6
Red	✗	✗	✗	✗	✗	✗
Blue	✗	✗	✗	✗	✗	✗
White	✗	✗	✗	✗	✗	✗

,b) i) $\frac{1}{18}$ ii) $\frac{6}{18}$ or $\frac{1}{3}$ iii) $\frac{2}{18}$ or $\frac{1}{9}$

Exercise 15.6

1 A standard six-sided dice is thrown. What is the probability of throwing:
  a) a 4
  b) a number that is not 4
  c) an odd number
  d) an even number
  e) a number more than 3
  f) a number less than 3?

2 When we choose a letter at random from the alphabet there are 26 possible outcomes. What is the probability that a letter chosen at random is:
  a) A 'b'
  b) A 'p' or a 'z'
  c) in **your** first name
  d) in **your** surname?

3 Each of the ten letters in the word CONNECTION are written on counters which are put in a bag and then a counter is picked out at random.

    a) List all the possible outcomes.

    b) What is the probability that a counter chosen at random shows:

        i) a 'C'   **ii)** an 'N'   **iii)** not an 'O'?

    Write your answers as decimals.

4 Twenty cards are numbered from 1 to 20. A card is then chosen at random.

    a) What is the probability of choosing an odd number?

    b) What is the probability of choosing a card showing a number below 5?

    c) What is the probability of choosing a card with a prime number?

    d) What is the probability of choosing a card with a number between (but not including) 11 and 15?

5 List all the possible outcomes when these two spinners are spun together:

6 List all the possible outcomes when this five-sided spinner and a coin are spun together.

7 Hannah wants to taste at least two different flavours and her mother says she can have two scoops of ice cream. What combinations of flavours can she have? What is the probability that she chooses vanilla and mint?

> **Ice cream flavours:**
> *Vanilla Chocolate Mint*

8 A lunchtime menu has two choices for the starter, the main course and the dessert.

    a) List all of the possible three-course combinations.

    b) What is the probability that a meal chosen at random will include:

        i) soup and cake

        ii) garlic bread

        iii) garlic bread, pizza and ice cream?

> **Starters:**
> *Soup*
> *Garlic Bread*

> **Main Course:**
> *Pizza*
> *Pasta*

> **Dessert:**
> *Ice cream*
> *Cake*

Investigation

9 Antonio, Bethany and Carlo always queue for lunch together. How many days can the children change the order in which they stand so that each day they are in a different order? What is the probability that Carlo will not be first in line on any particular day? Djabir comes to join them. How many days can the four children now change the order in which they stand so that each day they are in a different order?

15.7 Estimating probability

⊕ Estimate probabilities from the results of an experiment

We can use the results of an experiment to find approximate or **estimated probabilities**. We do this by dividing the **frequency** of a certain outcome (the number of times that a certain outcome occurs) by the total number of times that the experiment was carried out.

Example Bryn chooses ten counters of three different colours and puts them in a bag. Naomi is trying to guess how many of each colour counter are in the bag. She takes a counter from the bag without looking, records its colour and replaces it in the bag. She repeats this a total of 20 times. Here are her results:

a) Use the frequency table to calculate the estimated probabilities and decide how many of each coloured counter might be in the bag.

Colour	White	Red	Blue
Frequency	1	14	5

b) What can Naomi do to improve her chances of guessing the correct number of each colour counters in the bag?

a)

Colour	White	Red	Blue
Frequency	1	14	5
Estimated probability	$\frac{1}{20}$	$\frac{14}{20}$	$\frac{5}{20}$

It is **likely** that there are 7 red counters, 2 blue counters and 1 white counter.

b) To improve her chances of guessing the correct number of counters for each colour, Naomi should increase the number of times she carries out the experiment.

Red was picked 14 out of 20 times which is the same as 7 out of 10, so it is likely that there were 7 red counters. White was chosen just once, so there must be at least 1 white counter. It is likely that there was only 1 white counter. Blue was picked 5 out of 20 times which is $2\frac{1}{2}$ times out of 10. If there were 2 blue counters there would be 10 counters in total.

Exercise 15.7

1 A coin is spun 100 times and the side showing is recorded each time. Use the frequencies to work out the estimated probabilities.

	Head	Tail
Frequency	46	54
Estimated probability		

2 A three-coloured spinner is spun 25 times and the colour it lands on each time is recorded. Copy and complete the table.

Colour	Blue	Red	White
Frequency	14	9	2
Estimated probability (fraction)			
Estimated probability (decimal)			
Estimated probability (percentage)			

3 Five counters were put in a bag. A counter was chosen at random, its colour was recorded and the counter was returned to the bag. This was repeated 20 times with these results:

Colour	Blue	Yellow
Frequency	12	8

How many of each colour counter is likely to be in the bag?

4 Four letter cards are needed: A, B, C and D. Copy the table below, allowing space for 10 rows.

Experiment number	1st card	2nd card	3rd card	4th card
1				

Shuffle the cards. Lay them face down in a row. Without looking, guess the first card. If you are correct, put a tick in the first column. If you are wrong put a cross. Remove the card. Guess the next card. Put a tick or cross in the second column. Repeat until you have guessed all four cards.

Carry out this experiment ten times, recording your results each time in the table.

Use the words: **impossible   possible   equally likely   likely   certain**   to answer these questions.

a) It is _____ for the 1st guess to be correct.   **b)** It is _____ for the 2nd guess to be correct.

c) It is _____ for the 3rd guess to be correct.   **d)** It is _____ for the 4th guess to be correct.

5 Work with a partner. A bag and different colour counters are required.

One player chooses five counters of two different colours and puts them in a bag.

The other player takes one counter from the bag without looking, records its colour and replaces it in the bag. Repeat this ten times.

Record the colour each time in a frequency table with these headings:

Colour of counter	Tally	Frequency	Estimated probability

Use the table to decide how many of each colour of counter might be in the bag.

Now look in the bag to see if you were correct.

Repeat this activity using three different colours of counter.

What could you do to increase the chance of guessing correctly?

Investigation

6 You need a card, a cocktail stick and colouring pens.

Design and make a circular spinner with three sections of different sizes.

Choose a different colour for each section and colour in the sections.

Spin your spinner 40 times, recording the colour it lands on each time in a frequency table.

Estimate the probability of your spinner landing on each of the three colours.

15.8 Comparing probabilities

⊕ Compare probabilities from an experiment with the expected probabilities

We know that the probability of getting a *head* on a fair coin is $\frac{1}{2}$, so we would **expect** that if we spin a coin ten times we would get a *head* for half of those spins. So the **expected probability** of getting a *head* would be $\frac{1}{2}$. When we perform an experiment such as spinning a coin 100 times the fraction of *heads* we get is called the **experimental probability**. The experimental probability and the expected probability are roughly the same but become closer, the larger the sample of data taken.

Example 1   A four-coloured spinner is spun 20 times and the colour it lands on is recorded.

Colour	Orange	Blue	Purple	Green
Frequency	6	4	3	7

a)   What would we expect the probability to be of the spinner landing on each colour?

b)   Use the frequencies to find the estimated probabilities for each of the colours.

c)   The **estimated probabilities** are not the same as the **expected probabilities**. Does this mean that the spinner was not fair?

a)   As the spinner has four colours the expected probability of it landing on each colour is $\frac{1}{4}$ or 0.25.

b)

Colour	Orange	Blue	Purple	Green
Frequency	6	4	3	7
Estimated probability	$\frac{6}{20} = 0.3$	$\frac{4}{20} = 0.2$	$\frac{3}{20} = 0.15$	$\frac{7}{20} = 0.35$

c)   No. If the spinner was spun more times then this would give us a more accurate picture of whether or not the spinner was fair.

Example 2   Siobhan uses the RAN# key on her calculator to generate random numbers. She decides to find the experimental probability of the number generated ending with an odd or even digit. These are her random numbers:

0.871   0.046   0.079   0.825   0.980   0.540   0.127   0.923   0.234   0.385
0.856   0.700   0.119   0.923   0.241   0.550   0.972   0.357   0.216   0.984
0.633   0.570   0.122   0.679   0.626   0.400   0.219   0.038   0.875   0.134

Use her random numbers to estimate the probabilities of an odd or even last digit.

	Ends in an even	Ends in an odd
Tally	卌 卌 卌 I	卌 卌 IIII
Frequency	16	14
Estimated probability	$\frac{16}{30} = 0.53$	$\frac{14}{30} = 0.47$

This is quite close to what we would expect to happen.

The expected probability of an even = expected probability of an odd = $\frac{1}{2}$.

Exercise 15.8 .... Comparing probabilities

1 You will need a regular polygon to use as a template.

> Testing the spinner 30 times is a good idea for a hexagonal or pentagonal spinner as 5 and 6 divide exactly into 30.

  a) Design and make a spinner using a shape such as a pentagon or hexagon. Colour each section.

  b) Test your spinner to compare what you would expect to happen, with what really happens.

  c) Put a small piece of Blu-tack under one of the sections. Test your spinner again. Show these results to a friend. Can he/she tell where you have put the Blu-tack?

2 Use the Random feature on a scientific calculator to simulate a coin being spun 40 times. Compare the results of your experiment with the results you would expect to get when spinning a coin 40 times.

> Look at Example 2.

3 Work with a partner. You will need a blank six-sided dice.
Write any six numbers on the blank dice with a pencil. You may use the same numbers more than once if you wish. (This makes it more difficult.)

  a) Ask your partner to throw the dice six times and record the results in a tally chart.

  b) Ask your partner to guess the six numbers on the dice, including any that have been written on the dice more than once. Write these numbers down.

  c) Ask your partner to throw the dice a further 24 times and record the results in the tally chart.

  d) After these 30 throws ask your partner to guess the numbers on your dice again. Has he or she given a different set of answers to the ones given after only six throws? Which of the two guesses was the most accurate?

  e) Now repeat the activity with a different set of numbers. Swap roles with your partner.

4 Greta throws a dice twelve times with the following results:

Number	1	2	3	4	5	6
Frequency	3	2	1	2	3	1

Greta knows that her results would be more accurate if she carried out her experiment more times, so she decides to multiply the frequencies by five to show the results out of 60 throws. What is wrong with her idea?

5 Three pupils spin a fair, four-coloured square spinner 200 times with the following results:

Colour	Red	White	Green	Blue
Pupil 1	52	49	51	48
Pupil 2	50	50	50	50
Pupil 3	94	38	43	25

Explain why it is likely that only Pupil 1 carried out the experiment correctly.

16.1 Multiples

- Recognise the multiples of different numbers
- Find the lowest common multiple of two numbers

Key words
multiple
common multiple
lowest common multiple

The **multiples** of a given number are the product of all whole numbers and the given number. For example, the multiples of 6 are $6 \times 1 = 6$, $6 \times 2 = 12$, $6 \times 100 = 600$ and so on.

They appear in the rows and columns of a multiplication square.

Common multiples of two numbers are those which appear in the lists of multiples for both numbers.

For example: some multiples of 3 are 3, 6, 9, 12, ⑮, 18, 21, 24, 27, ㉚, 33, 36, ….
some multiples of 5 are 5, 10, ⑮, 20, 25, ㉚, 35, 40, ……
some common multiples of 3 and 5 are 15,㉚,㊺, …

1	2	3	4	5	6	7	8	9	10
2	4	6	8	10	12	14	16	18	20
3	6	9	12	⑮	18	21	24	27	㉚
4	8	12	16	20	24	28	32	36	40
5	10	⑮	20	25	㉚	35	40	㊺	50
6	12	18	24	㉚	36	42	48	54	(60)
7	14	21	28	35	42	49	56	63	70
8	16	24	32	40	48	56	64	72	80
9	18	27	36	㊺	54	63	72	81	(90)
10	20	㉚	40	50	(60)	70	80	(90)	100

The smallest of the common multiples is called the **lowest common multiple (LCM)**. The LCM of 3 and 5 is 15.

Example Find the lowest common multiple of 2, 4 and 5.

Multiples of 2: 2, 4, 6, 8, 10, 12, 14, 16, 18, 20, …
Multiples of 4: 4, 8, 12, 16, 20, 24, 28, 32, 36, 40, …
Multiples of 5: 5, 10, 15, 20, 25, 30, 35, 40, …
Common multiples of 2, 4 and 5 are: 20, 40, 60, 80, …
LCM of 2, 4 and 5 is 20.

Exercise 16.1

1. Write down the next five multiples for each of the following lists:
   a) 4, 8, 12, 16, … **b)** 9, 18, 27, 36, … **c)** 20, 40, 60, 80, …
   d) 7, 14, 21, 28, … **e)** 25, 50, 75, 100, … **f)** 8, 16, 24, 32, …

2. 42 36 28 27 39 16 52 54 100 85 60 72
   Which of these numbers are:
   a) multiples of 2 **b)** multiples of 5 **c)** multiples of 7 **d)** multiples of 4
   e) multiples of 9 **f)** multiples of 3 **g)** multiples of 6 **h)** multiples of 8?

3 Find the:
   a) fourth multiple of 7   **b)** third multiple of 11   **c)** fifth multiple of 9
   d) eighth multiple of 6   **e)** sixth multiple of 8   **f)** third multiple of 20
   g) fifth multiple of 15   **h)** eighth multiple of 29?

4 Find the lowest common multiple of:
   a) 2 and 3   **b)** 2 and 5   **c)** 3 and 5   **d)** 2 and 4   **e)** 3 and 4
   f) 5 and 6   **g)** 4 and 5   **h)** 6 and 7   **i)** 5 and 8   **j)** 4 and 6
   k) 2 and 7   **l)** 4 and 8   **m)** 6 and 8   **n)** 6 and 9   **o)** 8 and 10.

5 What do you notice about the following sets of numbers:
   a) the common multiples of 2 and 3   **b)** the common multiples of 3 and 5
   c) the common multiples of 4 and 8   **d)** the common multiples of 6 and 9
   e) the common multiples of 3 and 8?

6 Find the lowest common multiple of these sets of numbers:
   a) 2, 3 and 4   **b)** 3, 4 and 5   **c)** 4, 6 and 9   **d)** 5, 7 and 10   **e)** 3, 6 and 8
   f) 3, 5 and 9   **g)** 3, 4 and 6   **h)** 5, 6 and 9   **i)** 2, 7 and 3?

7 Use a set of 2 – 11 number cards.
Shuffle them and deal out five pairs.
The lowest common multiple for each pair is your
score for that pair.
Your overall score is the total score for the five pairs.
Can you get a score of less than 60? Record the pairs
you had and your scores.
Shuffle the cards and repeat several times. What is your highest score?

8 I am a number. Who am I?
   a) I am a common multiple of 3 and 5. I am a 2-digit number greater than 50 and my
   digits total 9.
   b) I am the square of one quarter of the LCM of 3 and 4.
   c) I am the fifth multiple of the LCM of 2, 3 and 5.
   d) I am the square of the number which is 66 less than the product of the LCM of 3 and 4
   and the LCM of 2 and 3.

Investigation

9 Use 0 – 9 digit cards. What is the maximum number of multiples of two you can make?
Here are five:

| 1 | 2 | | 8 |

| 3 | 4 | | 6 | (| 7 | 5 | not used.)

| 9 | 0 |

Investigate the maximum number of multiples of other numbers you can make with
the cards.

Tests for divisibility

⊕ Know tests for divisibility for the numbers 2 to 10

Key words
divisible
divisibility
multiple
common multiple

The tests for **divisibility** are:

    by 2 – is the last digit even?
    by 3 – is the digit total a **multiple** of 3?
    by 4 – do the last 2 digits make a two-digit multiple of 4?
    by 5 – is the last digit 0 or 5?
    by 6 – does it pass the tests for 2 and for 3?
    by 7 – compare it with near known multiples of 7.
    by 8 – halve it then test for divisibility by 4.
    by 9 – is the digit total a multiple of 9?
    by 10 – is last digit 0?

A **counter example** is an example that shows a statement is wrong.
For example: 'All multiples of 3 are also multiples of 9' is false as 6 is a multiple of 3 but is not a multiple of 9.

Example   44   75   152   357   419   326   428   782   948

    Which of the numbers in this list are divisible by 12?

To be divisible by 12 a number must be divisible by 4 and by 3.
Numbers divisible by 4: 44, 152, 428, 948
The numbers which are divisible by 3 in this list are: 152, 948.
The numbers which are divisible by 12 are therefore: **152** and **948**.

Check that the last two digits are multiples of 4.

Check the digit totals.

Exercise 16.2

1 Write 'True' or False' by the following statements.

  a) 67 is divisible by 3.   **b)** 785 is divisible by 5.

  c) 693 is divisible by 7.   **d)** 390 is divisible by 4.

  e) 621 is divisible by 9.   **f)** 190 is divisible by 2.

  g) 530 is divisible by 6.   **h)** 268 is divisible by 8.

  i) 640 is divisible by 10.   **j)** 185 is divisible by 3.

2 96   517   325   468   69   78   147   255   49   88   154

  Which of the numbers in this list are:

  a) divisible by 3   **b)** divisible by 4   **c)** divisible by 5

  d) divisible by 2   **e)** divisible by 6   **f)** divisible by 8

  g) divisible by 9   **h)** divisible by 7   **i)** divisible by 14

  j) divisible by 15   **k)** divisible by 18   **l)** divisible by 12?

3 Copy the table and tick to show divisibility:

	÷2	÷3	÷4	÷5	÷6	÷7	÷8	÷9	÷10
48	✓	✓	✓		✓		✓		
75									
167									
213									
156									
748									
310									
450									
654									
387									

4 Write 'True' or False' by the following statements. If a statement is false, give a counter example.
If a number is:

a) divisible by 3 and 4 it must be divisible by 6.

b) divisible by 2 and 3 it must be divisible by 12.

c) divisible by 4 and 5 it must be divisible by 20.

d) divisible by 2, 3 and 4 it must be divisible by 24.

e) divisible by 3 and 8 it must be divisible by 12.

f) divisible by 5 and 7 it must be odd.

g) divisible by 4 and 6 it must be even.

5 Use a set of 0 – 9 digit cards.
Shuffle them and deal out three. Arrange them to make a 3-digit number of your choice, such as 126.
Test the number for divisibility by each of the numbers from 2 to 10.
126 is divisible by 2, 3, 6, 7, 8 and 9.
Score the total of each of the numbers your choice is divisible by.

For example: $2 + 3 + 6 + 7 + 8 + 9 = 35$ points.

Repeat several times, and record the number and your score each time.
What is your highest score?

Investigation

6 Here is a test for divisibility by 12.
For a number to be divisible by 12 it must be divisible by 3 and by 4.

The test for divisibility by 3 – is digit total a multiple of 3?
The test for divisibility by 4 – are last 2 digits a multiple of 4?

A test for divisibility by 12 could therefore be:
'Is the digit total of the number a multiple of 3, **and** are its last two digits a multiple of 4?'

Devise some tests for divisibility by other numbers, for example by 20, 50, 15 and so on.

⊕ Know how to find the pairs of factors of a number

⊕ List the set of factors of a number

⊕ Find the highest common factor of two numbers

The **factors** of a number are all the whole numbers that will divide exactly into that number.

Check this.

28 is divisible by 1, 2, 4, 7, 14 and 28. These are its factors.
Factors of 28 are: 1, 2, 4, 7, 14 and 28.

They can be split into **factor pairs** : 1×28, 2×14, 4×7.

Factors of 42 are: 1, 2, 3, 6, 7, 14, 21 and 42.

The **common factors** of two numbers appear in the lists of factors for both numbers.
Common factors of 28 and 42 are: 1, 2, 7, 14.
The **highest common factor (HCF)** is the largest of these.
For example the HCF of 28 and 42 is 14.

Example   Find all the pairs of factors of 56.

Try dividing by 1, to give 1×56.

Next try dividing by 2, to give 2×28.

Next try dividing by 3: this can't be done without a remainder.

Next try dividing by 4 to give 4×14.

Next try dividing by 5: this can't be done without a remainder.

Next try dividing by 6: this can't be done without a remainder.

Next try dividing by 7 to give 7×8.

The pairs of factors of 56 are: 1×56, 2×28, 4×14, 7×8.

Exercise 16.3

1 Write 'True' or False' by the following statements.

   a) 3 is a factor of 42.
   b) 4 is a factor of 84.
   c) 6 is a factor of 76.
   d) 7 is a factor of 63.
   e) 5 is a factor of 135.
   f) 8 is a factor of 92.
   g) 2 is a factor of 170.
   h) 9 is a factor of 66.
   i) 10 is a factor of 1010.
   j) 12 is a factor of 74.

2 Find all the pairs of factors of the following numbers:

a) 10	**b)** 4	**c)** 16	**d)** 20	**e)** 8
f) 36	**g)** 28	**h)** 24	**i)** 38	**j)** 32
k) 50	**l)** 18	**m)** 42	**n)** 30	**o)** 48
p) 52	**q)** 40	**r)** 68	**s)** 57	**t)** 60

3 Find the missing factors:
  a) factors of 12: 1, 2, ☐, 4, ☐, 12
  b) factors of 34: 1, ☐, ☐, 34
  c) factors of 45: 1, 3, ☐, 9, 15, ☐
  d) factors of 32: 1, 2, ☐, ☐, 16, 32
  e) factors of 72: 1, 2, 3, 4, ☐, 8, ☐, 12, ☐, ☐, ☐, 72

4 Find the highest common factor of these pairs of numbers:
  a) 15 and 20   **b)** 6 and 8   **c)** 12 and 16   **d)** 20 and 16   **e)** 30 and 36
  f) 25 and 35   **g)** 6 and 9   **h)** 14 and 21   **i)** 10 and 20   **j)** 18 and 30
  k) 42 and 80   **l)** 72 and 45 **m)** 90 and 56   **n)** 84 and 48   **o)** 36 and 63

5 Draw a chart which shows all the factors of the numbers from 1 to 12.
Shade squares to show that the numbers are factors:

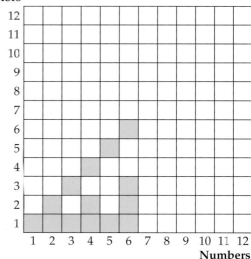

6 I am a number. Who am I?
  a) My factors have a total of 31. I am less than 20.
  b) I have an odd number of factors. I am between 20 and 35.
  c) I have 4 odd factors. I am less than 20.
  d) I am the highest common factor of 24, 40 and 48.
  e) I am a 2-digit number. I have more factors than any other 2-digit number.

Investigations

7 Investigate numbers up to 50.
Explore how many factors these numbers have.
For example: the factors of 34 are 1, 2, 17 and 34.
So, 34 has four factors.
Which other numbers have four factors?
Investigate patterns in the numbers which have two, three, four factors and so on.

8 Make 'factor chains'.
To make a factor chain, choose a starting number, then find the total of all its factors. Do not include the starting number. This gives the next number in the chain, for example:
    Factors of 16, except 16 itself: 1, 2, 4, 8   Total = 15
    Factors of 15, except 15 itself: 1, 3, 5   Total = 9
    Factors of 9, except 9 itself: 1, 3   Total = 4
    Factors of 4, except 4 itself: 1, 2   Total = 3
    Factors of 3, except 3 itself: 1   Total = 1

So, the chain is: 16 ⟶ 15 ⟶ 9 ⟶ 4 ⟶ 3 ⟶ 1

Make some more factor chains.

16.4 Prime numbers

◈ Recognise prime numbers up to 100

Prime numbers are numbers which have exactly two **factors**. The two factors will be the number itself and 1.

The first five prime numbers are 2, 3, 5, 7, 11, …

The first five non-prime numbers are 1, 4, 6, 8, 10, …

1 is not a prime number because it only has one factor. Its factor pair is 1×1.

There are 25 prime numbers less than 100.

Example   Which of these are prime numbers: 1, 5, 6, 14, 17?

5 and 17 are prime numbers.

1 is not a prime number because it only has one factor.

6 is not a prime number because it has four factors. Its factor pairs are 1×6 and 2×3.

14 is not a prime number because it has four factors. Its factor pairs are 1×14 and 2×7.

Exercise 16.4

1 Are these prime numbers? Write 'Yes' or 'No' by each of the following:

a) 14	**b)** 11	**c)** 7	**d)** 31	**e)** 37
f) 43	**g)** 39	**h)** 57	**i)** 65	**j)** 71
k) 93	**l)** 73	**m)** 97	**n)** 77	**o)** 91
p) 63	**q)** 51	**r)** 49	**s)** 81	**t)** 83

2 Find the next prime number after each of these:

a) 15	**b)** 64	**c)** 78	**d)** 90	**e)** 50
f) 18	**g)** 42	**h)** 32	**i)** 44	**j)** 74
k) 80	**l)** 48	**m)** 94	**n)** 62	**o)** 14

3 Find two prime numbers which have a total of:

a) 20	**b)** 12	**c)** 46	**d)** 50	**e)** 40
f) 80	**g)** 100	**h)** 18	**i)** 90	**j)** 50

4 Write 'True' or 'False' by the following statements.

a) The total of two prime numbers is always even.

b) The difference between two 2-digit prime numbers is always even.

c) The product of two prime number is always even.

d) Every 2-digit prime number is 1 more or 1 less than a multiple of 6.

e) If you double a prime number, then add 1, the result is always another prime number.

5. Roll two dice, and decide which will be the tens digit and which will be the units digit of a 2-digit number.
   If the number is a prime number, score points to match the digit total.
   If the number is not prime, lose three points.
   Repeat ten times, recording your number and score each time.
   What is your total score?
   Repeat the activity, and see if you can beat your score.

6. Use a set of 1–9 digit cards.
   Shuffle them and deal out five cards.
   Investigate how many different 2-digit prime numbers you can create with the five cards.
   Repeat for a different set of cards.

7. Who am I?
   a) I am a 2-digit prime number. My tens digit is 6, and my units digit is a prime number.
   b) I am a 2-digit prime number more than 25. My digit total is a prime number less than 7. Who am I?
   c) I am the difference between two consecutive prime numbers which both have a tens digit of 6.
   d) I am a 2-digit prime number. The total of my digits is a prime number greater than 13.

Investigations

8. Draw this six-column grid, and extend it down.
   Highlight the prime numbers.
   What pattern do you notice?

1	2	3	4	5	6
7	8	9	10	11	12
13	14	15	16	17	18
19	20	21	22	23	24
25	26				

9. Choose any prime number.
   Multiply it by itself.
   How many factors does the answer have?
   Investigate for different prime numbers.

10. 13 is a prime number, and so is its reverse, in this case 31.
    Investigate other 'reverse' prime numbers.

Squares and square roots

Key words
squared
square number
square root
power
inverse

- Know the squares of numbers 1 to 12
- Know the square roots of the squares of numbers 1 to 12
- Know how to work out squares of numbers greater than 12
- Use a calculator to find squares and square roots

Square numbers are found by multiplying a number by itself.

The square of 7 is $7 \times 7 = 49$.

We write $7^2 = 49$, and read it as:

'Seven **squared** is forty nine' or 'Seven to the power of two is forty nine'.

We can use a calculator to square a number by typing in the number and pressing this key: x^2

The reverse or **inverse** is $\sqrt{49} = 7$, which is read as:

'The **square root** of forty nine is seven'.

We can use a calculator to find the square root of a number by pressing this key and then typing in the number: $\sqrt{}$

The name 'square numbers' links to square arrangements of objects. For example:

$4^2 = 16$

16 counters can be placed in a square arrangement.

Example   Find the value of $\sqrt{3600}$.

$\sqrt{3600} = \sqrt{(36 \times 100)}$

$\phantom{\sqrt{3600}} = \sqrt{36} \times \sqrt{100}$

$\phantom{\sqrt{3600}} = 6 \times 10$

$\phantom{\sqrt{3600}} = 60$

Split 3600 into its factor pair of 36×100 to make the calculation easier.

Exercise 16.5

1 Find the value of:

   a) 9^2 **b)** 3^2 **c)** 8^2 **d)** 5^2 **e)** 7^2

   f) 12^2 **g)** 10^2 **h)** 20^2 **i)** 14^2 **j)** 100^2

   k) 80^2 **l)** 50^2 **m)** 600^2 **n)** 19^2 **o)** 21^2

Use a calculator to check your answers.

2 Write down the next square number after each of the following numbers:

   a) 20   **b)** 63   **c)** 78   **d)** 90

   e) 50   **f)** 11   **g)** 1   **h)** 32

   i) 44   **j)** 8   **k)** 140   **l)** 1000

3 Find the value of:
  a) $\sqrt{81}$ **b)** $\sqrt{36}$ **c)** $\sqrt{64}$ **d)** $\sqrt{1}$ **e)** $\sqrt{49}$
  f) $\sqrt{121}$ **g)** $\sqrt{4}$ **h)** $\sqrt{144}$ **i)** $\sqrt{25}$ **j)** $\sqrt{100}$
  k) $\sqrt{900}$ **l)** $\sqrt{400}$ **m)** $\sqrt{2500}$ **n)** $\sqrt{4900}$ **o)** $\sqrt{196}$

  Use a calculator to check your answers.

> You may find it helpful to split these numbers into factor pairs.

4 Use a calculator to find the value of:
  a) $\sqrt{1000}$ **b)** 26^2 **c)** $\sqrt{30}$ **d)** 83^2 **e)** $\sqrt{700}$
  f) 51^2 **g)** $\sqrt{5000}$ **h)** 37^2 **i)** $\sqrt{300}$ **j)** 104^2

> Round the decimal answers to two decimal places.

5 Use a set of 1–9 digit cards.
  Shuffle them and deal out five cards.
  Investigate how many different square numbers you can create with the five cards.
  Repeat with a different set of cards.

6 Who am I?
  a) I am a 2-digit square number. My digit total is a 2-digit prime number.
  b) I am a square number. I am 11 less than the next square number.
  c) I am the square root of a 2-digit number whose digit difference is even.
  d) I am a 2-digit number. I am the square of double a square number.

Investigations

7 These are triangular numbers:

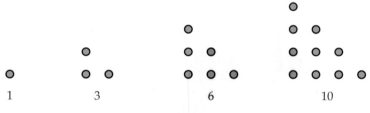

1   3   6   10

> You might find it helpful to draw out more triangles of dots.

  Find the next six triangular numbers.
  Investigate the total of pairs of consecutive triangular numbers.
  What pattern do you notice?
  Can you explain the pattern?

8 $15^2 = 225$
  $25^2 = 625$
  $35^2 =$

  Continue the sequence above. Can you spot a quicker way of finding these square numbers?

9 The square number 4 has three factors: 1, 2 and 4.
  Investigate the number of factors of other square numbers.
  What do you notice?

Subtraction

⊕ Subtract whole numbers using a standard written method

⊕ Subtract decimal numbers using a standard written method

Key words
estimate
subtraction
tenths
hundredths

When **subtracting** using the column method:

● write an **estimate** of the answer

● write the numbers in columns underneath each other, making sure each digit is in its correct column

● start subtracting from the right

● compare the answer with the estimate as a check.

Example 1   Subtract 3592 from 4679.

Write the digits in columns, making sure the unit digits line up. Start subtracting from the right.

Estimate : 4700 − 3600 = 1100

$$\begin{array}{r} 4\,\overset{5}{\cancel{6}}\,\overset{1}{7}\,9 \\ -\ 3\ 5\ 9\ 2 \\ \hline 1\ 0\ 8\ 7 \end{array}$$

6 hundred is the same as 5 hundred and 10 tens. We can leave 5 in the hundreds column and replace the 7 with 17 in the tens column.

Example 2   Subtract 65.82 from 93.6.

Estimate : 94 − 66 = 28

$$\begin{array}{r} \overset{8}{\cancel{9}}\,\overset{12}{\cancel{3}}\cdot\overset{15}{\cancel{6}}\,\overset{1}{0} \\ -\ 6\ 5\cdot8\ 2 \\ \hline 2\ 7\cdot7\ 8 \end{array}$$

Make sure the decimal points line up to check that the place value of the digits in each column is right.

93.60 is equal to 93.6.

Exercise 16.6

❶ Work out the following subtractions:

a) 4736 − 2879

b) 5134 − 2627

c) 6473 − 2868

d) 15 643 − 7671

e) 9325 − 489

Check each calculation by adding the smaller number to the answer. The result should match the larger number.

❷ Work out the following subtractions:

a) 86.35 − 14.79

b) 27.39 − 16.08

c) 53.74 − 29.48

d) 19.07 − 13.54

e) 53.7 − 26.48

Check each calculation by adding the smaller number to the answer. The result should match the larger number.

3 Copy and complete these difference pyramids.
The number in each brick is found by finding the difference between the two directly below it.

a)
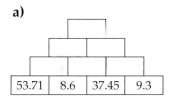

| 53.71 | 8.6 | 37.45 | 9.3 |

b)
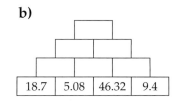

| 18.7 | 5.08 | 46.32 | 9.4 |

4 Claire went shopping and bought a handbag and a pair of shoes. What was the cost of the shoes if:

a) Total cost: £85.76, price of handbag: £9.38

b) Total cost: £79.43, price of handbag: £11.78

c) Total cost: £138.56, price of handbag: £13.85

5 Use a set of 0 – 9 digit cards.
Shuffle them and deal out two 4-digit numbers, such as 5672 and 3419.
Subtract the smaller number from the larger. In this case the answer is 2253.
Round the answer to the nearest thousand, in this case the answer is 2000.
The number of thousands in your number is your score. In this case score two points.
Play five rounds. Can you score more than 15 points?

6 Use a set of 0 – 9 digit cards.
Shuffle the cards and deal out two 2-digit numbers with 1 decimal place of the form 20.1.
Add them together and record the total.
Subtract the first number from the total. Check that it matches the second number.
Subtract the second number from the total. Check that it matches the first number.

7 Carrie went shopping with £38.72 in her purse. She bought a CD for £13.65, and a magazine for £2.74. How much money has she left in her purse?

8 6746 people attended the concert in the park on Saturday. Of these, 3829 were female. How many males were there at the concert?

9 Tommy's best score on his computer game 'Blongo' is 2748 points. In his current game he has 1635 points. How many more points does he need to beat his best score?

10 Invent a problem for which it would be necessary to do these calculations:

a) $9543 - 6275$

b) $87.52 - 36.67$

Investigation

11 Use 0 – 8 digit cards to create two 4-digit numbers.
Investigate arrangements of the digits that will give a difference close to 1000, 2000 or 3000.

16.7 Division

- Divide whole four-digit numbers by whole one-digit numbers using a standard written method
- Divide whole three-digit numbers by whole two-digit numbers using a standard written method

Key words
division
divisor
estimate
remainder

Division by a number is equivalent to repeated subtraction of that number. We call the number we are dividing by the **divisor**.

When dividing:

- write an **estimate** of the answer.
- start subtracting as many 1000s of the divisor as you can, then as many 100s of the divisor as you can, then as many 10s of the divisor as you can, and finally as many units of the divisor as you can.
- write the **remainder** as a fraction in its lowest terms.

Example 1 Divide 7679 by 4.

Estimate: 8000 ÷ 4 = 2000

$$
\begin{array}{r}
1\ 9\ 1\ 9\ \frac{3}{4} \\
4\overline{)7\ 6\ 7\ 9} \\
-\ 4\ 0\ 0\ 0 \quad 4 \times 1000 \\
\hline
3\ 6\ 7\ 9 \\
-\ 3\ 6\ 0\ 0 \quad 4 \times\ 900 \\
\hline
7\ 9 \\
-\quad\quad 4\ 0 \quad 4 \times\quad 10 \\
\hline
3\ 9 \\
-\quad\quad 3\ 6 \quad 4 \times\quad 9 \\
\hline
3
\end{array}
$$

Answer: **1919** $\frac{3}{4}$

Start by subtracting as many 1000s of 4 as you can and write down what is left.

The remainder is written as a fraction in its lowest terms.

Example 2 Divide 895 by 23.

Estimate: 900 ÷ 20 = 45

$$
\begin{array}{r}
3\ 8\ \frac{21}{23} \\
23\overline{)8\ 9\ 5} \\
6\ 9\ 0 \quad 23 \times\ 30 \\
\hline
2\ 0\ 5 \\
1\ 8\ 4 \quad 23 \times\ 8 \\
\hline
2\ 1
\end{array}
$$

Answer: **38** $\frac{21}{23}$

Exercise 16.7

1 Complete these exact divisions:
   a) $3066 \div 7$ **b)** $2635 \div 5$ **c)** $2556 \div 4$ **d)** $4192 \div 8$ **e)** $1602 \div 9$

Check each calculation by multiplying the answer by the divisor. The result should match the starting number.

2 Complete these exact divisions:
   a) $658 \div 14$ **b)** $736 \div 23$ **c)** $682 \div 22$ **d)** $432 \div 18$ **e)** $962 \div 26$

Check each calculation by multiplying the answer by the divisor. The result should match the starting number.

3 Complete these divisions, writing the remainders as fractions in their lowest terms:
   a) $4725 \div 4$ **b)** $1938 \div 7$ **c)** $487 \div 18$ **d)** $973 \div 26$ **e)** $7938 \div 5$ **f)** $876 \div 13$

4 For each salary, calculate: **i)** the average (mean) monthly earnings **ii)** the average (mean) weekly earnings.
   Round each answer to the nearest £.
   a) Jenny: £16,500 per year
   b) Jack: £19,725 per year
   c) Natalie: £45,165 per year
   d) Greg: £27,326 per year

> The average (mean) is found by dividing the total by the number of months (12) or weeks (52) in a year.

5 Here are the costs for a holiday for four people at different resorts:
   a) Florida £3250
   b) Cornwall £6756
   c) Spain £1864
   d) Dubai £2485

If you have 24 weeks to save, how much would you need to save per week for each holiday? Round each answer to the nearest £.

6 Division calculations can be made easier by halving both numbers.
   For example, $4268 \div 18$ is the same as $2134 \div 9$, which is an easier calculation.
   Use this trick to calculate each of the following divisions:
   a) $8626 \div 12$ **b)** $5282 \div 16$ **c)** $6484 \div 14$ **d)** $3670 \div 18$

7 Use a set of 0 – 9 digit cards.
   Shuffle them and deal out a 4-digit number and a 1-digit number.
   Multiply them together. Divide your answer by the 1-digit number.
   Check that it matches the original 4-digit number

8 Use a set of 2 – 9 digit cards.
   Shuffle them and deal a 3-digit number and a 2-digit number.
   Divide the larger number by the smaller one.
   The whole number part of the answer is your score.
   Shuffle the cards again and repeat.
   Play five rounds. Can you score a total of more than 60 points?

9 A school has 17 classes with a total of 472 pupils. What is the average (mean) class size?

10 Wanderers Football Club are playing away on Saturday. A total of 948 supporters wish to travel by coach. Each coach seats 42 passengers. How many coaches will the Club need?

11 Invent a problem for which this calculation is necessary: $6545 \div 7$.

Dividing decimals

⊕ Divide numbers with 1 decimal place using a standard written method
⊕ Divide numbers with 2 decimal places using a standard written method

Division by a number is equivalent to repeated subtraction of that number. We call the number we are dividing by the **divisor** .

When dividing:

- write an estimate of the answer
- start subtracting as many 100s of the divisor as you can, then as many 10s of the divisor as you can, then as many units of the divisor as you can, then as many tenths of the divisor, and so on
- round the **remainder** to the nearest whole number **tenth** or **hundredth** depending on the context of the problem.

Example 1   Divide 862.74 by 6.

Estimate: $900 \div 6 = 150$

```
      1 4 3 . 7 9
  6 ) 8 6 2 . 7 4
      6 0 0          6 × 1 0 0
      2 6 2 . 7 4
      2 4 0          6 ×    4 0
        2 2 . 7 4
        1 8          6 ×     3
          4 . 7 4
          4 . 2      6 ×     0 . 7
          0 . 5 4
          0 . 5 4    6 ×      . 0 9
          0 . 0
```

Subtract as many tenths of 6 as you can.

Subtract as many hundredths of 6 as you can.

Answer: **143.79**

Exercise 16.8

1 Complete these exact divisions:

a) $444.5 \div 7$ b) $413.5 \div 5$ c) $315.2 \div 8$ d) $341.4 \div 6$ e) $648.9 \div 9$

Check each calculation by multiplying the answer by the divisor. The result should match the starting number.

2 Complete these exact divisions:

a) $342.0 \div 8$ b) $159.15 \div 5$ c) $338.16 \div 6$ d) $576.94 \div 7$ e) $683.73 \div 9$

Check each calculation by multiplying the answer by the divisor. The result should match the starting number.

3 Complete these divisions, writing the answer to the nearest tenth or one decimal place:

    a) 537.4 ÷ 4   **b)** 467.35 ÷ 6   **c)** 712.8 ÷ 9   **d)** 837.12 ÷ 8

4 Calculate the cost per person for each of the following activities.

    a) helicopter ride for four people: £257.80

    b) balloon ride for five people: £241.75

    c) parachute jump for three people: £218.97

    d) sea-plane trip for six people: £236.40

    e) hang-gliding lessons for four people: £154.60.

5 A division trick for dividing by a multiple of 10 is to simplify the calculation first by dividing both numbers by 10.

For example, 6418.7 ÷ 30 is equivalent to 641.87 ÷ 3, which is an easier calculation.

Use this trick to calculate each of the following divisions, writing your answers to the nearest 1 decimal place:

    a) 523.6 ÷ 30   **b)** 871.4 ÷ 40   **c)** 97.8 ÷ 160

    d) 936.2 ÷ 80   **e)** 908.6 ÷ 70   **f)** 732.6 ÷ 50

6 Use a set of 0 – 9 digit cards.

Shuffle them and deal out four cards to make a 2-digit number with 1 decimal place of the form 20.1, and a 1-digit number.

Multiply the numbers together. Divide your answer by the 1-digit number.

Check that it matches the original decimal number.

7 Use a set of 2 – 9 digit cards.

Shuffle them and deal four cards to make a 4-digit number.

Divide the number by 4, 5, 6, 7 and 8, rounding each answer to the nearest tenth.

The tenths digit of each number is your score.

Play five rounds. Can you score a total of more than 25?

8 Five people are sharing the cost of a meal. The bill comes to £89.30.

How much does each person have to pay?

9 Rhona ran four laps round an athletics track. Her time was 7 minutes, 34.24 seconds. What is her average (mean) lap time in seconds?

> The average (mean) lap time is found by dividing the total time by the number of laps.

10 A regular hexagon has a perimeter of 343.8 mm.

Calculate the length of a side of the hexagon, in mm, to the nearest 1 decimal place.

11 Invent a problem for which this calculation is necessary: 37.35 ÷ 3.

Sequences in real life

⊕ Find the general term for sequences including ones that occur in real life

---

A **sequence** of numbers is a list of numbers in a given order. A sequence often follows a rule. For example, for the sequence: 7 9 11 13 15… the term-to-term rule is 'add two'.

The **general term** of a sequence tells us how to find each term.

For example, if the general term of a sequence is $2n + 5$:

1st term:	$2 \times 1 + 5 = 7$
2nd term:	$2 \times 2 + 5 = 9$
3rd term:	$2 \times 3 + 5 = 11$ etc.

To find each term, you substitute the term number into the expression $2n + 5$.

Example   Find the next few terms and the general term of this sequence:

3, 5, 7, 9 …

The sequence is going up by 2 each time so the next few terms are **11, 13, 15, 17**.

Term number	1	2	3	4	5	6	…	n
Sequence	3	5	7	9	11	13		

To find the general term of the sequence draw out a table.

Differences   2   2   2   2   2

Look at the differences.
The difference is $+2$ so the general term will include $2n$. Draw another row in the table.

Term number	1	2	3	4	5	6	…	n
Sequence	3	5	7	9	11	13		
$2n$	$2 \times 1 = 2$	$2 \times 2 = 4$	$2 \times 3 = 6$	$2 \times 4 = 8$	$2 \times 5 = 10$	$2 \times 6 = 12$		

The general term is: $2n + 1$.

Check: $2 \times 3 + 1 = 7$ ✓

How you can get from the new sequence ($2n$) to the old sequence? By adding 1.

Exercise 17.1

1 Find the general term of the following sequences:

    a) 3, 6, 9, 12, …   **b)** 5, 15, 25, 35, …   **c)** 8, 11, 14, 17, …

    d) 10, 8, 6, 4, …   **e)** $-12, -8, -4, 0$ …

2 Describe the following sequences in two ways:

    i) by giving the first term and the term-to-term rule

    ii) by giving the general term.

    a) 2, 4, 6, 8, …   **b)** 3, 5, 7, 9, …   **c)** 1, 3, 5, 7, …

    d) 1, 4, 7, 10, …   **e)** 9, 13, 17, 21, …   **f)** 6, 16, 26, 36, …

    g) 10, 15, 20, 25, …   **h)** 9, 6, 3, 0, …   **i)** 5, 4, 3, 2, 1, …

3 A taxi driver charges 70p per mile and a £2.00 standard charge.

a) Copy and complete the table below to show the cost of different journeys:

Length of journey (miles)	1	2	3	4	5
Cost (£)					

b) How much would a journey of 10 miles cost?

c) How much would a journey of 32 miles cost?

d) How much would a journey of *n* miles cost?

e) If the journey costs £10.40, how many miles is it?

> You are finding the general term of the sequence.

4 The cost of a mobile phone bill is £17.99 line rental per month and 50p per minute for calls.

a) How much does it cost if you spend 20 minutes on the telephone?

b) Copy and complete the table below:

Total time of calls (minutes)	1	2	3	4	5
Cost (£)					

c) If the monthly bill is £57.99, how long was spent on the telephone?

5 The Electricity Board's Price Plan A has a basic charge of £15.65 per month plus an extra 39p for every unit of electricity that is used.

a) Find a general term to calculate the cost of an electricity bill when *n* units are used.

b) Calculate the monthly cost of electricity for a family that uses 325 units per month.

c) If the electricity bill is £74.15 calculate the number of units used.

> You could draw up a table like the ones in Q3 and 4 to help you.

Investigation

6 Squares are made from matchsticks in the following way:

a) Investigate the number of matchsticks needed for different numbers of squares.

b) Find a general term that calculates the number of matchsticks needed for *n* squares. Give a reason for your answer.

> Find the general term.

c) Two rows of squares are now made:

Repeat parts **a** and **b** for two rows of squares.

d) Repeat parts **a** and **b** for three, four and five rows of squares.

e) Predict the general term for six rows of squares.

Key words
cell
column
row
generate
general term

A spreadsheet page looks like this.

	A	B	C	D	E
1					
2				$= 3 \times 5$	
3					
4					
5		■			$= A8 \times 5$
6					
7					
8		29			
9					
10					

- Each individual space in a spreadsheet is called a **cell** — the area shaded red in this spreadsheet is one of the cells.
- The area shaded in red is cell B5. You always write the **column** letter before the **row** number.
- You can enter information into a spreadsheet by moving to a particular cell and typing values in. (See cell A8.)
- If you want the spreadsheet to calculate a value, enter '=' and then the calculation you want the spreadsheet to do. (See cell D2.)
- You can enter calculations in cells that refer to other cells. (See cell E5.)
- Spreadsheets can be used to **generate** sequences.

Example   Use a spreadsheet to generate the following sequence: $5n + 2$.

There are two ways in which you can do this:
a) Enter the first term in the sequence in cell A1. The second term in the sequence is the first term plus 5, so enter '$=A1 + 5$' into cell A2 and so on.

b) Enter the term numbers into column A. Each term in the sequence is $5 \times$ term number $+ 2$. Enter '$=5 \times A1 + 2$' into cell B1 and so on.

a)

	A	B
1	7	
2	$= A1 + 5$	
3	$= A2 + 5$	
4	$= A3 + 5$	
5	$= A4 + 5$	
6	$= A5 + 5$	
7	$= A6 + 5$	
8	$= A7 + 5$	

b)

	A	B
1	1	$= 5 \times A1 + 2$
2	2	$= 5 \times A2 + 2$
3	3	$= 5 \times A3 + 2$
4	4	$= 5 \times A4 + 2$
5	5	$= 5 \times A5 + 2$
6	6	$= 5 \times A6 + 2$
7	7	$= 5 \times A7 + 2$
8	8	$= 5 \times A8 + 2$

Exercise 17.2

1 The first few terms of a sequence are 101, 151, 201, 251, 301, …

　　a) Describe the sequence by giving the first term and the term-to-term rule.

　　b) Using a spreadsheet package, generate the sequence as far as the tenth term, using the information from part **a**.

See Example part **a**.

　　c) What is the general term of the sequence?

　　d) Use the general term to generate the sequence on the spreadsheet up to the 15th term.

2 a) Write down the sequence of numbers generated when the following information is put into a spreadsheet:

　　b) Find the general term of the sequence.

	A	B	C	D	E
1	20				
2	= A1 − 2				
3	= A2 − 2				
4	= A3 − 2				
5	= A4 − 2				
6	= A5 − 2				
7	= A6 − 2				
8	= A7 − 2				
9	= A8 − 2				
10	= A9 − 2				

　　c) The same sequence of numbers is generated in column B using the general term of the sequence. Copy and complete columns A and B of the spreadsheet up to row 10:

	A	B
1	1	
2	2	

3 The first three terms of a sequence are generated in this spreadsheet:

　　a) What value will appear in
　　　i) cell B1?　　ii) cell B2?　　iii) cell B3?

　　b) Copy and complete the spreadsheet to continue the sequence up to row 10.

　　c) List the first ten terms of the sequence.

	A	B
1	1	= 7 × A1 + 10
2	2	= 7 × A2 + 10
3	3	= 7 × A3 + 10
4	4	

4 A mobile phone bill costs £10 line rental per month and 30p per minute for calls.

　　a) Find a general term to calculate the cost of the bill each month where t is the number of minutes spent on the telephone.

　　b) Use a spreadsheet package to help you generate the different possible monthly bills for customers.

Start with a customer who made one minute's worth of calls, then two minutes' worth etc.

　　c) The mobile phone company decides to lower its line rental to £8.99 per month. Change the relevant figures in your spreadsheet so that the new monthly bills can be calculated.

　　d) The mobile phone company increases the cost of calls to 45p per minute. Change the relevant figures in your spreadsheet so that the new monthly bills can be calculated.

Investigation

5 Using a spreadsheet package, investigate ways of generating the following sequences:

　　a) multiples of 12　　　　　　b) the square numbers

　　c) the triangular numbers　　　d) the prime numbers.

Properties of graphs

◈ Understand how a graph is related to its equation

Key words
equation
gradient
y-intercept
origin

To find a point on a graph, you need to draw lines to make sure you are accurate.
For example:

If we wanted to know the y-value when $x = 5$, find $x = 5$ on the x-axis and draw a vertical line from here to the graph. Next, draw a horizontal line from the graph to the y-axis, to find that $y = 13$.

We can draw graphs directly from their **equations** :

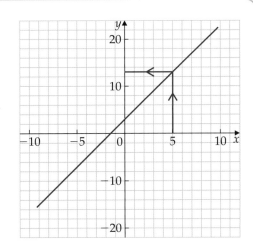

The **2** tells us that for every 1 we move in the x direction, we move 2 in the y direction. The fact that the **2** is positive tells us that the **gradient** is positive (it goes uphill).

$y = 2x + 3$

The **+3** tells us the graph crosses the y-axis at 3. This is called the **y-intercept** . If there is no value then the graph goes through the **origin** .

Example   Draw the graph of $y = 5x$ directly from the equation:

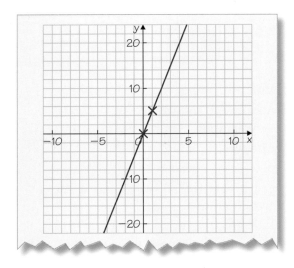

We know that the graph will go through the origin because there is no value for the y-intercept in the equation.

The 5 tells us that for every 1 we move in the x-direction, we move 5 in the y-direction.

When we join up these two points and continue the line, we can see the gradient is positive. This is correct, since the x-term is positive.

Exercise 17.3

❶ Draw a pair of axes from −10 to 10. Draw the following graphs directly from their equations:

a) $y = 2x$ b) $y = x + 2$ c) $y = x - 5$ d) $y = 3x$

2 Which of the following graphs go through the origin:

a) $y = x + 4$
b) $y = 3x$
c) $y = -x + 3$
d) $y = 5x$
e) $y = \frac{1}{2}x$
f) $y = 5 + x$

> You could use a graph sketching package to help you with this question.

3 For the graphs in Q2, write down the points where they cross the y-axis (the y-intercept.)

4 For the graphs in Q2, write down whether the gradient is positive or negative.

5 Draw each of the graphs in Q2 on separate axes.

> Look back at the Example.

6 Find the equation that matches each of the following graphs:

a) $y = 2x + 5$
b) $y = -x$
c) $y = 17$
d) $x = 3$
e) $y = -3x - 6$

1

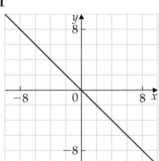

2

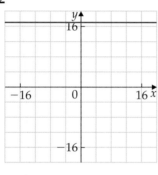

3

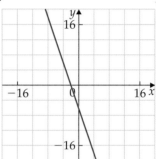

4

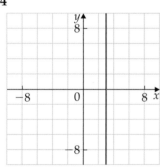

5

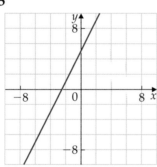

Investigation

7 Find the equations of the following lines:

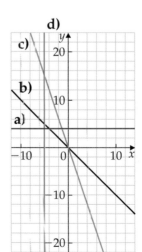

Plotting graphs

◈ Plot graphs to illustrate real life problems

The media uses graphs to show trends and patterns. Graphs are a good way of displaying a lot of information without taking up too much space. We can show a relationship between two **variables** by **plotting** a graph. For example, this graph shows some data about global warming.

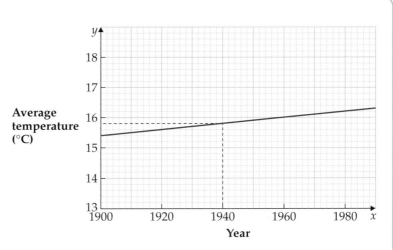

To find the average temperature in 1940, draw a vertical line from 1940 to the straight-line graph. Next, draw a horizontal line from the meeting point to the *y*-axis.

Example   A mobile phone company charges £0.50 per minute for calls.

    a) Calculate how much 10, 20 and 30 minutes of calls cost.

    b) Draw an appropriate set of axes and plot the points you've found.

    c) Use your graph to find the number of minutes spent on the telephone if the bill is £14.

a)

Time (minutes)	Cost (£)
10	5
20	10
30	15

b)

c) £28

When drawing a graph, you need to:

● Label the *x*-axis and the *y*-axis.
● Decide where your scale will start and finish on the *x*-axis and the *y*-axis.
● Keep the same space intervals between the numbers you mark on the axes.

Plot the points you know and draw a straight line through them. Draw a horizontal line from the point on the *y*-axis to meet the straight-line graph *y* = 14. Next, draw a vertical line from this meeting point to the *x*-axis and read off the value on the *x*-axis.

Exercise 17.4

1 There are two commonly used ways of measuring temperature: degrees Fahrenheit (°F) and degrees Celsius (°C).

Temperature in Fahrenheit	Temperature in degrees Celsius
50	10
77	25
95	35

   a) Draw an appropriate pair of axes and plot the points in the table.

   b) Join the points.

   c) Does this graph pass through the origin?

   d) Use your graph to find what 30°C is in °F.

   e) Use your graph to find what 40°F is in °C.

2 A bank displays the following information to give people a rough guide to exchanging money into euros.

Pounds (sterling)	Euros
£20	€30
£50	€75
£100	€150

   a) On graph paper draw a pair of axes with pounds on the x-axis and euros on the y-axis.

   b) Plot the three points on the axes and join them with a straight line.

   c) Use the graph to find how much you would have in euros if you exchanged:
   i) £75   **ii)** £43   **iii)** £10

   d) Use the graph to find how much you would have in pounds if you exchanged:
   i) €72   **ii)** €150   **iii)** €10.

3 A car accelerates from 0 km/h to 100 km/h. Each minute, the cars speed increases 10 km/h. Draw a graph to represent this information.

> Draw a table and find some values. Then plot these values and join the points with a straight line. Think about what your axes will represent.

4 On a factory production line, 300 toy cars can be manufactured in one hour. Draw a straight line graph to represent this information.

> How many cars have been made at 0 mins? How many cars have been made after 30 mins? And so on.

Investigation

5 Draw a pair of axes as shown:

   The Water Board offers two billing methods:
   Economy 1 – A standing charge of £8 per month and each unit costs 10p
   Economy 2 – Each unit costs 20p.

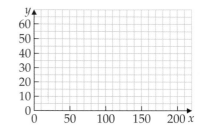

   a) Draw a table for each billing method and find some values.

   b) Plot the points you have found for the billing method 'Economy 1' and join them with a straight line. Repeat for 'Economy 2'.

   c) Look at the two straight-line graphs together. If you used 180 units, how much would this cost with: **i)** Economy 1   **ii)** Economy 2?

⊕ **Be able to read information off a graph representing a real life problem**

Graphs tell you about the relationship between two things.

If the graph has a **positive gradient**, then we can say that as the x-value increases, so does the y-value:

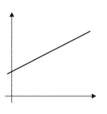

If a graph has a **negative gradient**, then we can say that as the x-value increases, the y-value decreases:

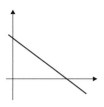

Example   Electricity is measured in units. The graph shows the cost of an electricity bill according to the number of units of electricity used. Find:

a)   the cost of ten units

b)   the number of units used if the cost is £30

c)   how the cost is related to the number of units used

d)   the cost of one unit.

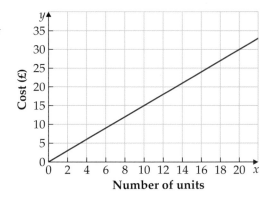

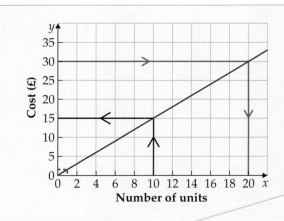

a)   The cost of 10 units is £15.

b)   20 units were used.

c)   The graph slopes upwards because as the number of units of electricity used increases, so does the cost.

d)   The cost of one unit is £1.50.

By drawing a vertical line up from 10 units to the straight-line graph and a horizontal line across from the meeting point, you can find the cost of 10 units (see the black line).

By drawing a horizontal line across from £30 to the straight-line graph and a vertical line down from the meeting point, you can find the number of units used (see blue line).

See dotted lines.

1 The graphs show the amount of rainfall in different areas.

a)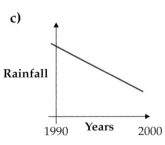

b)

c)

Match each of the three graphs with one of the descriptions below.
i) The amount of rainfall has increased over the past few years.
ii) The amount of rainfall has decreased over the past few years.
iii) The amount of rainfall has remained the same over the last few years.

2 The following information will be plotted against time, as in **Q1**. Decide whether the graphs should have a positive gradient, a negative gradient or have zero gradient.
a) The speed of a car as it accelerates.
b) The mass of a candle as it burns.

3 The graph shows the number of ice creams sold against the temperature on that day:

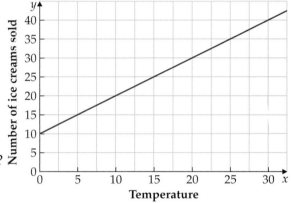

How many ice creams will be sold if the temperature is:
a) 20 °C **b)** 12 °C **c)** 0 °C?

What temperature was it if:
d) 25 **e)** 30 **f)** 10 ice creams were sold?
g) If the temperature goes up by 1 °C, how many more ice creams are sold?
h) What are the problems with this graph?

4 A shopkeeper alters the price of chocolate bars each day to see how many he will sell at each price. He draws up a graph to show the price against the number of chocolate bars sold:

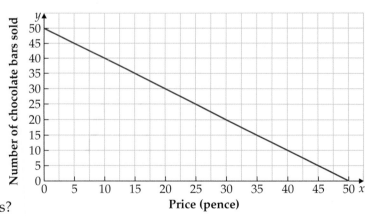

How many bars does he sell if the cost of the chocolate bar is
a) 30p **b)** 5p?

What is the cost of the chocolate bar if he sells **c)** 30 bars **d)** no bars?
e) Why does the graph have a negative gradient?
f) If the cost of a chocolate bar is 0p, how many does he sell?
g) Why do you think your answer to part **f** is unrealistic?

Graphs in real life

⊕ Draw and interpret graphs from real life

A century is 100 years.

This graph shows the world's population growth over three centuries.

We can see that the world's population has increased over the past three centuries.

We can also see that the world's population increased slowly between 1700 and 1800 but that it increased by a larger amount between 1800 and 1900.

In the twentieth century, the world's population increased dramatically, from 1 500 000 000 to 6 000 000 000.

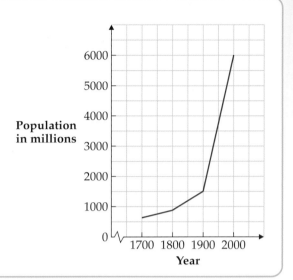

Example　This graph shows the time it takes Mr Zakira to drive from Wiltshire to Devon.

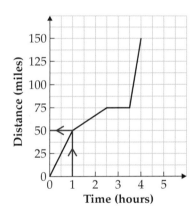

a)　How far has Mr Zakira travelled after 1 hour?

b)　What could Mr Zakira have been doing between $2\frac{1}{2}$ and $3\frac{1}{2}$ hours?

c)　How long did the journey take altogether?

d)　During which period was Mr Zakira driving fastest?

a)　50 miles. —————————————————————————— See the red line.

b)　Resting or stuck in traffic.

c)　4 hours.

d)　Between $3\frac{1}{2}$ and 4 hours.

Exercise 17.6

1 The following graph shows a walk taken by the Sherborne Rambling Association:

How far from their starting point were they after:

a) 25 mins **b)** 100 mins **c)** 150 mins?

d) What could they have been doing between 100 mins and 150 mins?

e) How far from their starting point were they after 200 mins?

f) How long did it take them to walk the first four miles?

g) How many miles did they walk altogether?

h) How long did it take them to walk the last stretch of their journey?

i) When were they walking the fastest?

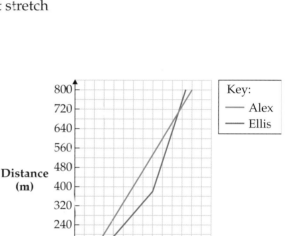

2 The following graph shows two swimmers over a distance of 800m.

a) How far has Alex swum after 400 secs?

b) How far has Ellis swum after 400 secs?

c) Who is in the lead after 200 secs?

d) How long does it take Ellis to swim the last 50 m?

e) Does Ellis swim faster during the first 400 secs or the last 200 secs?

f) How can you tell this just by looking at the graph?

g) Who wins the race?

3 **a)** Draw graphs to show Mr Egger and Miss Jameson's journeys to work on Friday. Make sure you label your axes appropriately.
   i) Mr Egger drives 2 miles in the first 5 minutes. He waits at traffic lights for 2 minutes before driving a further 6 miles which takes a further 15 minutes.
   ii) Miss Jameson drives 8 miles in the first 15 minutes and then gets on the motorway and drives 35 miles in half an hour. She then leaves the motorway and drives a futher 5 miles in 12 minutes.

b) Use your graph to find the distances Mr Egger and Miss Jameson travel.

c) How long did Mr Egger and Miss Jameson's journeys take them on Friday?

Investigation

4 Choose a graph in a Science or Geography text book or choose one from a newspaper. Make up some questions about it for someone else to answer. For example, ask them to read some values off it or to describe how the variable represented on the x-axis is related to the variable represented on the y-axis.

Solving real life problems

⊕ **Use algebra to solve everyday problems**

Key words
algebra
algebraically
equation
solve
unknown

We use **algebra** all the time without realising it. When we buy four oranges for £1.00 we can easily work out that each one costs 25p.

We could write this **algebraically** as: $4x = 100$

$$\frac{4x}{4} = \frac{100}{4}$$

$x = 25$, where x is the cost in pence of one orange.

Example 1 Solve this equation: $3x + 2 = 17$,

$3x + 2 - 2 = 17 - 2$ ——— First subtract 2 from both sides.

$3x = 15$

$$\frac{3x}{3} = \frac{15}{3}$$ ——— Now divide both sides by 3.

$x = 5$

Check by substituting back into the **equation**.
$3 \times 5 + 2 = 17$ ✓

Example 2 An offer in a supermarket reads: "Four yoghurts for the price of three." If one yoghurt usually costs 40p, find the new cost of one yoghurt.

$3 \times 40 = £1.20$ ——— First work out how much three yoghurts cost.

$4y = £1.20$

$$\frac{4y}{4} = \frac{£1.20}{4}$$

$y = £0.30$

One yoghurt now costs 30p.

Now four yoghurts cost £1.20.

Now **solve** the equation to find y.

Divide both sides by 4.

Exercise 17.7

1 Solve the following equations:

a) $x + 5 = 10$ b) $x - 12 = 30$ c) $2 + x = 2$

d) $x - 4 = 16$ e) $2x + 5 = 27$ f) $3x + 7 = 13$

g) $7 + 2x = 27$ h) $4 + 7x = 67$ i) $2x - 5 = 19$

j) $5x - 15 = 0$ k) $10x + 52 = 57$ l) $12x - 50 = 82$

2 In a supermarket, four apples cost 48p. Form an equation to help you calculate how much each apple costs.

3 In a corner shop, you buy three chocolate bars and a bag of crisps. The crisps cost 22p. The total bill is £1.39.
Form an equation to calculate the cost of a chocolate bar.

4 A telephone company calculates its bills using the following equation:

$$B = 12.99 + 0.2m$$

where B is the total bill in pounds and m is the number of minutes spent on the telephone.

Calculate the bill if a customer spends:
a) 36 minutes
b) 3 hours 45 minutes on the telephone.

> First change hours and minutes to minutes.

Find to the nearest minute the length of time a customer spent on the telephone if the bill is **c)** £34.99   **d)** £82.00.

5 A shop owner (Mr A) calculates the cost of his chocolate bars by adding 10p to the price he pays in the *Cash and Carry* and then multiplying this number by 2.

> Remember to use brackets.

a) Write an equation to calculate the shop price of the chocolate (S) in terms of the *Cash and Carry* price (C).

Another shop owner (Mrs B) calculates the cost of her chocolate bars by multiplying the *Cash and Carry* price by 2.5 and then adding 7p.

b) Form an equation to calculate the shop price of the chocolate (S) in terms of the *Cash and Carry* price (C).

c) Copy and complete this table using your equations to calculate the missing prices:

Chocolate bar	*Cash and Carry* price	Mr A's price	Mrs B's price
Pluto Bar	12p		
Nebula	10p		
Sprint	14p		
Chewy K	16p		
Caramunch	8p		

d) Which shop would you rather shop at?

Investigations

6 Three consecutive numbers add up to 27. The first number is x.
a) Represent the other two numbers algebraically.
b) Form an equation to show the above information.
c) Solve the equation to find x.
d) What are the three numbers?

7 Two consecutive odd numbers add to give 104. Using the system you used for Q6, find the two numbers.

8 Repeat Q6 but this time use x to stand in for the third number.

17.8 **Using formulae**

⊕ Use formulae from maths and other subjects to solve problems

Key words
formula
formulae
variable
substitute

In March 2003, one pound sterling was worth 1.5 euros. To convert pounds to euros, we need to multiply by 1.5. So we can express this as $e = 1.5 \times p$, where e = number of euros and
p = number of pounds.

This is called a **formula** . We call e and p **variables** because we can use them to stand in for a range of different values. A formula links two variables.

Remember that when using **formulae** , you must ensure your information is in the correct units. When converting between pounds and euros, you must make sure you have the amount in pounds and not in pence.

Example 1 **a)** Hasif is going on holiday to France. He has £230. How much is this in euros?

b) When he returns, he has €115 left. How much is this in pounds sterling?

a) $e = 1.5 \times p$

$= 1.5 \times 230$

Answer: **€345**

> Substitute the values you know into the formula.
> e = euros and
> p = pounds sterling.

b) $e = 1.5 \times p$

$115 = 1.5 \times p$

$\dfrac{115}{1.5} = p$

$76.6666667 = p$

Answer: **£76.67**

> Substitute the values you know into the formula.

> This is the amount in £, so round to the nearest penny.

Example 2 To calculate the amount of tax he owes, Kumar uses a formula. He multiplies what he earns by 0.22.

a) Find the formula Kumar uses to calculate the tax (t) he owes on his earnings (e).

b) Calculate the amount of tax Kumar pays if he earns £13 000.

a) $t = 0.22 \times e$

b) $t = 0.22e$

$= 0.22 \times 13\,000$

$= £2860$

> Tax $= 0.22 \times$ earnings

> Substitute the values you know into the formula.

Exercise 17.8

1 A helicopter uses fuel at a rate of 300 kg per hour.
To calculate how much fuel he uses, the pilot uses the following formula:
Fuel = 300 × time in hours
Find the amount of fuel used by the helicopter for the following periods of time:

a) 2 hrs   **b)** 10 hrs   **c)** 30 mins   **d)** 45 mins   **e)** 1.5 hrs.

2 The ages of these babies are given in weeks. Give their age in days, and explain how you have worked these out.

a) 6 weeks   **b)** 31 weeks   **c)** 17 weeks.

3 Speed $= \dfrac{\text{Distance}}{\text{Time}}$

Find the speed of the following in km/h (remember your distance must be in km and your time in hours):

a) a car that travels 600 km in 6 hrs

b) a man who jogs 4 km in 30 mins

c) a van that travels 90000 m in $1\frac{1}{2}$ hrs

d) a cyclist who cycles 1200 m in 15 mins.

4 Using the formula given in Q1, calculate the length of time the pilot spends flying if he uses: **a)** 600 kg of fuel   **b)** 150 kg of fuel   **c)** 100 kg of fuel   **d)** 1200 kg of fuel.

5 a) Form formulae to find the yearly cost of each type of insurance. Choose letters to represent the variables. For example, use *H* to stand in for the cost of Household Insurance and *d* to stand in for the number of extra bedrooms.

> **Car Insurance**
> Car Insurance usually costs £300. However, we're offering you £5 discount for every year of no-claims-bonus you have.

> **Household Insurance**
> Yearly household insurance for a one bedroom house is £45. Each extra bedroom costs £3 extra.

> **Health Insurance**
> Health insurance with BAPA costs £300 per year plus a £1 supplement for every year of age for those over 25.
> (A 30 year old man would pay a £5 supplement.)

> If you're having problems working out the formula, try it out for a specific value. For example, to find out how much car insurance you would pay if you had a 10 year no-claims-bonus, you would calculate:
> £300 − 10 × £5 = **£250**

b) Using your formulae, calculate the total insurance cost for a 36 year old man who has five years no-claims-bonus and a house with four bedrooms.

Investigation

6 Look up the current exchange rates for Europe, America and Australia.
A bank charges £10 commission for changing pounds into foreign currency.
Form formulae to tell you how much of each currency you will receive for a given amount of pounds (£).

◈ **Use known facts to describe 2-D shapes**

Polygons can be identified by describing their sides, angles, and the kind of symmetry they have. A clear description is one that has no room for misunderstanding. For example, this description: 'A polygon has four sides with two sides the same length' could be:

a kite   a rectangle 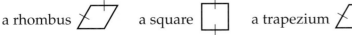   a parallelogram

a rhombus   a square   a trapezium

an arrowhead 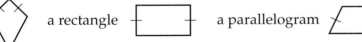   or just an irregular quadrilateral 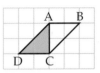 .

We need more information to be able to say exactly what the polygon is.

Example 1   Name the polygon ACD, giving reasons for your answer.

> Polygon ACD is an isosceles right-angled triangle.
>
> It is a right-angled triangle because it is on a square grid, so angle ACD must be 90°.
>
> It is isosceles because on a square grid the sides of the squares are the same. AC = CD.

Example 2   Name the polygon ABCD, giving reasons for your answer.

> Polygon ABCD is a parallelogram.
>
> AB is parallel to DC; AD is parallel to BC.
>
> AB = DC (2 units from the grid) and BC = AD. That means the two pairs of opposite sides are equal, which makes the polygon a parallelogram.

Exercise 18.1

1 Name the polygons on the grids, giving reasons for your answers.

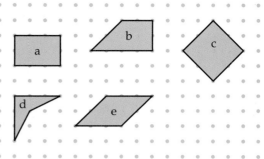

> Look back to page 114 for help with naming the polygons.

2 Name the polygons on the grids, giving reasons for your answers.

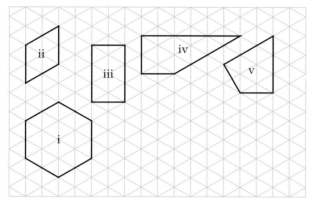

3 In a polygon ABCDE, AB = DE = EA and BC = CD and AB is parallel to ED. Sketch the polygon and name ABDE and BCD, giving reasons for your answers.

4 On triangular paper, draw a regular hexagon. Join alternate vertices. What polygons are formed? Explain how you know.

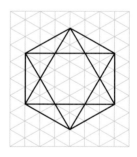

5 Using triangular paper, draw as many regular polygons as possible. Show how you **know** they are regular.

> Remember a regular polygon has equal angles and sides of equal length.

6 Using squared paper, draw as many regular polygons as possible. Show how you **know** they are regular.

Investigation

7 On a square grid draw a right-angled triangle with sides of 1 and 2 units
Investigate the polygons you can make by joining two, three and four triangles. Give the polygons you make their correct names.
Two examples have been drawn for you.

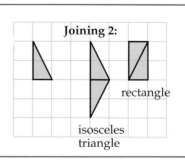

Joining 2:

rectangle

isosceles triangle

Folded shapes

⊕ Use side, angle and symmetry properties of shapes to solve problems

We can fold and rotate shapes to find out information about their properties. We do not always need to make measurements in order to identify and describe shapes.

Example 1   Fold each side of an isosceles triangle onto its adjacent side. Crease firmly and then draw along the creases. What polygons are made? Justify your answers..

① and ② are identical right-angled triangles: AD is a line of

symmetry so it is perpendicular to the base.

③, ④, ⑤, ⑥ are all scalene. (We can check by folding that they are

not isosceles or right-angled.) ③ is identical to ⑥, and

④ is identical to ⑤ because AD is a line of symmetry.

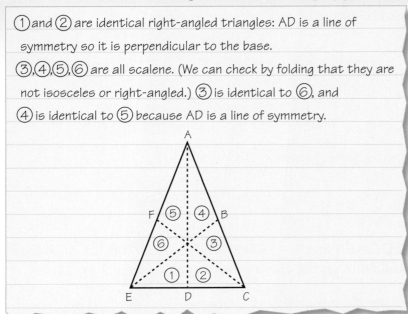

Example 2   Make four different polygons by overlapping these two shapes. Describe each polygon that is made, justifying your answer.

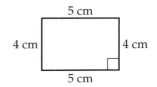
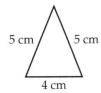

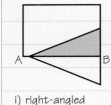
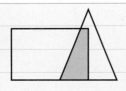

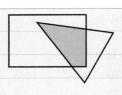

| i) right-angled triangle | ii) trapezium | iii) symmetrical trapezium | iv) irregular quadrilateral |

i)   right-angled triangle (AB is a line of symmetry so is perpendicular to the base)

ii)   trapezium (sides of a rectangle are parallel so the opposite sides of this
quadrilateral are parallel)

iii)   trapezium (see above)

iv)   irregular quadrilateral (no sides or angles equal)

Exercise 18.2

1 Fold each side of an equilateral triangle on to its adjacent side. Crease firmly and then draw along the creases.
What polygons are made?
Justify your answers.

> Adjacent sides are sides that are next to each other.

2 Make five different polygons by overlapping these two shapes. Describe each one, justifying your statements.

> You may find it helpful to use tracing paper.

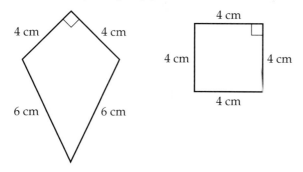

3 **a)** Fold one vertex of a rectangle to its opposite vertex. Unfold and draw along the fold line. What polygons are made?

b) Repeat with the other two vertices. What polygons do you have? Check by folding that you have identified your polygons correctly.

4 Start with a five by five square.
Divide the square into the following polygons, leaving no space unaccounted for:
A smaller square, a rectangle, an isosceles triangle, two right-angled scalene triangles and three right-angled isosceles triangles.

Investigation

5 Starting each time with a fresh piece of paper, fold it into a:
square;
rhombus;
parallelogram;
kite;
isosceles triangle;
equilateral triangle.
For each polygon, give a short explanation of your method, using either words or diagrams.

> Try sketching each one first, including the diagonals.

⊕ Explore reflection, rotation and translation using ICT

> In Unit 14 we looked at three **transformations** : **reflection** , **rotation** and **translation** .
> Remember:
>
> A reflection produces an image of the shape in a mirror line.
>
> A rotation turns a shape through an angle about a centre of rotation.
>
> A translation moves a shape up, down or across.

Example 1   Using a dynamic geometry package, construct a square ABCD. Rotate it through 180° about one vertex and draw in the rotated image.

a)   What polygon have you made?
Reflect your shape using the bottom longest side as the mirror line. Draw in the reflected image.
b)   What polygon is made now?
c)   Describe its symmetry.

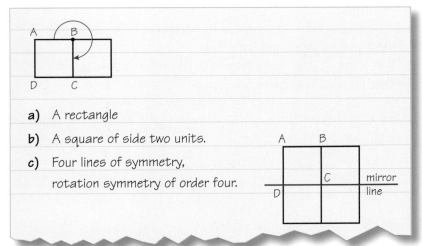

a)   A rectangle

b)   A square of side two units.

c)   Four lines of symmetry,
rotation symmetry of order four.

Example 2   Using a coordinate grid on your screen, plot the parallelogram A(1,1) B(4,1) C(3,0) D(0,0). Rotate it using (0,0) as the centre of rotation through 90° and draw in the image. Repeat 3 times. Describe the symmetry of your new picture.

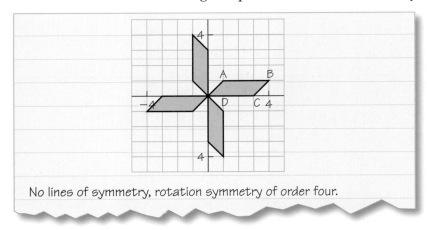

No lines of symmetry, rotation symmetry of order four.

Exercise 18.3 ....

1 Draw an isosceles triangle. Predict what will happen if you:

   a) reflect it along one of its sides

   b) rotate it about one of its vertices.

   Use your dynamic geometry package programme to check whether you are correct.

2 Use a dynamic geometry package to draw a polygon which has rotation symmetry of order three but no lines of symmetry.

> Sketch your idea first and mark in all the measurements you know.

3 Use a dynamic geometry package to draw a triangle PQR where angle PQR = 45° and angle PRQ is 55°. Choose a suitable length for RQ. Rotate your triangle using Q as the centre and turning through 45° each time. How many triangles do you need to draw to complete the circle? Describe the symmetry of the new shape that is made. Repeat for different triangles and then for different angles of rotation.

Investigation

4 Start with a square and cut it in half diagonally.

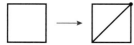

   a) What shapes are made? Keep one shape still and rotate the other using a vertex of the square as the centre, until it touches the other shape.

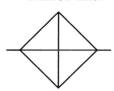

   b) How far have you rotated it? Reflect your new shape using the longest side as the mirror line.

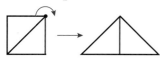

   c) What shape is made? Cut it in half diagonally. Keep one half still and rotate the other using a vertex of the square as the centre, until it touches the other shape.

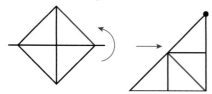

   Reflect your new shape using the longest side as the mirror line. Continue until you notice a repeating pattern. Each time a square is made, calculate its area.

   d) What do you notice? Explain why this is the case.

⊕ **Construct triangles and quadrilaterals using a ruler and protractor**

To **construct** a **quadrilateral** we need information about the sides and angles.
When drawing accurate diagrams, a rough sketch can be useful.
We can draw fairly accurate right angles and parallel lines using a ruler and set square.

Example 1 Construct a parallelogram PQRS with sides RS = 6 cm and PS = 3 cm and
∠RSP = 60°.

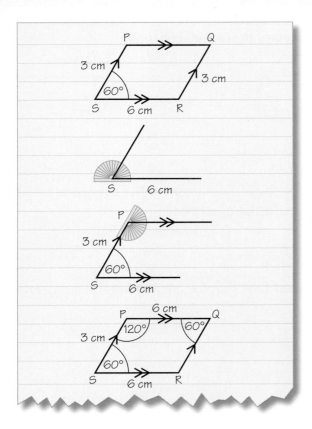

1) Draw a sketch first and mark on all the measurements.

2) Draw a base line RS of 6 cm. Mark on a vertex for the angle at S. Draw an angle of 60° at S with a long line.

3) Mark a second line PS of 3 cm. Mark on a vertex for the angle at P. Since the opposite angles in a parallelogram are equal and the angles in a quadrilateral sum to 360°, the two missing angles must equal 360 − 2 × 60. 360 − 120 = 240 therefore each angle is 240 ÷ 2 = 120°. Draw an angle of 120° at P with a long line.

4) Mark a third line PQ of 6 cm. Mark on a vertex for the angle at Q. Draw an angle of 60° at Q and extend the line until it intersects with R.

Exercise 18.4

① Construct these quadrilaterals:

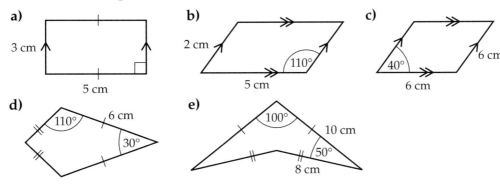

2 Draw rhombus PQRS where PQ = 5 cm, ∠PQR = 120°.
Measure PR.

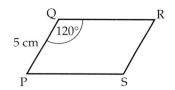

3 Draw kite DEFG where DE = 5 cm, EF = 6 cm and ∠DEF = 110°.
Measure DF.

4 Draw parallelogram JKLM where JK = 65 mm, KL = 45 mm and ∠KLM = 134°.
Measure KM.

Investigations

5 Draw any quadrilateral, measure it and mark on your choice of measurements (both angles and sides). Construct another identical quadrilateral with one side in common. (It could be a rotation, reflection or translation of the original shape.)

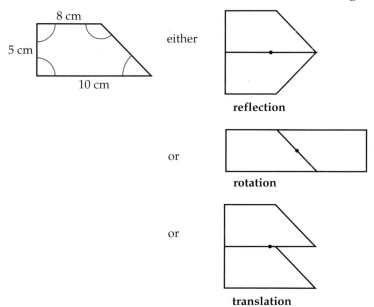

Construct more quadrilaterals to form a repeating pattern. Can you design a pattern that leaves no gaps?

6 Take any quadrilateral. Rotate it through 180° about the mid-point of each side. What do you notice? Will this work with any other polygon?

Constructing nets

⊕ **Use other 2-D shapes to visualise and describe 3-D shapes and consider their properties**

Key words
net
cuboid
tetrahedron
prism

A **net** folds up to make a 3-D shape. After sketching a net we can draw it accurately using a ruler and protractor, if we know enough facts about the 3-D shape we want to make. Look back at page 32 for a reminder about nets.

Example   Construct the net of a regular tetrahedron with sides of length 5 cm.

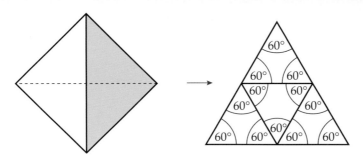

Sketch the net. We know that the faces are all equilateral triangles, so all the angles must be 60°. Mark on the measurements. Decide where to start. Use a set square and ruler to draw parallel lines wherever you can.

This is a suggested order of drawing but there are others.

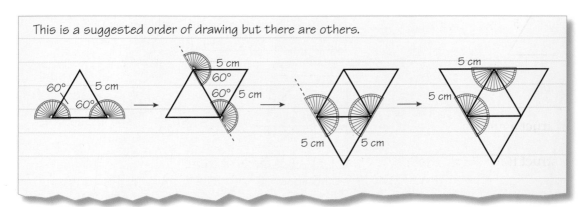

Exercise 18.5

1 Construct the nets for these cuboids:

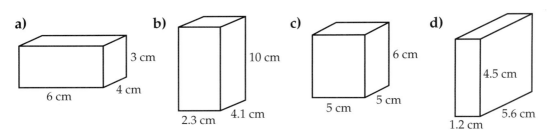

a) 6 cm, 4 cm, 3 cm

b) 2.3 cm, 4.1 cm, 10 cm

c) 5 cm, 5 cm, 6 cm

d) 1.2 cm, 5.6 cm, 4.5 cm

First sketch the nets with all the dimensions you know. This will also help you fit it on the page.

2 Construct the nets for these regular tetrahedra and prisms:

a)

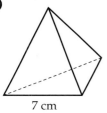

7 cm

b)

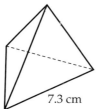

7.3 cm

> First sketch the nets with all the dimensions you know.

c)

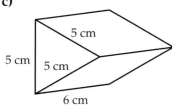

5 cm
5 cm
5 cm
6 cm

d)

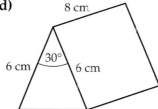

8 cm
6 cm   30°   6 cm

3 What 3-D shapes will these nets make? Copy them accurately and assemble them.

a)

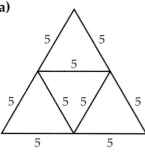

5 5
5
5 5 5 5
5 5

b)

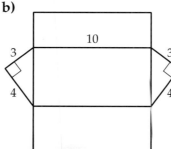

10
3   3
4   4

c)

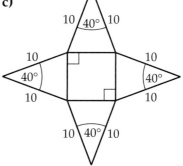

10 40° 10
10   10
40°   40°
10   10
10 40° 10

4 Construct a net for a cuboid with dimensions 2 cm, 3 cm and 4 cm.

5 Construct the net for a regular tetrahedron with sides of 8 cm.

Investigation

6 A shoe box measures 10 cm by 10 cm by 30 cm. Sketch the net. Sketch the net for a box which is twice as wide, twice as long and twice as deep. Calculate the area of card needed to make the two nets and write down anything you notice.

Investigating nets

Key words
net
surface area
cube
cuboid
tetrahedron

- ◈ Use other 2-D shapes to visualise and describe 3-D shapes and consider their properties
- ◈ Know what the nets of cubes, cuboids and tetrahedrons look like
- ◈ Calculate the surface area of shapes made from cuboids
- ◈ Use the formula for the surface area of a cuboid

We can use 2-D representations of 3-D shapes to help us to visualise them. We can also construct **nets** in order to make solid shapes.

We can use what we know about the net for a 3-D shape to help us work out some of its properties. For example, we can find the **surface area** of a 3-D shape by adding together the area of all its faces.

The formula for the surface area S of a cuboid with length l, width w and height h is:
$S = 2 \text{ (length} \times \text{width)} + 2 \text{ (length} \times \text{height)} + 2 \text{ (height} \times \text{width)} = 2lw + 2lh + 2hw$

Example 1 A cuboid has length 4 cm, width 5 cm and height 6 cm. What is its surface area?

$S = 2lw + 2lh + 2hw$
$= 2 \times 4 \times 5 + 2 \times 4 \times 6 + 2 \times 6 \times 5$
$= 148 \text{ cm}^2$

Use the formula for finding the surface area of a cuboid. Substitute in the values $l = 4$, $w = 5$ and $h = 6$.

Example 2 Draw a net for a cuboid. Use coloured pens to show which edges will meet when it is folded up.

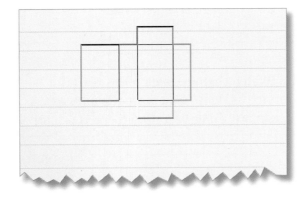

Use what you know about the dimensions of the different faces of the cuboid to help you work out which edges will meet.

Exercise 18.6

1 Estimate the surface area of these objects. Match the object to the correct area:

A CD case; a computer monitor; a garden shed; a 1 kg packet of sugar.
28 m²;   520 cm²;   180 cm²;   7800 cm².

2 Use the formula for surface area to calculate the surface area of the following shapes:

  a) A cube with 3 cm sides

  b) A cuboid with dimensions 1 cm, 5 cm, 6 cm

  c) A cube with 1.5 m sides

  d) A shoe box with dimensions 30 cm, 10 cm, 10 cm.

3 Draw a net for a cube. Write the number 2 on any one of the faces. Now, choose numbers for each of the other faces so that when the net is folded up, the opposite faces add up to 6.

4 Rajeev and Aroosa are decorating their living room. The room is 5 m wide, 6 m long and 3 m high.

  a) What is the area of the floor?

  b) Aroosa buys tiles for the floor, which measure 0.6 m by 0.5 m. How many tiles will she need to cover the floor?

  c) What is the total surface area of the room?

  d) Rajeev buys wallpaper for the walls. He buys 30 m². Has he bought enough?

> Remember, Rajeev does not need to put wallpaper on the ceiling or the floor.

5 Rajeev and Aroosa decide to paint the room instead. However, Aroosa is worried that Rajeev is going to get paint on her sculpture collection. In Aroosa's sculpture collection is a cube, a regular tetrahedron and a cuboid. She asks him to make paper nets for them so that they are completely covered. What is wrong with each of Rajeev's attempts?

> If you can't tell, make up the nets and test them.

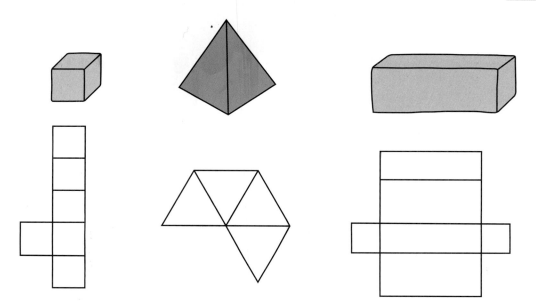

Investigations

6 Help Rajeev cover the sculptures. Sketch as many different nets as you can think of for a cube, a tetrahedron and a cuboid.

Index